those amazing NEWFOUNDLAND DOGS

THE BOOK SUPPORTING THE CHARITY NEWFOUND FRIENDS

JAN BONDESON

Edited by Jonathan Downes
Typeset/Layout by Jessica Heard
Cover and Internal Layout by Jon Downes for CFZ Communications
Using Microsoft Word 2000, Microsoft Publisher 2000, Adobe Photoshop.

First edition published 2012 by CFZ Publications

**CFZ PRESS
Myrtle Cottage
Woolfardisworthy
Bideford
North Devon
EX39 5QR**

© CFZ MMXII

All rights reserved. Without limiting the rights under copyright reserved above, no part of this publication may be reproduced, stored in or introduced into a retrieval system, or transmitted, in any form of by any means (electronic, mechanical, photocopying, recording or otherwise), without the prior written permission of both the copyright owners and the publishers of this book.

ISBN: 978-1-905723-96-6

CONTENTS

5.		PREFACE
7.	CHAPTER 1.	INTRODUCTION
9.	CHAPTER 2.	THE ORIGINS AND EARLY HISTORY OF THE NEWFOUNDLAND DOG
15.	CHAPTER 3.	SOME EARLY NEWFOUNDLAND DOGS IN BRITAIN
27.	CHAPTER 4.	NEW LIGHT ON LORD BYRON AND 'BOATSWAIN'
41.	CHAPTER 5.	NEWFOUNDLAND DOGS IN THE NEWS 1750-1800
49.	CHAPTER 6.	EDWARD JESSE'S ANECDOTES ON NEWFOUNDLAND DOGS
61.	CHAPTER 7.	CARLO THE ACTING NEWFOUNDLAND DOG
69.	CHAPTER 8.	SOME OTHER ACTING NEWFOUNDLAND DOGS
83.	CHAPTER 9.	NEWFOUNDLAND DOGS IN THE NEWS 1800-1850
97.	CHAPTER 10.	THE CULT OF THE NEWFOUNDLAND DOG
117.	CHAPTER 11.	SIR EDWIN LANDSEER AND THE NEWFOUNDLAND DOG
133.	CHAPTER 12.	WILLIAM GORDON STABLES AND SOME OTHER VICTORIAN NEWFOUNDLAND DOG FANCIERS
141.	CHAPTER 13.	A HISTORICAL ANALYSIS OF NEWFOUNDLAND DOG FUR COLOUR GENETICS
151.	CHAPTER 14.	NEWFOUNDLAND DOGS IN THE NEWS 1850-1900
165.	CHAPTER 15.	NEWFOUNDLAND DOG MEMORABILIA BY DI SELLERS
181.	CHAPTER 16.	SOME SPECTRAL NEWFOUNDLAND DOGS
193.	CHAPTER 17.	THE LIFESAVING NEWFOUNDLAND DOGS OF PARIS
209.	CHAPTER 18.	NEWFOUNDLAND DOG WATER RESCUE BY MR DAVID PUGH OF NEWFOUND FRIENDS
229.	CHAPTER 19.	THE CHANGING NEWFOUNDLAND DOG
237.		NOTES

THOSE AMAZING NEWFOUNDLAND DOGS

ABOUT THIS BOOK
The Newfoundland dog is one of the most majestic and impressive breeds of dogs. Originally bred as water dogs and draught dogs, Newfoundland dogs have been known in Britain at least since the 1730s. Considered a very superior breed of dogs, they soon became expensive and sought after: many noblemen and magnates wanted a specimen. Newfoundland dogs were also highly regarded for their ability to save human lives during shipwrecks or bathing accidents. Heroic Newfoundland dogs were depicted in schoolbooks, on popular engravings, and in books on natural history. These dogs were considered not just brave and altruistic, but also extremely intelligent; a large proportion of the anecdotes of dogs told by the Victorian dog-fanciers were related to the extraordinary sagacity of the Newfoundland. This book will resurrect the forgotten history of the Newfoundland dog, using original sources and illustrations to shed new light on this magnificent breed.

ABOUT THE AUTHOR
Jan Bondeson is a senior lecturer at Cardiff University and the author of *Amazing Dogs*, *Greyfriars Bobby*, and nine other critically praised books. He has been researching the history of Newfoundland dogs for six years. This book supports the charity Newfound Friends, dedicated to Newfoundland dog water rescue and hospital work, as well as helping critically ill children.

PREFACE
BY MR DAVID PUGH OF NEWFOUND FRIENDS

Intelligent, versatile and immensely strong, the Newfoundland is one of the most distinguished of all dog breeds, steeped in history with tales of bravery and tantalizing endeavours. This book is a must for all canine enthusiasts.

The Newfoundland, be warned, will change the life of its owner. I often say that most new owners make all their mistakes with their first dog, and time after time I have been proved right. I look back and see the mistakes I made too. When the second Newfoundland joins the family home, the approach to the new arrival is markedly different from the first, since the lessons of owning a Newfoundland only come from experience. A very astute and calculating animal, the Newfoundland will always give the impression that the world is just passing it by, but don't be taken in by this false sense of security: they know all that is going on, it's just the fact that they very often don't want their human counterparts to understand just what's going on in their own private world. My dogs can tell which day of the week it is, and know if it is swimming day. Oh yes they know, they know the moves you make and these tell them if you are leaving them at home, or if it's time for their daily walks, meal time, or someone coming to visit.

Jan Bondeson, a very distinguished and prolific writer, has brought together a number of stories and tales that illustrate the importance in history of this the most noble of all dogs. Jan's previous book *Amazing Dogs* uncovered untold tales of the Newfoundland and it is a wonderful gesture that Jan has chosen to put this new research into this very different book about *Those Amazing Newfoundland Dogs*.

CHAPTER 1.
INTRODUCTION

N is for Newfoundland, of all dogs the best;
Just give me this dog, you may keep all the rest.
In the water he'll jump and will struggle to save
A dear little child from a watery grave.
A lover of children, a boy's closest friend,
A servant of man on which to depend.
He'll carry a basket or drive home the cow,
Or keep back a tramp with his fierce
Bow-wow-wow!

From *The Natural History A*B*C**,
printed by M.A. Donahue and Co., Chicago.

The Newfoundland dog is one of the most majestic and impressive breeds, today known for their placid temperament and friendly nature.[1] Originally bred as water dogs and draught dogs, Newfoundland dogs have been known in Britain at least since the 1730s. Considered a very superior breed of dogs, they soon became expensive and sought after: many noblemen and magnates wanted a specimen. Lord Byron's Newfoundland dog 'Boatswain' was not the only member of his breed to be immortalized in a painting and given a grand funerary monument. Already in 1803, the extraordinary acting Newfoundland dog 'Carlo' enjoyed success as an actor on the London stage; he was followed by other canine thespians, some of them having special plays written for them.

In Victorian collections of dog stories, and altruistic Newfoundland dogs make use of their superior intellects to protect children, catch thieves, and rescue people from various calamities. If an imprudent child is in danger from drowning, fire, or falling down a precipice, a sagacious Newfoundland dog is never far away. If burglars or robbers are up to mischief, the watchful Newfoundland drives them away with his fierce Bow-wow-wow! or teaches them a lesson with his powerful fangs. If a yapping little dog annoys the lordly Newfoundland, he grabs it by the scruff of the neck and drops it into the water from the quayside, but he then benevolently leaps into the water himself to rescue the struggling little wretch.

Newfoundland dogs were also highly regarded for their ability to save human lives during shipwrecks or bathing accidents. The struggle between life and death, with the helpless human in the hands of the hostile elements, when a compassionate brute creature takes his side and brings him to safety, was a subject that fascinated the Victorians. Heroic Newfoundland dogs were depicted in schoolbooks, on popular engravings, and in books on natural history. These dogs were considered not just brave and altruistic, but also extremely intelligent; a large proportion of the anecdotes of dogs told and re-told by the Victorian dog-fanciers were related to the extraordinary sagacity of the Newfoundland.

The Cult of the Newfoundland dog in popular culture reigned supreme throughout the nineteenth century. Some authors have suspected that this cult rest on far from solid foundations. Some of the unreferenced old yarns about super-intelligent Newfoundland dogs read more or less like fairy tales; were they equally devoid of factual foundation? Or could it be that these extraordinary Victorian Newfoundland dogs really capable of deductive intelligence and constructive thinking superior to what we today associate with dogs?

If you want to read about practical aspects of Newfoundland dog ownership, and get advice how to feed, groom and educate these animals, this book is not for you. Instead, it will resurrect the forgotten history of the Newfoundland dog, using original sources and illustrations to shed new light on this magnificent breed.[2]

CHAPTER 2.
THE ORIGINS AND EARLY HISTORY OF THE NEWFOUNDLAND DOG

> Form'd to dare the drifted snow,
> Or to breast the briny wave;
> Thine is merit passing show,
> Faithful, and acute, and brave!
>
> On the Newfoundland dog, from
> *Natural History of the Holy Land,*
> by Bernard Barton.

The Newfoundland dog is not an ancient breed, like the Chow Chow or the Saluki, but a relatively recent creation.[1] The province of Newfoundland was discovered by Vikings around the year 1000 AD, but there is no evidence that they were in possession of any dogs resembling Newfoundland dogs. There are a number of present-day Scandinavian breeds of hunting dogs, used for tracking bears and moose, like the Norsk Elghund (Norwegian Moose Dog) and the Karelsk Björnhund (Karelian Bear Dog). But these are medium-sized spitz breeds, and do not resemble Newfoundland dogs in the slightest. The animals were called 'bear dogs' because they were useful for hunting bears, not because the dogs were particularly bear-like themselves. It would not have been illogical for the Vikings to bring a few dogs along when they went out exploring, but it would not have made any sense for them to leave any of these animals behind when they departed. And even if a dog or two escaped, they would soon have been devoured by the Newfoundland wolves and bears.

In 1497, Newfoundland was rediscovered by John Cabot, who gave it its name; he mentions nothing about any indigenous breed of dogs. Not does Captain Richard Whitbourne in his 1620 *Discourse and Discovery of Newfoundland,* a most exhaustive treatise; had there been a distinctive breed of large dogs in Newfoundland at this time, he would surely have mentioned it. In particular, although he described the natives and their habits in great detail, he mentioned nothing about them possessing any dogs. Although many native American tribes kept dogs, there is nothing to suggest that the Beothuk, Newfoundland's indigenous people, kept any of those animals. Army captain George Cartwright, who made a report on the Beothuk in 1768, remarked that "providence has even denied them the pleasing services and companionship of the faithful dog." No dog remains have been found at Beothuk burial sites, and an examination of bones from Beothuk settlements has indicated that these have not been gnawed by dogs.[2]

As early as 1506, Europeans established fisheries at Rougnose and elsewhere in Newfoundland. It is reasonable to suggest that during the sixteenth and seventeenth centuries, dogs were regularly brought

THOSE AMAZING NEWFOUNDLAND DOGS

A Newfoundland dog, from Thomas Bewick's 1790 *History of Quadrupeds*.

to Newfoundland, by fishermen and various visitors. The local inhabitants soon found that large, strong dogs could be extremely useful allies, particularly if they were also good swimmers, enabling them to retrieve objects from the water, and to help with the fishing nets. The dogs needed a thick, water resistant coat to be able to swim in the icy waters. These early Newfoundland dogs were large, muscular beasts, useful as draught dogs and excellent in the water. The hardy animals were far from picky about their food, and liked eating raw fish from the nets. With time, the dogs developed, becoming more homogenous, with thicker fur, and greater prowess at swimming. The Newfoundlanders are likely to have appreciated that dogs with webbed feet swum better, and selected their breeding accordingly.

A Newfoundland dog by Philip Reinagle, from the *Sportsman's Cabinet* of 1803.

Similarly, double coats of fur insulated the dogs from the icy cold water, and an oily outer coat made them more buoyant. The dogs bred on the mainland were bulkier, often with white and black or white and brown spotted fur. Those bred on the St. Pierre and Miquelon islands were smaller and more retriever-like, and often solid black. The island of St. John had its own breed of dog: the St. John's water dog, which is the ancestor of today's Labrador and flat-coated retrievers.

* * *

Many cynologists have pondered which breeds of dog constitute the ancestors of the Newfoundland dog. Pyrenean mountain dogs were certainly used as ship's dogs in those days, and look not unlike early Newfoundland dogs, but they have double hind dew claws, a characteristic lacking in the Newfoundland. Another likely contributor is the Portuguese water dog, sharing the typical Newfoundland trait of having webbed feet. This breed today has both curly-haired and wavy-haired variants; the latter one is more Newfoundland-like. The today extinct Great Rough water dog looked quite Newfoundland-like, with long, curly fur and a large tail. It had webbed feet and was known as an excellent swimmer. In his *General History of Quadrupeds*, Thomas Bewick stated that the Great Rough water dog was web-footed and swam with great ease; it was used in hunting docks and other aquatic birds. From its aptness to retrieve, it was often used on board ship, for the purpose of recovering any object that has fallen overboard. It would have made perfect sense for the French and Basque fishermen to bring these dogs from these three breeds with them to Newfoundland as ship's dogs. Not only could the dogs make themselves useful on board ship, but they could also guard the nets and deal with snapping codfish that fell off the hook when they were dragged aboard the dory. In 1763, not less than 250 French fishing-boats were plying the Grand Banks off Newfoundland.

A study of the genetic structure of the purebred domestic dog clusters the Newfoundland with some other large mastiff-like breeds, like the rottweiler, bullmastiff and Bernese mountain dog, but provides no further clue about their ancestry.[3] Another study adds that the Newfoundland and several other large breeds are likely to be of the same blood lineage as the Tibetan mastiff. A believer in large-scale warfare, Genghis Khan brought not less than 30 000 of these mastiffs with him to Europe, for use as war dogs, and their descendants are the forefathers of Europe's mastiff-like large breeds.[4]

It is very likely, from the looks and behaviour of the early Newfoundland dogs, that there was also significant cross-breeding with Eskimo dogs. After all, one of the main early uses for Newfoundland dogs was as draught dogs, pulling sledges. For example, it is said of the early Newfoundlands that if one of them gave a howl, the rest of the pack immediately joined in. This sometimes works with today's Newfoundlands as well: try playing the popular Youtube recording of 'Lulu, the Singing Newfoundland' to a Newfoundland male, and you might be amazed at the result. But it should also be noted that many contemporary writers contrasted the fierce and unpredictable husky with the docile and intelligent Newfoundland dog.

In 1765, Major Robert Rogers' *Concise Account of North America* states that Newfoundland has few horses, but that the inhabitants instead make use of dogs "for the drawing of wood and other conveyances which they manage with great dexterity, fixing them in leather collars, to any number they please". Ten years later, the aforementioned George Cartwright also makes mention of a Newfoundland dog drawing a sled.[5]

* * *

The first certain mention of a Newfoundland dog in Britain is in the *Gentleman Farrier* from 1732, which states that "The Bear Dog is of a very large Size, commonly sluggish in his Looks, but he is very watchful, he comes from *Newfoundland*, his Business is to guard a Court or House, and has a thundering Voice when Strangers come near him, and does well to turn a Water Wheel."[6] Then there is a curious 1739 letter from Captain William Cleland, commanding the *Seahorse*. He wrote to the Navy Board about the loss of the imprest for his lieutenant, which he had put on his "cabbin table" and never seen again. "I can no ways account for this loss, but having a Newfoundland dog on board, which I believe must have destroyed it." The tale of this omnivorous dog, which obviously had access to Captain Cleland's 'cabbin', provides the first recorded use of the term 'Newfoundland dog'.[7]

A painting dated 1742, depicting what may well be an early Newfoundland dog, is kept at Ripley Castle in Yorkshire. The dog is white with a few large black spots; it has one brown eye and one blue one. The painting's inscription 'Windsor, Newfoundland' may well refer to where the dog was seen. A dog in John Zoffany's 1762 group portrait of the Rosoman family, with white fur and a black face mask, may well be a young Newfoundland.[8]

The earliest mention of a Newfoundland dog in the British Library's Burney Collection of early newspapers is from the *Daily Advertiser* of January 16, 1752: "Lost, a white rough puppy of the Newfoundland Breed". The year after, a Fulham gentleman lost "a large black Dog of the Newfoundland Breed, with some white spots about his head", answering to the name of Fearnought. In 1759, "A large black Dog of the Newfoundland Breed, with a white Star on his Breast, and a large Brass Collar" was lost; it was added that "he answers to the name of Ipswich". The earliest newspaper use of the term 'Newfoundland dog' took place in March 1760, according to the same collection of newspapers.

The early Newfoundland dogs imported into Britain were considered a distinct breed, although they were quite heterogenous: some were retriever-like, others were bulkier and had longer fur, and a few even resembled today's Newfoundlands. Many fur colour variations existed: white and black, white and brown, pure white, and even white and yellow. In his *General History of Quadrupeds*, Thomas Bewick described a Newfoundland dog he had encountered at Eslington, Northumberland. The dog was webfooted and could swim very fast and dive with great ease. It was very adept at retrieving objects from the bottom of the water. It was naturally fond of eating fish, both cooked and raw. In Newfoundland, Bewick wrote, these dogs were often used for draught, being able to pull large sledges loaded with timber without any human intervention. After delivering their load, they returned to the woods after being rewarded with some dried fish.

The English nobility and gentry were very much impressed with these early Newfoundland dogs: they were brave, strong and majestic in appearance, but also intelligent, affectionate and gentle. The dogs soon became fashionable and expensive. Keeping a Newfoundland dog seems to have been something of a status symbol in those days. The Earl of Home had a Newfoundland dog celebrated for catching salmon, sometimes retrieving twenty in a morning, a success rate that clearly annoyed Lord Tankerville, the owner of the fishing rights. He instituted a process against the dog, but when the case went to court, it was won by the four-legged defendant.[9]

A Newfoundland dog by J. Tookey, from John Church's 1798 *Cabinet of Quadrupeds*.

A Great Rough water dog.

CHAPTER 3.
SOME EARLY NEWFOUNDLAND DOGS IN BRITAIN

> Thus when a little forward puppy meets
> A noble Newfoundland dog in the streets,
> He barks impotently – then stops:
> Now barks again, then on he pops;
> Runs up and smells, and then
> Stops – barks – and runs again;
> Takes another smell, and seems t'intreat him
> To pass politely, or else he'll eat him.
>
> The Newfoundland dog, conscious of his might,
> Cocks high his tail and ears, his state to show;
> Then lifts his leg (a little unpolite)
> And almost drowns the saucy dog below; -
>
> Then seems in full blown majesty to say,
> 'Great is my power, but lo! I'll not abuse it;
> I'm *Criticus*! – Go, *Leonard*, on thy way
> But mind, I can devour thee, if I chose it!
>
> A dog-gerel poem by 'Juvenis Canicula',
> from the *Hull Packet*, September 17,
> 1810. It was inspired by a quarrel between
> two newspaper writers calling themselves
> Criticus and Leonard, and Juvenis
> Canicula took the part of the former.

In October 1789, the young student William Phillips was visiting Portsmouth. He came from a wealthy family and studied theology in Oxford. For some reason or other, he wanted to go bathing in the sea, although he could not swim. The consequences of his actions were graphically described by the *London Chronicle*:

> "A few days ago Mr. Phillips, of Northumberland-street, was bathing in the sea at Portsmouth, he was suddenly seized with the cramp, and sunk twice; which being perceived by the man attending the bathing machine, he jumped in to his assistance. Mr. Phillips caught hold of him, and so entangled both, that it was with great difficulty the man could preserve even his own life. A large Newfoundland dog seeing the danger Mr. Phillips was in, after the man had left him, jumped in and caught hold of his bathing-cap, and with the assistance of the tide, which was

flowing, brought him safe to shore. Mr. Phillips purchased the dog, and liberally rewarded the man who had endeavoured to save him." [1]

The *Bath Chronicle* agrees that Mr Phillips had got out of his depth while bathing in the sea, that a large Newfoundland pulled by to shore by his bathing-cap, and that Mr Phillips purchased the noble animal.[2] But according to another newspaper, the dog actually grabbed Mr Phillips by the hair:

"Fortunately, however, a person who had a Newfoundland dog with him, learning of the dreadful situation of the gentleman, directed the dog to the place where he was sinking, who dived after him, seized him by part of the hair, and brought him to shore. The necessary steps being taken, his recovery was soon effected. – Thus a valuable life was saved by the sagacity and power of that useful animal, which in this case as in many others, proved superior to human endeavours."[3]

MR PHILLIPPS'S DOG FRIEND.
Who rescued Him from the Sea in Portsmouth Harbour, October 4th 1789.

Mr Phillips' dog 'Friend'; a print after George Morland's painting.

The Newfoundland dog that saved Mr Phillips was named 'Tiger', but the student did not think that such a fierce-sounding name suited the philanthropic animal, so he renamed his canine rescuer 'Friend'. When he became Vicar of Eling, in Hampshire not far from Southampton, in 1803, he brought the dog with him. He commissioned the artist George Morland to paint the dog's portrait; it was later engraved by Bartolozzi as 'Mr Phillips' Dog Friend'.[4] The painting shows the dog looking out over the water, perhaps searching for other wealthy young theology students to rescue. Friend's pointed muzzle and pricked ears are not very Newfoundland-like. When Morland's painting of Friend was exhibited in London in 1894, it was still owned by the Phillips family.[5]

After Friend had died, the Rev. Mr Phillips had him buried in the vicarage grounds, overlooking the Southampton water. Perhaps inspired by Lord Byron and 'Boatswain', he later erected a fine monument to his life-saving dog, with a stone statue of Friend and the inscription:

> In Memory
> of a Newfoundland dog
> Formerly called 'Tiger', afterwards 'Friend',
> Eminently qualified
> By acuteness of sight, quickness of eye,
> Strength of body, and peculiar sagacity
> For every duty of his species.

> Who on the fourteenth day of October, 1789,
> When one to whom he was yet a stranger,
> But was in a short time to be his master,
> Had unconsciously been carried out of his depth
> While bathing in the sea at Portsmouth,
> And being unable to swim
> His strength became exhausted and his senses
> Overpowered
> By long struggling with the waves,
> Rushed spontaneously to his assistance,
> Seized him by the hair.
> Brought him cautiously and steadily to the shore,
> And thus saved him from imminent death,
> From gratitude
> ------ the preserver -----
>   ------ guardian of -----
> who ----- age, the 6th -----
> ----- Phillips,
> Caused this monument to be erected
>   Over his remains which are here deposited, A.D. 1810.

Himself, the Rev. Mr Phillips lived to be very old, serving as Vicar for not less than 43 years before his death in 1853. Thus the fortunate rescue by Friend back in 1789 had prolonged his life by not less than 64 years.

It is notable that in memory of their ancestor's escape, a branch of the Phillips family took the crest of a Newfoundland dog, and the motto of "Auspice Deo extuli maro", meaning "God being my leader, I brought him out of the sea", in memory of the rescue of their ancestor.[6] An Internet version gives a different, possibly garbled account:

> "A Mr. William Phillips, while bathing at Portsmouth, ventured out too far, and was in imminent peril. Two boatmen, instead of starting off to assist him, selfishly strove to make a hard bargain with some of the bystanders, who urged them. While the parley was going on, a Newfoundland dog, seeing the danger, plunged into the water, and saved the struggling swimmer.

The Eling monument to a heroic Newfoundland dog, from *Animal World*, April 1908.

It is pleasantly told that Mr. Phillips, in gratitude for his deliverance, bought the dog from his owner, a butcher, and thereafter gave an annual festival, at which the dog was assigned the place of honour, with a good ration of beefsteaks.

He had a picture of the dog painted by Morland, and engraved by Bartolozzi; and on all his table linen he had this picture worked in the tissue, with the motto, 'Virum extuli mari.' Several paintings of the dog by Morland are still in the possession of various family members, not only descendants of William but also those of his brother George. In addition to the paintings William had a crest designed (not to be confused with the arms) that showed a dog saving a drowning man."[7]

In 1908, when the Rev. Thomas Thistle submitted a photograph of Friend's monument to the RSPCA's journal *Animal World*, the inscription was fast disappearing. Presuming that Friend had died in 1810, the year his monument was erected, Thistle presumed that the dog had survived to a very unusual age.[8] But the truth is likely to be that the monument had been erected several years after Friend died and was buried in the vicarage grounds. In the 1990s, when Newfoundland dog enthusiasts Freda Pratt and Carol Cooper made inquiries what had happened to Friend's monument, they found that the vicarage had been turned into flats and the grounds 'developed'. A modern bungalow stood where Friend's monument had once been. It was rumoured, however, that the stone dog had been taken care of by a descendant of the Rev. Mr Phillips, and erected in the grounds of a house in Kent.[9]

* * *

During a winter storm in 1799, a ship out of Newcastle was driven onto the rocks and wrecked near Yarmouth. The only survivor was a Newfoundland dog, which had swum to shore carrying the captain's pocket-book in his mouth. Several of the bystanders attempted to take it from him, but he would not part with it. At length, selecting one person from the crowd, whose appearance probably pleased him, he leaped against his breast in a fawning manner, and delivered the book to his care. The dog immediately returned to the place where he had landed, watching for all the things that came from

The Newfoundland dog brings the Captain's wallet ashore from the ship, a vignette from the 1873 edition of Edward Jesse's *Anecdotes of Dogs*.

the wrecked vessel, seizing them and endeavouring to bring them to land. For days, he remained on guard on the beach, plunging into the waves to retrieve various large pieces of wreckage. Politician Lord Grenville, who was in the area on some business or other, went to see the shipwrecked dog. He was the son of Whig Prime Minister George Grenville, and himself entered the House of Commons in 1782. In 1789, Grenville briefly served as Speaker of the House of Commons, before he entered the cabinet as Home Secretary. He became Leader of the House of Lords when he was raised to the peerage the next year as Baron Grenville. In 1791, he succeeded the Duke of Leeds as Foreign Secretary.

Lord Grenville decided to take care of the shipwrecked dog, renamed him Tippo, and installed him at stately Dropmore Park, near Cliveden in Buckinghamshire. When Tippo expired several years later, Lord Grenville built him an elaborate monument, with an eloquent Latin inscription written by the erudite Peer himself. It was translated in Edward Jesse's *Anecdotes of Dogs*:

> Here, stranger, pause, nor view with scornful eyes
> The stone which marks where faithful Tippo lies.
> Freely kind Nature gave each liberal grace,
> Which most ennobles and exalts our race,
> Excelling strength and beauty joined in me,
> Ingenuous worth, and firm fidelity.
> Nor shame I to have borne a tyrant's name,
> Cast by a fatal storm on Tenby's coast,
> Reckless of life, I wailed my master lost.
> Whom long contending with the o'erwhelming wave
> In vain with fruitless love I strove to save.
> I, only I, alas! surviving bore,
> His dying trust, his tablets, to the shore.
> Kind welcome from the Belgian race I found,
> Who, once in times remote, to British ground
> Strangers like me came from a foreign strand.
> I loved at large along the extended sand
> To roam, and oft beneath the swelling wave,
> Tho' known so fatal once, my limbs to lave;
> Or join the children in their summer play,
> First in their sports, companion of their way.
> Thus while from many a hand a meal I sought,
> Winter and age had certain misery brought;
> But Fortune smiled, a safe and blest abode
> A new-found master's generous love bestowed,
> And midst these shades, where smiling flow'rets bloom.[10]

Following Pitt's death in 1806, Lord Grenville became the head of the 'Ministry of All the Talents', a short-lived coalition between various scheming politicians that was overthrown in March 1807. In the years after the fall of the ministry, Grenville continued in opposition, but he never again returned to the cabinet. His political career was ended by a stroke in 1823, but he served as Chancellor of the University of Oxford from 1810 until his death in 1834. Dropmore Park faced hard times after the Grenvilles left, with various later owners not taking proper care of the grand old stately home. In the 1990s, it was ravaged by fire and well-nigh derelict, but the restoration company Corporate Estates purchased the building and converted it into luxury flats. Although the estate was also developed, with 57 new homes built, the monument to Tippo is still present in the grounds. A list of monuments at Dropmore describes it as a "carved stone sarcophagus with garlands and long Latin inscription now illegible and ram's heads at corners"[11]

In contrast to these canophilic English gentlemen, the Newfoundlanders themselves were not overly concerned about their dogs. The animals were worked hard and fed the most unpromising diet, like the offal of cod. Since the dogs bred like rabbits, there was soon significant canine overpopulation in these parts. Some of the more unscrupulous and penurious Newfoundlanders allowed their dogs to roam free, to scavenge for scraps and terrorize the neighbours. The problem with the unruly dogs soon amounted to such proportions that in 1780, the Governor prohibited the keeping of more than one dog, and authorized the destruction of ownerless animals scavenging for food. When they learnt that Newfoundland dogs were quite highly valued in England, the Newfoundlanders exported the dogs in increasing quantities. When the timber ships from Newfoundland arrived in Poole and other harbours, they were met by crowds of dog-fanciers, eager to snap up a fine specimen.

* * *

James Macnamara, a young Irish gentleman, joined the Royal Navy at the age of just fourteen. Being promoted to lieutenant in 1788, and to post-captain in 1795, he served with distinction in the American War of Independence, and in the French Revolutionary and Napoleonic wars, under admirals such as Lord Hood and Lord Nelson. In February 1803, Captain Macnamara was put on half-pay after the Peace of Amiens. He was a Newfoundland dog enthusiast, and kept one of these animals on board his latest command, the frigate Cerberus. The dog accompanied him as he went ashore and settled in London.

On the afternoon of April 6 1803, Captain Macnamara went for a ride in Hyde Park, accompanied by his Newfoundland dog. As ill-luck would have it, Colonel Montgomery, of the 9th Regiment of Guards, was also taking a ride that particular day, accompanied by another large Newfoundland. The dogs took an instant dislike to each other, and started a furious fight. Captain Macnamara's dog got the upper hand in the fracas, but the Colonel bravely managed to separate the animals, striking the Captain's dog with a small cane as he did so. A witness heard Colonel Montgomery call out 'Whose dog is this?' Captain Macnamara answered 'It is my dog.' Colonel Montgomery said 'If you do not call your dog off I shall send him sprawling.' Captain Macnamara replied 'Have you the arrogance, Sir, to say you will send my dog sprawling? 'I certainly shall, Sir, if he falls on my dog!' asserted the Colonel. 'If you send my dog sprawling, Sir, I will send *you* sprawling!' the Captain replied. Those were fighting words.

Lord Buckhurst, who was also taking exercise in Hyde Park, came up to calm the two angry officers down. His Lordship heard Captain Macnamara say that the way in which Colonel Montgomery had desired him to call off his dog was arrogant, and not in language fit to be used by one gentleman towards another. Captain Macnamara said he would as soon revenge an insult as any man, and would fight Colonel Montgomery as well as any other man who offered him an injury. Captain Macnamara was shaking his stick, but it appeared to be an involuntary action, the consequence of his anger and excitement, and not intended as an insult. Together, the three gentlemen proceeded to Piccadilly, where Colonel Montgomery and Captain Macnamara gave their names to each other, with the intention to fight a duel. A witness heard Colonel Montgomery say 'It is not my intention to quarrel with you, but if your dog falls on mine I shall knock him down.'

The two gentlemen arranged to meet, with pistols, at Primrose Hill, at half past six the very same day. Neither Lord Buckhurst nor any other person was able to talk any sense into them, or to impart the message that it was foolhardy to risk their lives because of a scrap between two Newfoundland dogs. Duelling was outlawed in Britain at this time, so the victor would face a trial for murder or manslaughter. Both officers were tough, battle-hardened veterans, who took their honour as gentlemen very seriously indeed. They were also crack shots: in the first exchange of fire, the Captain was wounded in the groin, but the Colonel received a lethal shot in the chest.

For this regrettable duel over two Newfoundland dogs, Captain Macnamara was tried for manslaughter at the Old Bailey on April 22. He could not deny that he had shot Colonel Montgomery in a duel, but he eloquently addressed the jury:

> "Gentlemen, I am a captain in the British Navy. My character you can hear only from others; but to maintain any character in that station I must be respected. When called upon to lead others into honourable dangers I must not be supposed to be a man who had sought safety by submitting to what custom has taught others to consider as a disgrace. I am not presuming to urge anything against the laws of God, or of this land. I know that, in the eye of religion and reason, obedience to the law, though against the general feelings of the world, is the first duty, and ought to be the rule of action; but in putting a construction upon my motives, so as to ascertain the quality of my actions, you will make allowance for my situation."

Both Lord Hood and Lord Nelson appeared in court as character witnesses, speaking highly of Captain Macnamara, as did some of the Lords of the Admirality. As a result, common sense prevailed on this occasion, and the Captain was acquitted.[12]

Captain Macnamara returned to sea on the renewal of the war, presumably bringing his pugnacious Newfoundland dog with him. He served with distinction in the Baltic, and in 1811, his flotilla of cruising frigates drove on shore and destroyed a French frigate. In 1814, Macnamara was promoted to rear-admiral, although he saw no further active service. Admiral Macnamara married in 1818, but died prematurely at Clifton, Bristol, in 1826.

* * *

Princess Frederica Charlotte was born in 1767, formally the only daughter of Crown Prince Frederick William of Prussia, and his first wife Elisabeth Christine of Brunswick-Lüneburg. Whether she was really the daughter of Frederick William is a matter of conjecture, since her mother led an immoral life and enjoyed many affairs with various men. In 1769, when the Crown Princess again became pregnant, she planned to escape from Prussia with her lover, but she was betrayed and captured. After the divorce had quickly been granted, she was placed under house arrest in the castle of Stettin, where she remained for the next 71 years until her death in 1840, aged 93. Frederica Charlotte never saw her mother again. According to the custom of the time, an arranged marriage was negotiated for Princess Frederica Charlotte; it was her misfortune that she was betrothed to Frederick Duke of York, the second son of George III. This was the notorious 'Grand Old' Duke of York, who once commanded ten thousand men and marched them about in a random manner during the disastrous Flanders campaign of 1793. The short but eloquent poem:

> My name is York, I draw a cork
> Much better than I fight,
> The soldiers know and so do you
> That what I say is right!

gives a fair reflection of what the soldiers thought of him. The Duke later disgraced himself further through getting involved in a swindle to sell military commissions, run by his mistress Mary Ann Clarke. Since this

The 1805 engraving of Nelson's head, by George Orme after Charles Turner, after H.B. Chalon.

THOSE AMAZING NEWFOUNDLAND DOGS

A print of George Stubbs' painting of Nelson.

dismal Duke kept several other mistresses, and sired a number of bastard children, the Duchess soon had enough of him: they separated, and she settled down at Oatlands Park in Weybridge. Their relationship after separation appears to have been amicable, but there was never any question of reconciliation.

Frederica Duchess of York was reasonably clever and well-informed. She did not care for fashionable London life, preferring the rural surroundings at Oatlands. She disliked all form and ceremony, but in the midst of the most familiar intercourse she always preserves a certain dignity of manner. A great friend of animals, Frederica was particularly fond of dogs. At Oatlands, she kept at least forty of these animals, from the massive Newfoundland dog Nelson to the most diminutive breeds. Nelson is said to have been imported from Newfoundland, and to have been one of the largest dogs in Britain. Henry Grenville wrote that: "Her dogs are her greatest interest and amusement, and she has at least forty of various kinds ... it is impossible to offend her or annoy her more than by ill-using any of the dogs, and if she was to see anybody beat or kick any one of them she would never forgive it." The Oatlands dogs ran free at all times, to the detriment of the night's sleep of the house-guests of the Duchess, as expressed by dandy and diarist Thomas Raikes: "many a morning have I, to my annoyance, been awakened from an incipient slumber, by the noisy pack rushing along the gallery next to my bedroom, at the call of old Dawe the footman to their morning meal." The notorious bully and duellist Baron Hompesch tried to insinuate himself into the favours of the Duchess, by giving her a black dog named Satan, with the poem:

> Satan! at her feet we depose our wiles
> All must be good when Frederica smiles
> The very saints rejoice and chant aloud in Heaven
> By Hompesch Satan's self is to an angel given.

A print depicting the Duchess of York with some of her dogs, the large Newfoundland Nelson prominent among them, a rather worn print (or book illustration) from Stroehling's

It is not known whether he had any success in this intrigue, but at least she accepted the dog: Satan's inscribed collar is today kept at the Weybridge Museum.

The Duchess of York was of course keen that the likeness of her favourite Nelson would be preserved for posterity, by the leading animal painters in the land. The first to come was the 79-year-old George Stubbs, who had enjoyed a long and lucrative career painting the favourite animals of various wealthy magnates. Stubbs is today recognized as one of the greatest British painters of horses and dogs. The massive Nelson was probably the biggest dog Stubbs had ever painted. In his remarkable 'Portrait of a Newfoundland dog', the scale of the sturdy animal is indicated by the primroses and briars that grow beneath his feet. Interestingly, this very impressive dog looks very much like a present-day Newfoundland, except that his tail is rather curved over his back. Like Morland and Taplin before him, Stubbs indicated Nelson's Newfoundland heritage by portraying him looking out over a lake. At the sale of the Duke of York's effects at Christie's in April 1827, Stubbs' 'Portrait of a Newfoundland dog, size of life' was sold for just £18 18s. to the Duke's friend (Sir) Thomas Sherlock Gooch MP. Remarkably, it stayed in the same family for many years. It was believed lost before being exhibited at Gainsborough House, Sudbury, in the 1980s.[13] It passed by direct descent to Sir John Gooch, 12th Baronet, and was sold by his executors at Sotheby's in 1999, fetching a cool £2.2 million.

The next painter to give Nelson attention was the 35-year-old Henry Bernard Chalon, who had studied at the Royal Academy Schools and become a specialist in sporting and animal painting. He had been appointed Animal Painter to the Duchess of York in 1795. Chalon admired Stubbs and tried to imitate his style, with a variable degree of success. He is likely to have visited Oatlands in 1804, to add to Nelson's iconography. His painting of Nelson may well have been the one exhibited at the Royal Academy in 1816 as 'Portrait of Nelson, a famous Newfoundland dog, the property of His R.H. the Duke of York'. At the sale of the Duke of York's effects in 1827, it fetched just £6 6s. In June 1832, it was part of the collection of the wealthy magnate George Watson Taylor, at stately Erlestoke Park in Wiltshire. It was seen there by the visiting William Beckford, and according to a newspaper article, the Fonthill aesthete "was also much struck with a Newfoundland dog in the dining-room, painted by H.B. Chalon, from one of the largest of its kind in the kingdom. This painting was a great favourite of the late Duke of York, and is strikingly correct."[14] It is a great pity that this important painting cannot be traced today. Another painter, Charles Turner, copied the dog's head and had it engraved by George Orme in January 1805.

Peter Edward Stroehling, a German portrait painter, had come to London in 1803 to seek his fortune. He soon managed to get some notable commissions, including a portrait of King George III at Windsor Castle with an adoring spaniel, and a singularly unflattering portrait of Queen Charlotte. In 1807, he came to Oatlands to paint Duchess Frederica. In Stroehling's felicitous portrait, she is portrayed with some of her dogs: the massive Nelson, a poodle, and a little lap-dog. The dog's colouring shows that this is clearly the same Nelson that was painted by Stubbs. The Stroehling painting belongs to the Royal Collection. It is another important image of one of the finest Newfoundland dogs in Britain at the time, again showing Nelson looking very much like a present-day Newfoundland, with his large head, luxuriant fur and long tail. The dog tilting his head as the Duchess scratches him behind the ear adds realism and charm to the painting.

The obscure Leeds artist Charles Henry Schwanfelder had started out helping his father paint decorated clock faces and snuff boxes, before achieving some success as an artist, being appointed animal painter to the Prince Regent in 1816. It is not known when he painted the portrait 'Nelson with a Terrier', showing a sturdy Newfoundland dog carrying a tree branch in its mouth, and playing with a small terrier. The dog looks quite like the Nelson painted by Stubbs and Stroehling, but cannot be conclusively stated to be the same animal. Finally, the Bavarian artist Benjamin Zobel painted 'Nelson, the favourite dog of the Duke of York'. The image of this large and sturdy Newfoundland was stated to have been "very singularly and naturally executed in marble dust by Zobel." Sold along with other of the Duke's paintings in 1827, it found its way into the collection of the Southampton eccentric William Burrough Hill in the 1920s.[15] This dog's colouring is clearly quite different from that of the original Nelson, proving that the Duke and Duchess of York had (at least) two Newfoundlands, both named Nelson, and that Zobel (and possibly also Chalon) painted Nelson II. It may well be that Chalon painted both Nelson I and Nelson II; it seems odd that a painting finished in 1804 would not be exhibited until 1816. The Duchess of York buried her dogs in the still preserved dog cemetery at Oatlands Park, and a list of the names of the dogs shows that there were two Nelsons.[16]

CHAPTER 4.
NEW LIGHT ON LORD BYRON AND 'BOATSWAIN'

When some proud Son of Man returns to Earth,
Unknown by Glory, but upheld by Birth,
The sculptor's art exhausts the pomp of woe,
And storied urns record who rests below.
When all is done, upon the Tomb is seen,
Not what he was, but what he should have been.
But the poor Dog, in life the firmest friend,
The first to welcome, foremost to defend,
Whose honest heart is still his Master's own,
Who labours, fights, lives, breathes for him alone,
Unhonoured falls, unnoticed all his worth,
Denied in heaven the Soul he held on earth –
While man, vain insect! hopes to be forgiven,
And claims himself a sole exclusive heaven.

From Lord Byron's epitaph to Boatswain.

Lord Byron was another of the many upper-class Englishmen who wanted a Newfoundland dog. He had been very fond of animals, particularly dogs, from an early age. When he was a Cambridge undergraduate, he was annoyed that the university regulations prohibited the keeping of dogs. Since the statutes made no mention of bears, he installed a tame bear in his rooms instead, without the authorities being able to interfere. The bear seems to have conducted itself with decorum; in a letter, Byron even suggested that his ursine friend should sit for a fellowship.

At his family seat, the rambling Newstead Abbey, Lord Byron kept quite a menagerie of animals. His predecessor, the fifth Baron, had kept a tame wolf, and a descendent of this animal, named Lyon, was in residence. Noted for his fierceness, this bad-tempered wolf-dog hybrid had once torn the backside off Byron's breeches. Lord Byron also kept two Newfoundland dogs, named Boatswain and Thunder, and the canine population at Newstead sometimes also included the fierce mastiff Nelson and Mrs Byron's fox-terrier Gilpin. Both Boatswain and Thunder are likely to have been imported from Newfoundland. According to Byron, Boatswain had been born there in May 1803, and was resident at Newstead at least since early 1806. A tenant farmer at Newstead told that at the Upper Lake, he sometimes saw the poet get into the boat with his two noble Newfoundland dogs, row into the middle of the lake, and tumble into the water, having the two dogs seize him by the coat and drag him away to land. When Byron went to visit his friend Edward Long at Little Hampton in Sussex, he was accompanied by his favourite Boatswain. When the poet practiced with pistols, shooting at oyster shells by a tall pier, Boatswain

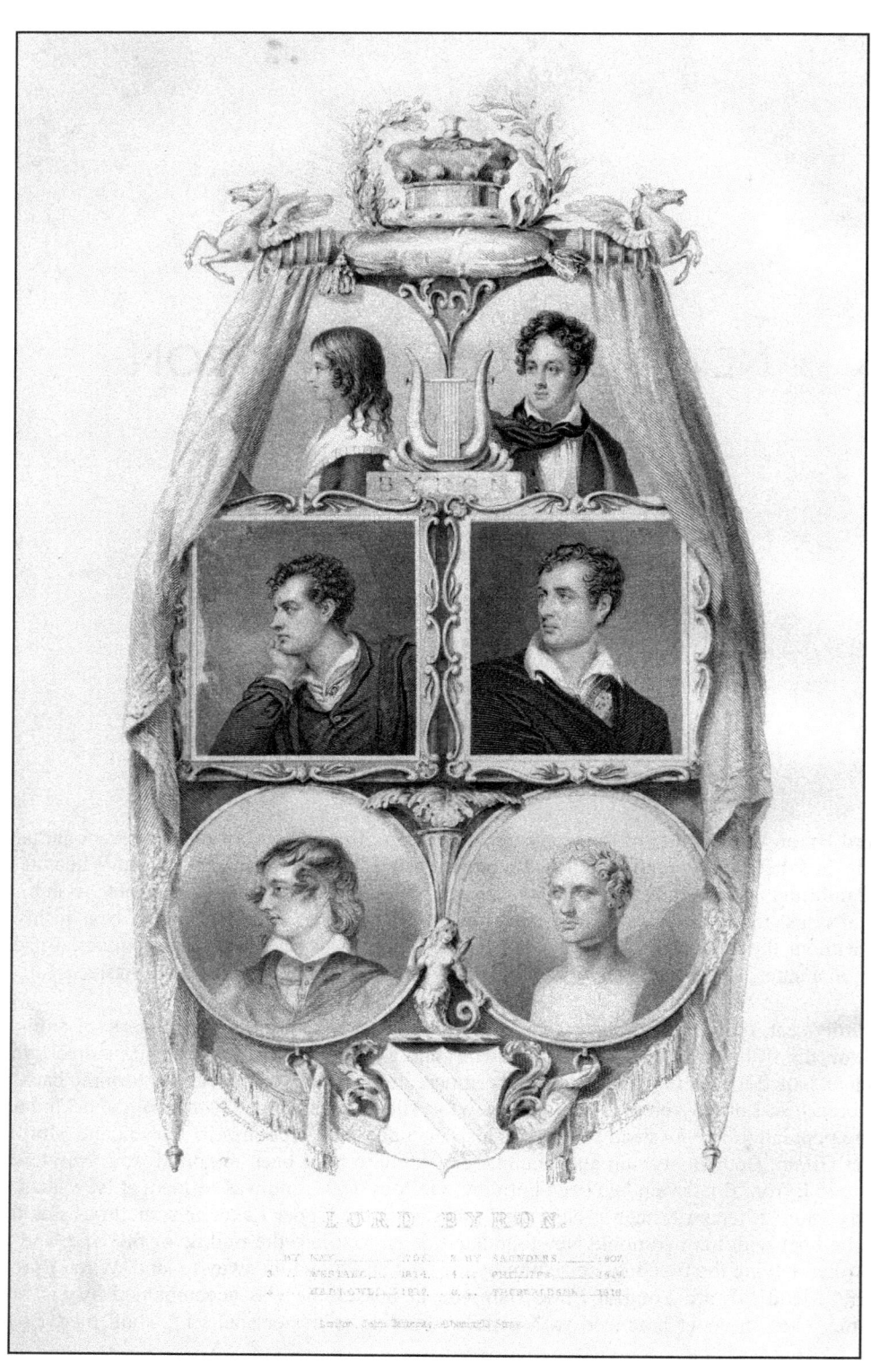

Various images of Lord Byron, from Byron's *Life and Letters*.

Lord Byron and Boatswain, a fanciful representation reproduced by permission of Nottingham City Museums and Galleries, Newstead Abbey.

leapt into the water from the pier, a feat Long could not persuade his own dog to perform.

Less valorously, Byron used his two Newfoundland dogs to bait the tame bear. A former Newstead servant remembered that Thunder, although the larger of the two dogs, was less courageous than Boatswain. The brass collars of both dogs, which were sold by auction at Newstead in 1903 for twenty-one and four guineas respectively, are still kept at Newstead Abbey.[1] They have been severely battered, probably through the dogs' scraps with the bear, with each other, and with other large dogs. It does not appear as if Boatswain was ever chained or put in a kennel. He went where it pleased him to go, seeking out other large dogs to fight, or bitches to mate with. Byron's friend Elizabeth Pigot once wrote that Boatswain had enjoyed another battle with a dog named Tippoo, at the House of Correction, coming off the conqueror. Mrs Byron's fox-terrier Gilpin was Boatswain's particular enemy. When Byron lived with his mother at Burgage Manor in Southwell, Boatswain fought Gilpin all over Burgage Green, until the opponents were finally separated by Elizabeth Pigot's brother Henry.

Since Boatswain took every opportunity to attack and worry his fierce little opponent, Mrs Byron was fearful her little dog would be killed. She sent Boatswain and her son's other two dogs away to a servant when Lord Byron went back to university. But one morning, the servant was alarmed to find that Boatswain had gone missing. It turned out that he had gone all the way to Newstead to fetch Gilpin, and that the two had become good friends. Byron's biographers have used this story to illustrate Boatswain's magnanimous nature, but an explanation more consistent with modern notions of canine behaviour is that there had been some fighting between the two dogs before Gilpin had been forced to accept a lower position in the canine hierarchy. When Boatswain returned to Newstead, probably to look for his generously filled food-bowl there, he met Gilpin, whose nature was to follow the pack leader. Later, Boatswain protected the pack member Gilpin against other dogs, a task which the quarrelsome nature of the little terrier rendered no sinecure.[2]

* * *

Lord Byron seems to have been quite an irresponsible dog owner, even by Georgian standards, allowing his large, fierce dogs to roam free and terrorize the neighbourhood. The concept that it was advisable to have some degree of control over a large and potentially aggressive dog seems to have been entirely alien to the poet's mind. The mastiff Nelson had to wear a muzzle most of the time, since he was quite ferocious and intractable. Once, Byron amused himself by removing the muzzle and helping Nelson to wreck the room of a friend of the poet's, who was staying at Newstead. There was a jealous feud between Nelson and Boatswain, which one day exploded into a ferocious fight when Nelson was unmuzzled. If Lord Byron and his friends had not parted the dogs, by thrusting pokers and tongs into the mouth of each, either dog might have died. Boatswain's feud with Nelson continued until the unpredictable mastiff was shot dead, after he had tried to kill one of Lord Byron's horses.

After returning to Cambridge in the summer of 1807, Byron left his dogs Boatswain and Bran (a replacement for Nelson) at Southwell, where they were taken care of by the groom Charles Monk. Byron's friend and neighbour Elizabeth Pigot, who regularly corresponded with him about the dogs, also seems to have been very fond of Boatswain. The great dog, who roamed free as always, often visited Elizabeth and her brother at their cottage nearby. Once, when Elizabeth Pigot was having tea with some elderly lady friends, Boatswain frightened them by suddenly jumping in through an open window. He approached them wagging his tail, perhaps hoping to share their meal, but since the timid old ladies objected to his presence, Elizabeth managed to decoy the great dog out of the room by opening the door and exclaiming 'Cat Bos'n!'

The best likeness of Lord Byron's favourite dog is the portrait of Boatswain by the Nottingham artist

Boatswain's collar, reproduced by permission of Nottingham City Museums and Galleries, Newstead Abbey.

Clifton Tomson, painted in the summer of 1808. It depicts a very strange-looking animal indeed; today, Boatswain would not have won the five-hundreth prize at a Newfoundland dog show. His head is too small, his fur too short, his ears the wrong shape, and his tail too curled. It was sometimes said at the time that any dog as big as a donkey and as furry as a bear could be called a Newfoundland dog. But although the Newfoundlands were quite heterogenous at the time, Boatswain was certainly an extreme, perhaps even a Newfoundland-husky cross. In contrast to the shrewd Duchess of York, who had selected Nelson, perhaps the finest Newfoundland available in Britain at the time, Lord Byron had been 'sold a pup' in more ways than one by some unscrupulous dog dealer!

Since the dog in the 'Boatswain' portrait looks so very unlike a Newfoundland, there has been speculation that perhaps there had been a mix-up or substitution of paintings at some stage. Tomson's portrait is well authenticated, however, and Lord Byron would hardly have valued a portrait of his favourite that looked quite unlike the dog in real life. What settles the matter is a series of drawings of Byron and Boatswain, made by their friend Elizabeth Pigot in March 1807. In one of these, Byron comes back from playing cricket, to find Boatswain eating his dinner from a large plate. The dog looks just like the animal depicted by Tomson. Elizabeth Pigot calls Byron and Boatswain 'the wonderful pair': Byron was a person of fame and renown, and his favourite Boatswain was well known in town.[3]

The portrait of Boatswain at Newstead Abbey, reproduced by permission of Nottingham City Museums and Galleries, Newstead Abbey.

She also emphasizes the close relationship between them:

> Lord Byron look's pleas'd, I know what he saw,
> 'Twas Bo'sen, who instantly gave him his paw,
> He patted his head with affectionate hand.
> Says he, 'You're the very best dog in the Land.'

* * *

In spite of their idealization of their hero's relation with his favourite dog, Lord Byron's biographers are right that their hero, who treated the women in his life so very caddishly, was remarkably fond of his Newfoundland dog. When at university, he often wrote to his mother and to Elizabeth Pigot, asking for news about Boatswain, the 'Phoenix of Canine Quadrupeds'.

It has been speculated by the descendants of Lord Byron's publisher John Murray that when asked for a lock of his hair by his female admirers, the poetical peer cut off some of Boatswain's fur instead.[4] If this is at all true, Byron must have made sure that he used only black fur, since otherwise his lady friends would have become fearful that his hair had gone white overnight, an obscure medical phenomenon mentioned by Byron himself in his poem about the Prisoner of Chillon.

Boatswain sometimes went into Mansfield, to do mischief and to fight other large dogs. In November 1808, he fought one too many, at Mansfield market-place, and caught hydrophobia. Returning to Newstead, Boatswain was seized by "a fit of madness". It is recorded that Byron, who was unaware of the nature of the malady, wiped the slaver from Boatswain's jaws more than once during his paroxysms. Poor Boatswain died on November 11 (not on November 18, as claimed on his monument). In a letter to his friend Francis Hodson, to announce the death of his favourite dog, Byron assured him that Boatswain had retained all the gentleness of his nature to the last, and did not attempt to do any injury to the people surrounding him.

Lord Byron's friend John Cam Hobhouse wrote a prose epitaph to Boatswain, pointing out Boatswain's undaunted courage and belligerent nature. Being of a nature truly heroic, the great dog had emerged victorious from fifty pitched battles. He had died in his fifth year, but still lived long enough for his glory. Lord Byron only used the bottom four lines, however, and substituted a better epitaph of his own:

Boatswain being given a hearty meal by Lord Byron's servants, an amusing vignette from the children's book *Memoires d'un Caniche*.

> Near this Spot
> Are deposited the Remains of one
> Who possessed Beauty without Vanity
> Strength without Insolence
> Courage without Ferocity
> And all the virtues of Man without his Vices
> This praise which would be unmeaning Flattery
> If inscribed over human Ashes
> Is but a just tribute to the Memory of
> BOATSWAIN, a DOG,
> Who was born in Newfoundland May 1803
> and died at Newstead Nov. 18, 1808.

Lord Byron had a fine monument and vault constructed at Newstead, inscribed with Boatswain's epitaph, in poetry and prose:

> Oh man! thou feeble tenant of an hour,
> Debased by slavery, or corrupt by power –
> Who knows thee well must quit thee with disgust,
> Degraded mass of animated dust!
> Thy love is lust, thy friendship all a cheat,
> Thy tongue hypocrisy, thy heart deceit!
> By nature vile, ennobled but by name,
> Each kindred brute might bid thee blush for shame.
> Ye, who perchance behold this simple urn,
> Pass on – it honors none you wish to mourn.
> To mark a friend's remains these stones arise;
> I never knew but one – and here he lies.

Another view of Boatswain's Tomb, from an old postcard

The inscription on Boatswain's monument, from an early postcard. Reproduced by permission of Nottingham City Museums and Galleries, Newstead Abbey.

Boatswain's monument at Newstead Abbey, from an old postcard.

Boatswain's Tomb, from a postcard stamped and posted in 1913.

Since Lord Byron had been so remarkably fond of the great dog, he instructed that his own remains should one day be interred in Boatswain's tomb, but this did not happen, since the debt-ridden Peer had to sell Newstead in 1817. After the poet's untimely demise in Greece, his remains were embalmed and brought back to London, where his body lay in state for two days. The Deans of St Paul's and Westminster Abbey both refused to take it, due to Byron's reputation for immorality. Instead, Lord Byron was buried in the family vault in the church of Saint Mary Magdalene, Hucknall. Boatswain's Tomb is still standing today, and has not changed since Lord Byron's days. When it was opened for restoration purposes in 1987, some bones from a dog were found; Boatswain was still waiting for his master to join him in their Newstead tomb.

* * *

There has been much conjecture why Byron was inspired to write such an elaborate epitaph for his favourite dog.[5] Epitaphs on deceased pet animals, either humorous or sentimental, were actually quite popular at the time. The monumental tomb of Serpent, a favourite dog of Lady Stepney, had an epitaph dated 1750; the Earl of Carlisle wrote a poem for the monument to a favourite spaniel; and John Gay wrote the *Elegy of a Lap-dog*. The *Poems* of G.D. Harley, published in 1796, contained a 14-page elegy on his Newfoundland dog Dash.

Nor was Byron the first to use the theme of contrasting human faithlessness with canine virtue; it occurs already in Matthew Prior's 1693 epitaph on True, Her Majesty's dog:

> Ye murmurers, let *True* evince,
> That Men are Beasts and Dogs have Sense.
> His Faith and Truth all *White-hall* knows,
> He ne're could fawn, or flatter those
> Whom he believ'd were *Mary's* Foes ...

Dr John Arbuthnot's epitaph for Earl Temple's greyhound Signor Fido describes the dog as "an Italian of good extraction, who came to England not to bite us, like most of his countrymen, but to gain a honest livelihood." Fido was a perfect philosopher, a faithful friend, and an agreeable companion: "Reader – This stone is guiltness of flattery, for he to whom it is inscribed, was not a Man, but a Greyhound." Dr Percival's prose epitaph to Sylvia, published in the *Annual Register* for 1777, may well have inspired Byron further, since it introduces the theme of perfect brute and imperfect man even clearer. Sylvia "mingled in all companies, yet preserved her native simplicity of manners; and was caressed by the profligate, while she reproved their Vices ... This Monument blazons no feigned virtues of the Dead, to flatter the Vanity of the Living; for it is erected not to a Woman, but to a Spaniel."[6]

* * *

At the time he kept Boatswain, Lord Byron was just an obscure young nobleman with literary ambitions. But after he had published *Childe Harold* in 1812, he acquired the great fame he had always aspired to. Although his literary output remained considerable throughout his time, he had plenty of time for travel and womanizing. He went to Italy in 1816 and remained there many years. In Ravenna, he kept eight large dogs, five cats, three monkeys, an eagle, a crow, and a falcon. Lord Byron had visited Greece, becoming a proponent of that country gaining independence from Turkey. In 1823, he decided to travel to Greece in person, to join the Greeks in their fight for freedom.

It was just about that time, fifteen years after Boatswain's death, that Lord Byron was given another Newfoundland dog by the retired naval lieutenant Edward Le Mesurier. Byron wrote back from Italy, thanking him for the great dog, and expressing his admiration for the Newfoundland breed. Lord Byron's other dogs did not at all appreciate the newcomer. Indeed, Byron had to send for some cheap wine to wash his dogs with, to prevent their wounds becoming infected after they had had a scrap. Both Lyon and the bulldog Moretto accompanied Byron to Greece. The poet travelled to Missolonghi, where he financed ships and armaments for the Greek freedom fighters, and set up a rather indisciplined troop of irregular soldiers. When he rode out to inspect his men, Lyon followed him, and when he practiced pistol-shooting at bottles, Lyon retrieved the bottles for him. One of Byron's companions wrote that "With Lyon, Lord Byron was accustomed, not only to associate, but to commune very much, and very often. His most usual phrase was, 'Lyon, you are no rogue' or, 'Lyon, thou art an honest fellow, Lyon.' The dog's eyes sparkled, and his tail swept the floor as he sat with his haunches on the ground. 'Thou art more faithful than men, Lyon; I trust thee more.' Lyon sprang up, and barked and bounded round his master, as much as to say, 'You may trust me; I will watch actively on every side.' 'Lyon, I love thee; thou art my faithful dog!' And Lyon jumped and kissed his master's hand as an acknowledgment of his homage."[7]

After Lord Byron's death in April 1824, his two dogs, Lyon and the bulldog Moretto, returned to England on board the *Florida*, the same ship that carried his remains. When his friend John Cam Hobhouse, who had once helped to compose Boatswain's epitaph, came on board at London Docks, he stood by Lord Byron's coffin, quite overcome with emotion. In his diary, he wrote that "Lord Byron's large Newfoundland dog was lying quite to my feet. I wished I was as unconscious of my loss as he was."[8] Later in 1824, Lyon was given to John Cam Hobhouse by Byron's sister Mrs Augusta Leigh. In the spring of 1825, Lyon fell ill. Hobhouse consulted the veterinarian William Youatt, who treated the dog and returned him as cured. But poor Lyon died just a few days later. In June 1825, Hobhouse wrote in his diary that "Lion, Lord Byron's Newfoundland dog that accompanied him to Greece and was given to me by Mrs Leigh died at Whitton some day this last week. he had long been ill, and at last broke a blood vessel, poor fellow he is to be buried under the willow-tree near the water at Whitton."[9] Youatt the veterinarian was quick to send his servant with a bill when he heard that Lyon had died, but Hobhouse sent this individual packing with a few choice words for company. Youatt first reacted angrily when he heard that he had been referred to as 'a fool, an ass and a dolt', although he later wrote Hobhouse a grovelling letter, emphasizing that the case had been a complicated one, and that Lyon's death was quite unexpected. It appears as if he was eventually paid.[10]

It is curious that around the same time, another Newfoundland dog was kept at Newstead Abbey, then owned by Colonel Thomas Wildman, but often visited by Lord Byron's many admirers. When the American writer Washington Irving came to Newstead in 1824, he was greeted by "a memento of Lord Byron, a great black and white Newfoundland dog who accompanied his remains from Greece. He was descended from the famous Boatswain... a cherished inmate of the Abbey...honoured and caressed by every visitor." The impostor 'Lyon' was regularly fed by the 'White Lady of Newstead', Sophia Hyatt, a great admirer of Lord Byron who liked to ramble in the gardens and grounds at Newstead. She was very short, quite stone deaf, and like to wear old-fashioned white dresses. The Newstead servants referred to her as the 'White Lady'. On September 20 1825, Sophia Hyatt visited Newstead and fed the Newfoundland dog. She cut off a small lock of his fur, which she placed in a handkerchief. The very next day, 'the White Lady of Newstead' was knocked down by a coach and killed.[11]

The statue of Lord Byron and Boatswain, from *Animal World*, October 1879

CHAPTER 5.
NEWFOUNDLAND DOGS IN THE NEWS 1750-1800

Stop, traveller, ere you farther jog;
Know, here lies entomb'd, poor honest Grog!
A quadruped, whose merit stood
In high esteem, with Captain H--d.
But Death, whose never-erring dart,
Makes Dogs, and Cats, and Men, to part,
This friend to realms of silence bore,
And faithful Grog will bark – no more!

No more his Master's ship defend,
Nor strike the deck from end to end
A failing scheme of observation,
To him (in love) was detestation.
Eager, perhaps, his flame to meet,
He threw himself 200 feet.
Come then, ye brethren of the howl,
Around his tomb dull dirges growl,
But if dog-matical you grow,
Or of this dog would further know,
Reader, apply to D--o--.

This poem was lately put on a stone at Torkey, to commemorate the unfortunate event of the loss of a favourite Newfoundland dog, who, in walking with his master, Captain Hood, fell over a precipice near 200 feet. His name was Grog. [Star, July 17, 1792]

Lost on Saturday last, between Tavistock-Street and Covent-Garden, a white rough Puppy Dog of the Newfoundland Breed, with a Sandy Mark near his Loins, a second coat on his fore Part, and long Hair on his hind. Whoever will bring him to the Black Swan in Ryder's Court, near Cranbourn-Alley, Leicester-Fields, shall have Half a Crown Reward. No greater Reward will be offered. [*Daily Advertiser*, January 16, 1752][1]

Lost on the 24th Instant near Horsley-down, a large black Dog of the Newfoundland Breed, with some white Spots about his Head, and very remarkable, having but one Ear when Pupp'd, and since that cut off; he

Answers to the name of *Fearnought*. [*Public Advertiser*, May 29, 1753] Lost at Fulham the 20th of this Month, a large black Dog of the Newfoundland Breed, with a white Star on his Breast, and a Large Brass Collar, he answers to the Name of Ipswich. Whoever brings him to the Sign of the *Black Bull* in Fulham, shall have Half a Guinea Reward for their Trouble. [*Public Advertiser*, February 28, 1759]

Lost, a Newfoundland Dog, answers to the name of Dick. [*Public Ledger*, March 28, 1760][2]

This morning a Woman was found drowned in a Ditch, on the Side of the New Road between Old-street and Islington. She was discovered by Means of a Newfoundland Dog, which was sporting in the Water. [*St. James's Chronicle*, April 24, 1762]

Corke, Feb. 18. A few days ago a Newfoundland dog, diving in the river above North-bridge, stayed so long under water, that it was imagined that he was drowned; but, to the great surprize of several who were present, he appeared with a salmon in his mouth, which bled fresh when he brought it on shore. [*Gazetteer and New Daily Advertiser,* March 2, 1768]

ADVERTISEMENT EXTRAORDINARY – MISSED from St. Paul's church on Saturday last, during divine service, a rough Newfoundland dog, very remarkable for his snarling, (but does nothing but show his teeth.) He was seen running towards the Mansion House, with a calve's head in his mouth. Note, Whoever will bring him to the dog-whipper of St. Paul's aforesaid, shall be very rewarded with a dog of King Charles's breed in lieu of him. [*Morning Chronicle* and *London Advertiser*, February 1, 1773]

A few Months ago a certain Cornish Member going down to his Country Seat, stopped at a noted Inn on the Western Road, and as the Chaises were getting ready, a fine Newfoundland Dog he had with him was assaulted by a Mastiff belonging to the Inn and severely torn. The same Dog, soon after his Arrival

An old German schoolbook print from 1806, depicting a life-saving Newfoundland dog.

in Devonshire, was, with another, missing for near a Forthnight. Upon the gentleman's return to Town, happening to stop at the same Inn, he was asked by the Landlord if his Newfoundland Dog, with another, had not been absent from his House, when the Gentleman answered in the Affimative, the Landlord informed him of their killing his Mastiff that Morning, and that they afterwards, with the greatest Composure, set out immediately for Devonshire. [*St. James's Chronicle*, March 11, 1773][3]

As soon as the Triton Indiaman, from Bengal, arrived off Dover, Mr. Larkins, the Chief Mate, and the Doctor, got a boat to go to shore; the wind being very high, and the sea rough, soon after the boat left the ship, she overset; the boatman saved themselves by getting on the keel of the boat; Mr. Larkins, who could swim extremely well, saved himself by getting onto the mast; and the Doctor, who could swim but little, was saved in the following miraculous manner: with great difficulty he got hold of one of the oars, and a gentleman, having a large Newfoundland dog, observing his distress, ordering him to go immediately to his assistance; on which he plunged into the sea, and swam directly to him, and then turned with his tail towards him, which he rubbed against him three or four times, but the Doctor, not having been used to this kind of company, suffered the dog to swim away without attempting to lay hold of him; he then made a short trip, and came to him a second time, on which the Doctor laid hold of his tail, and in a very few minutes was brought safely on shore. [*Middlesex Journal,* October 28, 1773][4]

A smuggling cutter, with a very valuable cargo of India goods on board, is lost off Penzance in Cornwall, and only one man saved, and that by means of a large Newfoundland dog he had on board, who brought him safe to shore, though at the distance of two miles from the place where the vessel struck. [*Morning Chronicle*, January 3, 1780]

The following whimsical Incident happened a few Days ago, and which is a Fact: A Butcher's Boy walking down Fish-street-hill, with a Newfoundland Dog with him, stopt at a Fishmonger's Shop opposite the Monument; being struck with the Appearance of some live Fish swimming in a Tub, among the rest particularly a large Jack drew his Attention, which the Fishmonger observing, bid him to put his Hand into its Mouth. No, said the Boy, after pausing, but if you will, I'll put Tom's (the Dog's name) Tail in, which the Fishmonger consented to, whereon the Jack seized it, and the Dog no sooner feeling, but took off over London-bridge with the Boy after, and the Fishmonger in vain after them all, to the great Diversion of the Spectators. [*Public Advertiser*, September 2, 1780]

Friday a young Man leapt from the Centre of Battersea-bridge, to swim up the River against Time for a Wager of five Guineas, but he was instantly followed by a Newfoundland Dog, belonging to a casual passenger, which seized him by the Arm, and without drawing Blood, dragged him to Shore, to the infinite Merriment of a large number of Spectators, who joined in paying a Tribute of Praise to this sagacious and generous Animal. [*Public Advertiser* August 19 1782]

As two gentlemen on Sunday evening were returning from Hampstead, they were attacked between Mother Red Cap's and the Adam and Eve by a footpad, who demanded their money; a large Newfoundland dog belonging to one of the Gentlemen seized the villain by the throat, whilst one of the gentlemen knocked him down and held him until the horse patrol came up. [*Parker's General Intelligencer and Morning Advertiser* January 27 1784]

Saturday morning early some villains attempted to rob a toyman's shop in Oxford-street, having broken out a panel from the street-door, but were prevented executing their Design by a Newfoundland dog that was kept in the house, and alarmed the family. [*General Advertiser* April 18 1785]

Thursday morning died Mrs. Walker, of Laurence Pountey-Hill. Her death was occasioned by the wanton behaviour of a neighbour, who in a joke set a large Newfoundland dog at her; the fright it occasioned threw her into fits, and notwithstanding the immediate assistance of the faculty, she died in less than two hours. [*Times*, July 9, 1785]

Extract of a Letter from Chatham.
Saturday Morning last between Six and Seven o'Clock, the Son of Mr Bartholomew, a Master Gardener of this Town, about 21 Years of Age, was bathing in a Creek near Princess's Bridge, he was unfortunately drowned. He had a very narrow Escape of the same Nature the Day before, when he was saved by the Assistance of his father's Newfoundland Dog. And what is remarkable, the poor Animal only was again with him when the Accident happened, and it is supposed that young Bartholomew caught hold of the Dog's Collar, which accidentally came off, and so he was drowned. The Dog going directly Home, led the unhappy Father to a Suspicion of what had happened, and he was unfortunately met by the Corps of his Son bringing home when he was going to see for him. [*St James's Chronicle*, September 15, 1787]

Theatrical anecdote: The bill-sticker to the Dublin Theatre, whose name is Morris, possesses so strong a penchant for the stage, that, notwithstanding he stutters in a most remarkable manner, he is never so happy as when requested to spout. The performers, to indulge him, and to laugh at his folly, frequently ask him to go through a scene. – One day last summer, whilst he was roaring out Othello (as far as his imperfection of utterance would permit) a large Newfoundland dog, seeing Morris violently seize his master by the collar, who stood up for Iago, flew at the ill fated representative of the Moor with a horrible growl, and pinned him immoveable against a wall. – After Morris was with some difficulty released, and recovered from his fright, he with much good humour declared, that, at that moment, he would retire from the stage, finding the new actor so much his superior in voice and power. [*Morning Chronicle*, January 9, 1788]

A few days since, as a Gentleman was passing along the Quay at Monkswearmouth Shore, Sunderland, followed by a terrier, and a dog of the Newfoundland breed, when the former was attacked by another terrier of a larger size, that proved too hard for him, which the Newfoundland dog observing, he seized the latter by the back of the neck, and carrying him in his mouth to the Quay-side, threw him over into the River, to the great entertainment of many spectators. [*World*, August 2, 1788]

Sunday night a gentleman returning from Dolphin's-barn-lane, in Ireland, where had supped, with no other companions than a case of good pocket-pistols, and a stout dog, of the Newfoundland breed, was attacked at Cork-bridge, near Mr Thwaite's brewery, by three desperate villains, who cried out 'Silence or death! Your money or your soul!' The gentleman made no reply, but grappling one of them, and twisting a hanger from his hand, the faithful Newfoundlander, looking on this as a signal, instantly seized another of them by the breast, which he tore in a shocking manner. [*Star*, January 9, 1789]

On Friday afternoon, the 14th of this Month, a large Newfoundland Dog of mine went after a Wild Duck that had been shot, into a large lake near my house. The water may, perhaps, be more than a mile in circumference. After swimming for some time, he went into a large bed of Reeds that grew in the middle of the water. Not finding him on shore, I concluded that he had gone home, but the dog not appearing, I sent on the day following to the neighbouring Villages, to find out if he had strayed thither. On the evening of the 24th, as Mr T. Cocke, to whom the lake belongs, was riding in the hills surrounding it, he heard the howling of a Dog at a distance, and recollecting that my Dog had been lost, he took one of his Boats and made his way through the Rushes, where he found the Dog, who had supported himself on an old nest which a Swan had build formerly, and was howling for assistance. When the Dog was taken into the Boat, he was so worn out and emaciated that he could not stand. Nor will this be wondered at, when it is recollected that he had had no other Sustenance, than Water, for the space of Ten Days! By giving him provision in small quantities, he has now recovered his strength; but as he cannot himself tell the tale, I have taken that trouble, Mr Conductor, upon myself. I have the Honour to be, Yours &c. &c. Edward Topham [*World*, August 28, 1789]

Two foot-pads have infested the road, between Rudgdy and Abbot's Bromley, and Mr. Ball, of the latter place, who was attacked by them and pulled off his horse, would have been robbed, had he not with him a Newfoundland dog, who seized and much worried one of the villains. [*Argus*, November 11, 1789]

A few days ago a Tar, accompanied by a large Newfoundland dog, went into a Baptist Meeting, the back door of which opens, for convenience, into a branch of the river Lee, where several persons were to be immersed; as this ceremony was an entire novelty to the stranger, he had arranged himself as near as possible, when the animal seeing the first person, a young female, plunge into the water, he sprang over the rails, and fetched her up again, not doing her the least damage, the fright excepted; this officious prevention was likewise exercised upon another patient, while it was not without some difficulty that the Tar was persuaded to withdraw, when he observed, that it would be much more service to the poor mad folks to be taken down to the salt water at once. [*Public Advertiser* July 13 1790]

On Monday last, a desperate battle was fought in a field on the Banks of the Thames, near Wandsworth, between a bull-dog and a large Newfoundland-dog (their owners had made a bet of ten guineas a side); when, after a most severe contest, which lasted five and twenty minutes, and in which the bull-dog had

A Newfoundland dog retrieving a stick, a print by Howitt from the *Sporting Magazine* of 1814.

evidently the advantage, the other by degrees, and after hard struggling, obtained the victory by getting his adversary into the water, where he held him under until the bull-dog was actually drowned. [*Star*, November 17, 1791][5]

Last week, a Newfoundland dog, the property of a gentleman in Glasgow, observing a cat (with which he had lived on good terms for some years) running off with a favourite starling, which she had torn from a cage, immediately seized her, and, without hurting, obliged her to relinquish the prey. He then took up the astonished bird very tenderly in his mouth, and carried it to the house-maid, who was in use to feed him. [*Star*, April 10, 1792]

EXTRACT OF A LETTER FROM BATH.—Sunday last the following melancholy accident happened in our river: John Payne, a servant to Mr. Monk, gardener, being bathing, called into the water a large Newfoundland dog, which after playing with him for some time, got upon the man's shoulders, and by keeping him under water, drowned him. As soon as the dog missed the man, he howled very much, and dived under water several times in search of him. [*Public Advertiser*, June 22, 1792]

A few days since some boys were collected on Blackfriars-bridge for the purpose of drowning a miserable cur dog, which from the centre arch they threw into the river; a large Newfoundland dog passing at the instant, and on looking through the balustrades observing the little animal splashing below; it instantly leaped on the parapet and plunged from thence into the river, took it in its mouth, and carried it in safety to the shore. [*Times*, August 12, 1793]

At the commencement of the late action between the Nymph and the Cleopatra, there was a large Newfoundland dog on board the former vessel, who, the moment the firing began, ran from below deck in spite of the men to keep him down, and climbing into the main chains, he there kept up a continued barking, and exhibited the most violent rage, the whole of the engagement. When the Cleopatra struck, he was among the foremost that boarded her, and there walked up and down the decks, seemingly conscious of the victory we had gained. [*Morning Post*, October 29, 1793]

He afterwards lived very miserably; and in walking once in a distressed situation through the streets of Paris, he was overthrown by a large Newfoundland dog, when he exclaimed 'I hope I shall live to see this city overturned as I now am!' [Star, February 27, 1796][6]

CANINE HUMANITY – In the course of last week a boy passing between some barges at Hull, unfortunately fell over one of them, where he must inevitably have perished, but for the voluntary interference of a Newfoundland Dog, who magnanimously brought him out safe, though he was an utter *stranger* to the boy, and had never been regularly admitted a *Member of the Humane Society*. [*Oracle*, August 4, 1796]

A poor woman, on Friday, threw herself in the river Avon; a Newfoundland dog immediately followed her, and dragged her to the shore, but although she was only immersed in the water a few minutes, all means used for her recovery proved ineffectual. [*Morning Post*, August 23, 1796]

Sunday last, about three o'clock, a large dog, belonging to a coal vessel at Dunleary Pier, tore a young boy near that place in a frightful manner; but whether from any provocation, we know not. Being pursued, he took to the water, and swam from Dunleary near a league into the sea, where he was followed by a party of sailors in a boat, and killed. It was of the Newfoundland breed, and swam amazingly well. [*Star*, August 31, 1796]

THOSE AMAZING NEWFOUNDLAND DOGS

About six weeks since, a Newfoundland dog, the property of Bryan Crowther, Esq., of Henwick, near Worcester, being taken down by his servant to the Severn to wash, he instantly (on approaching the river) plunged into it, and diving to the bottom continued there near three minutes, when, to the no small surprise of the man, he brought up an iron cast-ball, weighing four pounds, and leaping over three five-bar gates with it, conveyed it to his kennel, where he kept it a whole day, before any of the family could prevail on him to part with it, which he did at last, with much reluctance. It is supposed that this ball has been in the river Severn since the siege of Worcester, by Oliver Cromwell. [*London Packet*, December 9, 1796]

The King's chase on Tuesday was but of short duration; for the Deer having with great difficulty been forced to quit the Forest, proceeded to Mr Welch's Park, which he got into, and leaped over the paling near the house, where a large Newfoundland dog seized him, and put an end to the day's sport. [*True Briton*, November 17, 1797]

Head of a Newfoundland dog, a print after the 1815 painting by Abraham Cooper R.A.

CHAPTER 6.
EDWARD JESSE'S ANECDOTES ON NEWFOUNDLAND DOGS

> You who wander thither,
> Pass not unheeded
> The spot where poor Cæsar is deposited.
> To his rank among created beings
> The power of reasoning is denied!
> Cæsar manifested joy,
> For days before his master
> Arrived at Encombe;
> Cæsar manifested grief
> For days before his master left it.
> What name shall be given
> To that faculty,
> Which thus made expectation
> A source of joy,
> Which thus made expectation
> A source of grief?
>
> The epitaph of a favourite
> Newfoundland dog, by the
> Earl of Eldon, published in his
> biography by Horace Twiss.

Edward Jesse was born in 1780, the son of a Yorkshire vicar. He became a clerk in the Office of Woods and Forests, and later deputy surveyor of the royal parks and palaces, before retiring in 1851. Although lacking a formal zoological education, he was a copious writer of books of anecdotes on this subject, like *Gleanings in Natural History* (three series, 1832-1835), *An Angler's Rambles* (1836), *Scenes and Tales of Country Life; with Recollections of Natural History* (1844) and *Favourite Haunts and Rural Studies* (1847). He edited Izaak Walton's *The Compleat Angler*, Gilbert White's *Selborne*, and Leitch Ritchie's *Windsor Castle*.[1] In 1846, he published his *Anecdotes of Dogs*, with a long chapter on Newfoundland dogs, which deserves being reprinted here, in a slightly edited version.

THE NEWFOUNDLAND DOG
When we reflect on the docility of the Newfoundland dog, his affectionate disposition, his aptitude in receiving instruction, and his instantaneous sense of impending danger, we shall no longer wonder at

his being called the friend of his master, whom he is at all times ready to defend at the risk of his own life. How noble is his appearance, and at the same time how serene is his countenance!

No animal, perhaps, can show more real courage than this dog. His perseverance in what he undertakes is so great, that he never relinquishes an attempt which has been enjoined him as long as there is a chance of success. I allude more particularly to storms at sea and consequent shipwreck, when his services, his courage, and indefatigable exertions, have been truly wonderful. Numerous persons have been saved from a watery grave by these dogs, and ropes have been conveyed by them from a sinking ship to the shore amidst foaming billows, by which means whole crews have been saved from destruction. Their feet are particularly well adapted to enable them to swim, being webbed very much like those of a duck, and they are at all times ready to plunge into the water to save a human being from drowning. Some dogs delight in following a fox, others in hunting the hare, or killing vermin. The delight of the Newfoundland dog appears to be in the preservation of the lives of the human race. A story is related on good authority of one of these dogs being in the habit, when he saw persons swimming in the Seine at Paris, of seizing them and bringing hem to the shore. In the immediate neighbourhood of Windsor a servant was saved from drowning by a Newfoundland dog, who seized him by the collar of his coat when he was almost exhausted, and brought him to the banks, where some of the family were assembled watching with great anxiety the exertions of the noble animal.

Those who were much at Windsor, not many years since, must have seen a fine Newfoundland dog, called Baby, reposing occasionally in front of the White Hart Hotel. Baby was a general favourite, and he deserved to be so; for he was very mild in his disposition, brave as a lion, and very sensible. When he was thirsty, and could not procure water at the pump in the yard, he has frequently been seen to go to the stable, fetch an empty bucket, and stand with it in his mouth at the pump till some one came for water. He then, by wagging his tail and expressive looks, made his want known, and had his bucket filled. Exposed as Baby was to the attacks of all sorts of curs, as he slumbered in the sun in front of the hotel, he seemed to think that a pat with his powerful paws was quit sufficient punishment for them, but he never tamely submitted to insult from a dog approaching his own size, and his courage was only equalled by his gentleness.[2]

The following anecdote, which is well authenticated, shows the sagacity as well as the kindliness of disposition of these dogs. In the city of Worcester, one of the principal streets leads by a gentle declivity to the river Severn. One day a child, in crossing the street, fell down in the middle of it, and a horse and cart, which were descending the hill, would have passed over it, had not a Newfoundland dog, rushed to the rescue of the child, caught it up in his mouth, and conveyed it in safety to the foot pavement.

My kind friend, Mr. T—, took a Newfoundland dog and a small spaniel into a boat with him on the river Thames, and when he got into the middle of the river, he turned them into the water. They swam different ways, but the spaniel got into the current, and after struggling some time was in danger of being drowned. As soon as the Newfoundland dog perceived the predicament of his companion, he swam to his assistance, and brought him safe to the shore.

A vessel went down in a gale of wind near Liverpool, and every one on board perished. A Newfoundland dog was seen swimming about the place where the vessel was lost for some time, and at last came on shore very much exhausted. For three days he swam off to the same spot, and was evidently trying to find his lost master, so strong was his affection.

THOSE AMAZING NEWFOUNDLAND DOGS

I have always been pleased with that charming remark of Sir Edwin Landseer, that the Newfoundland dog was a "Distinguished Member of the Humane Society." How delightfully has that distinguished artist portrayed the character of dogs in his pictures! and what justice has he done to their noble qualities! We see in them honesty, fidelity, courage, and sense — no exaggeration — no flattery. He makes us feel that his dogs will love us without selfishness, and defend us at the risk of their lives; that though friends may forsake us, they never will — and that in misfortune, poverty, and death, their affection will be unchanged, and their gratitude unceasing. But to return to the Newfoundland dog, and we shall again find him acting his part as a Member of the Humane Society.

There can be no doubt but that dogs calculate, and almost reason. A dog who had been in the habit of stealing from a kitchen, which had two doors opening into it, would never do so if one of them was shut, as he was afraid of being caught. If both the doors were open, his chance of escape was greater, and he therefore seized what he could. This sort of calculation, if I may call it so, was shown by a Newfoundland bitch. She had suckled two whelps until they were able to take care of themselves. They were, however, constantly following and disturbing her in order to be suckled, when she had little or no milk to give them. She was confined in a shed, which was separated from another by a wooden partition some feet high. Into this shed she conveyed her puppies, and left them there while she returned to the other to enjoy a night's rest unmolested. This shows that the animal was capable of reflecting to a degree beyond what would have been the result of mere instinct.

The late Rev. James Simpson, of the Potterrow congregation, Edinburgh, had a large dog of the Newfoundland breed. At that time he lived at Libberton, a distance of two miles from Edinburgh, in a house to which was attached a garden. One Sacrament Sunday the servant, who was left at home in charge of the house, thought it a good opportunity to entertain her friends, as he master and mistress were not likely to return home till after the evening's service, about nine o'clock. During the day the dog accompanied them through the garden, and indeed wherever they went. In the evening, when the time arrived that the party meant to separate, they proceeded to do so; but the dog, the instant they went to the door, interposed, and placing himself before it, would not allow one of them to touch the handle. On their persisting and attempting to use force, he became furious, and in a menacing manner drove them back into the kitchen, where he kept them until the arrival of Mr. and Mrs. Simpson, who were surprised to find the party at so late an hour, and more so to see the dog standing sentinel over them. Being thus detected, the servant acknowledged the whole circumstance, when were her friends were allowed to depart, after being admonished by the worthy divine in regard to the proper use of the Sabbath. They could not but consider the dog as an instrument in the hand of Providence to point out the impropriety of spending this holy day in feasting rather than in the duties of religion.

After the above circumstance, it became necessary for Mr. Simpson, on account of his children's education, to leave his country residence, when he took a house in Edinburgh in a common stair. Speaking of this, one day, to a friend who had visited him, he concluded that he would be obliged to part with his dog, as he was too large an animal to be kept in such a house. The animal was present, and heard him say so, and must have understood what he meant, as he disappeared that evening, and was never afterwards heard of. These circumstances have been related to me by an elder of Mr. Simpson's congregation, who had them from himself.[3]

I am indebted to the late amiable Lord Stowell for the following anecdote, which has since been verified by Mr. Henry Wix, brother of the archdeacon: A Newfoundland dog belonging to Archdeacon Wix, which had never quitted the island, was brought over to London by him in January, 1834, and when he and his family landed at Blackwall the dog was left on board the vessel. A few days afterwards the Archdeacon went from the Borough side of the Thames in a boat to the vessel, which was then in

The sagacious Newfoundland dog 'Baby' asking for some water, from *Chatterbox* May 26 1879.

St. Katherine's docs, to see about his luggage, but did not intend at that time to take the dog from the ship; however, on his leaving he vessel the dog succeeded in extricating himself from his confinement, jumped overboard, and swam after the boat across the Thames, followed his master into a courting-house on Gun-shot Wharf, Tooley street, and then over London Bride and through the City to St. Bartholomew's Hospital. The dog was shut within the square whilst the Archdeacon went into his father's house, and he then followed him on his way to Russell Square, but strayed somewhere in Holborn; and as several gentlemen stopped to admire him in the street, saying he was worth a great deal of money, the archdeacon concluded that some dog-stealer had enticed him away. He however wrote to the captain of the vessel to mention his loss, and made inquiries on the following morning at St. Bartholomew's Hospital, when he learnt that the dog had come to the gates late in the evening, and howled most piteously for admission, but was driven away. Two days afterwards the captain of the vessel waited on the Archdeacon with the dog, who had not only found his way back to the water's edge, on the Borough side, but, what is more surprising, swam across the Thames, where no scent could have directed him, and found out the vessel in St. Katharine's Docks. This sagacious and affectionate creature, had, previous to his leaving Newfoundland, saved his master's life by directing his way home when lost in a snowstorm many miles from any shelter. The dog was presented to the Archdeacon's uncle, Thomas Poynder, Esq., Clapham Common, in whose possession it continued until its death.

A gentleman of Suffolk, on an excursion with his friend, was attended by a Newfoundland dog, which soon became the subject of conversation. The master, after a warm eulogium upon the perfections of his canine favourite, assured his companion that he would, upon receiving the order, return and fetch any article he should leave behind, from any distance. To confirm this assertion, a marked shilling was put under a large square stone by the side of the road, being first shown to the dog. The gentlemen then rode for three miles, when the dog received his signal from the master to return for the shilling he has seen put under the stone. The dog turned back; the gentlemen rode on, and reached home; but to their surprise and disappointment the hitherto faithful messenger did not return during the day. It afterwards appeared that he had gone to the place where the shilling was deposited, but the stone being too large for his strength to remove, he had stayed howling at the place till two horsemen riding by, and attracted by his seeming distress, stopped to look at him, when one of them alighting, removed the stone, and seeing the shilling, put it into his pocket, not at the time conceiving it to be the object of the dog's search. The dog followed their horses for twenty miles, remained undisturbed in the room where they supped, followed the chambermaid into the bedchamber, and secreted himself under one of the beds. The possessor of the shilling hung his trousers upon a nail by the bed-side; but when the travellers were both asleep, the dog took them in his mouth, and leaping out of the window, which was left open on account of the sultry heat, reached the house of his master at four o-clock in the morning, with the prize he had made free with, in the pocket of which were found a watch and money, that were returned upon being advertised, when the whole mystery was mutually unravelled, to the admiration of all the parties.

Mrs. Kaye, residing opposite Windsor Park Wall, Datchet, had a beautiful Newfoundland dog. For the convenience of the family a boat was kept, that they might at time cross the water without the inconvenience of going a considerable way round to Datchet Bridge. The dog was so delighted with the aquatic trips, that he very rarely permitted the boat to go without him. It happened that the coachman, who had been but little accustomed to the depths and shallows of the water, intending a forcible push with the punt pole, which was not long enough to reach the bottom, fell over the side of the boat in the deepest part of the water, and in the central part of the current, which accident was observed by a part of the family then at the front windows of the house; sudden and dreadful as the alarm was, they had the consolation of seeing the sagacious animal instantaneously follow his companion, when after diving, and making two or three abortive attempts, by laying hold of different parts of his apparel, which as repeatedly gave way or overpowered his exertions, he then, with the most determined and energetic fortitude, seized him by the arm, and brought him to the edge of the bank, where the domestics of the terrified family were ready to assist in extricating him from his perilous situation.

I have mentioned that revenge had been shown by dogs, and the following is an instance of it. A gentleman was staying at Worthing, where his Newfoundland dog was teased and annoyed by a small cur, which snapped and barked at him. This he bore, without appearing to notice it, for some time; but at last the Newfoundland dog seemed to lose his usual patience and forbearance, and he one day, in the presence of several spectators, took the cur up by his back, swam with it into the sea, held it under the water, and would probably have drowned it, had not a boat been put off and rescued it. There was another instance communicated to me. A fine Newfoundland dog had been constantly annoyed by a small spaniel. The former, seizing the opportunity when they were on a terrace under which a river flowed, took up the spaniel in his mouth, and dropped it over the parapet into the river.

Jukes, in his *Excursions in and about Newfoundland*, says, "A thin, short-haired black dog, belonging to George Harvey, came off to us to-day; this animal was of a breed very different form what we understand by the term Newfoundland dog in England. He had a thin tapering snout, a long thin tail, and rather thin but powerful legs, with a lank body, the hair short and smooth. These are the most abundant dogs of the country, the long-haired curly dogs being comparatively rare. They are by no handsome, but are generally more intelligent and useful than the others. This one caught his own fish; he sat on a projecting rock beneath a fish-lake or stage, where the fish are laid to dry, watching the water, which had a depth of six or eight feet, the bottom of which was white with fish-bones. On throwing a piece of codfish into the water, three or four heavy, clumsy-looking fish, called in Newfoundland sculpins, with great heads and mouths, and many spines about them, and generally about a foot long, would swim to catch it. These he would 'set' attentively, and the moment one turned his broadside to him, he darted down like a fish-hawk, and seldom came up without the fish in his mouth. As he caught them he carried them regularly to a place a few yards off, where he laid them down; and they told us that in the summer he would sometimes make a pile of fifty or sixty a-day just at that place. He never attempted to eat them, but seemed to be fishing purely for his own amusement. I watched him for about two hours, and when the fish did not come I observed he once or twice put his right foot in the water, and paddled it about. This foot was white, and Harvey said he did it to toll or entice the fish; but whether it was for that specific reason, or merely a motion of impatience, I could not exactly decide."

Extraordinary as the following anecdote may appear to some persons, it is strictly true, and strongly shows the sense, and I am almost inclined to add, reason of the Newfoundland dog. A friend of mine, while shooting wild fowl with his brother, was attended by a sagacious dog of this breed. In getting near some reeds by the side of a river, they threw down their hats, and crept to the edge of the water, when they fired at some birds. They soon afterwards sent the dog to bring their hats, one of which was smaller than the other. After several attempts to bring them both together in his mouth, the dog at last placed the smaller hat in the larger one, pressed it down with his foot, and thus was able to bring them both at the same time.

A gentleman residing in Fifeshire, and not far from the city of St. Andrews, was in possession of a very fine Newfoundland dog, which was remarkable alike for its tractability and its trustworthiness. At two other points, each distant about a mile, and at the same distance from this gentleman's mansion, there were two dogs of great power, but of less tractable breeds than the Newfoundland one. One of these was a large mastiff, kept as a watch-dog by a farmer, and the other a stanch bull-dog, that kept guard over the parish mill. As each of these three was lord-ascendant of all animals at his master's residence, they all had a good deal of aristocratic pride and pugnacity, so that two of them seldom met without attempting to settle their respective dignities by a wager of battle. The Newfoundland dog was of some service in the domestic arrangements, besides his guardianship of the house; for every forenoon he was sent to the baker's shop in the village, about half-a-mile distant, with a towel containing money in the corner, and he returned with the value of the money in bread. There were many useless and not over-civil curs in the village, as there are in too many villages throughout the country; but generally the haughty Newfoundland treated this ignoble race in that contemptuous style in which great dogs are wont to treat little ones. When the dog returned from the baker's shop, he used to be regularly served with his dinner, and went peaceably on house-duty for the rest of the day.

One day, however, he returned with his coat dirtied and his ears scratched, having been subjected to a combined attack of the curs while he had charge of his towel and bread, and so could not defend himself. Instead of waiting for his dinner as usual, he laid down his charge somewhat sulkily, and marched off; and, upon looking after him, it was observed that he was crossing the intervening hollow in a straight line for the house of the farmer, or rather on an embassy to the farmer's mastiff. The farmer's people noticed this unusual visit, which they were induced to do from its being a meeting of peace between those who had habitually been belligerents. After some intercourse, of which no interpretation could be given, the two set off together in the direction of the mill; and having arrived there, they in brief space engaged the miller's bull-dog as an ally. The straight road to the village where the indignity had been offered to the Newfoundland dog passed immediately in front of his master's house, but there was a more private and more circuitous road by the back of the mill. The three took this road, reached the village, scoured it in great wrath, putting to the tooth every cur they could get sight of; and having taken their revenge, and washed themselves in a ditch, they returned, each dog to the abode of his master; and, when any two of them happened to meet afterwards, they displayed the same pugnacity as they had done previous to their joint expedition.

There is a well-authenticated anecdote of two dogs at Donaghadee, in which the instinctive daring of the one by the other caused a friendship, and, as it should seem, a kind of lamentation for the dead, after one of them had paid the debt of nature. This happened while the Government harbour or pier for the packets at Donaghadee was in the course of building, and it took place in the sight of several witnesses. The one dog in this case was also a Newfoundland, and the other was a mastiff. They were both powerful dogs; and though each was good-natured when alone, hey were very much in the habit of fighting when they met. One day they had a fierce and prolonged battle on the pier, from the point of which they both fell into the sea; and as the pier was long and steep, they had no means of escape but by swimming a considerable distance. Throwing water upon fighting dogs is an approved means of putting an end to their hostilities; and it is natural to suppose that two combatants of the same species tumbling themselves into the sea would have the same effect. It had; and each began to make for the land as best he could. The Newfoundland being an excellent swimmer, very speedily gained the pier, on which he stood shaking himself; but at the same time watching the motions of his late antagonist, which, being no swimmer, was struggling exhausted in the water, and just about to sink. In dashed the Newfoundland dog, took the other gently by the collar, kept his head above water, and brought him safely on shore. There was a peculiar kind of recognition between the two animals; they never fought again; they were always together; and when the Newfoundland dog had been accidentally killed by the passage of a stone wagon on the railway over him, the other languished and lamented for a long time.

A gentleman had a pointer and Newfoundland dog, which were great friends. The former broke his leg, and was confined to the kennel. During that time the Newfoundland never failed bringing bones and other food to the pointer, and would sit for hours together by the side of his suffering friend.

THOSE AMAZING NEWFOUNDLAND DOGS

During a period of very hot weather, the Mayor of Plymouth gave orders that all dogs found wandering in the public streets should be secured by the police and removed to the prison-yard. Among them was a Newfoundland dog belonging to a ship-owner of the port, who, with several others, was tied up in the yard. The Newfoundland soon gnawed the rope which confined him, and then hearing the cries of his companions to be released, he set to work to gnaw the ropes which confined them, and had succeeded in three or four instances, when he was interrupted by the entrance of the jailer. A nearly similar case has frequently occurred in the Cumberland Gardens, Windsor Great Park. Two dogs of the Newfoundland breed were confined in kennels at that place. When one of them was let loose, he has been frequently seen to set his companion free.

A boatman once plunged into the water to swim with another man for a wager. His Newfoundland dog, mistaking the purpose, and supposing that his master was in danger, plunged after him, and dragged him to the shore by his hair, to the great diversion of the spectators. Mr. Peter Macarthur informs me, that in the year 1821, when opposite to Falmouth, he was at breakfast with a gentleman, when a large Newfoundland dog, all dripping with water, entered the room, and laid a newspaper on the table. The gentleman (who was one of the Society of Friends) informed, the party, that this dog swam regularly across the ferry every morning, and went to the post-office, and fetched the papers of the day.

Dr. Abell, in one of his lectures on phrenology, related a very striking anecdote of a Newfoundland dog at Cork. This dog was of a noble and generous disposition, and when he left his master's house was often assailed by a number of little noisy dogs in the street. He usually passed them with apparent unconcern, as if they were beneath his notice. One little cur, however, was particularly troublesome, and at length carried his petulance so far as to bite the Newfoundland dog in the back of his foot. This was too much to be patiently endured. He instantly turned round, ran after the offender, and seized him by the skin of his back. In this way he carried him in his mouth to the quay, and holding him some time over the water, at length dropped him into it. He did not seem, however, to wish to punish the culprit too much, for he waited a little while the poor animal, who was unused to the element, was not only well ducked, but near sinking, when he plunged in himself, and brought the other safe to land.

A vessel was driven by a storm on the beach of Lydd, in Kent. The surf was rolling furiously. Eight men were calling for help, but not a boat could be got off to their assistance. At length a gentleman came on the beach, accompanied by his Newfoundland dog. He directed the attention of the noble animal to the vessel, and put a short stick in his mouth. The intelligent and courageous dog at once understood his meaning, and sprung into the sea, fighting his way through the foaming waves. He could not, however, get close enough to the vessel to deliver that which he was charged, but the crew joyfully made fast a rope to another piece of wood, and threw it towards him. The sagacious dog saw the whole business in an instant; he dropped his own piece, and immediately seized that which had been cast to him; and then, with a degree of strength and determination almost incredible, he dragged it through the surge and delivered it to his master. By this means a line of communication was formed, and every man on board saved.

The keeper of a ferry on the banks of the Severn had a sagacious Newfoundland dog. If a dog was left behind by his owner in crossing, and was afraid of taking to the water, the Newfoundland dog has been frequently known to take the yelping animal in his mouth and convey it into the river. A person while rowing a boat, pushed his Newfoundland dog into the stream. The animal followed the boat for some time, till, probably finding himself fatigued, he endeavoured to get into it by placing his feet on the side. His owner repeatedly pushed the dog away, and in one of his efforts to do so he overbalanced himself and fell into the river, and would probably have been drowned, had not the noble and generous animal immediately seized and held him above water till assistance arrived from the shore.

A Newfoundland dog and a spaniel, from the 1873 edition of Edward Jesse's *Anecdotes of Dogs*.

THOSE AMAZING NEWFOUNDLAND DOGS

The following is another instance of extraordinary sagacity. A Newfoundland dog, belonging to a grocer, had observed one of the porters of the house, and who was often in the shop, frequently take money from the till, and which the man was in the habit of concealing in the stable. The dog, having witnessed these thefts, became restless, pulling persons by the skirts of their coats, and apparently wishing them to follow him. At length, an apprentice had occasion to go to the stable; the dog followed him, and having drawn his attention to the heap of rubbish under which the money was buried, began to scratch till he had brought the booty to view. The apprentice brought it to his master, who marked the money and restored it to the place where it had been hidden. Some of the marked money was soon afterwards found on the porter, who was taken before a magistrate, and convicted of the theft.

A Newfoundland dog, which was frequently to be seen in a tavern in the High Street of Glasgow, lay generally at the door. When any person came to the house, he trotted before them into an apartment, rang the bell, and then resumed his station at the door.

On Thursday evening, January 28, 1858, as the play of "Jessie Vere" was being performed at Woolwich Theatre, and when a scene in the third act had been reached, in which a "terrific struggle" for the possession of a child takes place between the fond mother and two "hired ruffians," a large Newfoundland dog, which had by some means gained admittance with its owner into the pit, leaped over the heads of the musicians in the orchestra, and flew to the rescue, seizing one of the assassins, and almost dragging him to the ground. It was with difficulty removed, and dragged off the stage. The dog, which is the property of the chief engineer of Her Majesty's ship Buffalo, has been habitually accustomed to the society of children, for whom he has on many occasions evinced strong proofs of affection.

In Newfoundland, this dog if invaluable, and answers the purpose of a horse. He is docile, capable of strong attachment, and is easy to please in the quality of his food, as he will live on scraps of boiled

A vignette of a Newfoundland dog saving a child, from the 1873 edition of Edward Jesse's *Anecdotes of Dogs*.

fish, either salted or fresh, and on boiled potatoes, and cabbage. The natural colour of this dog is black, with the exception of a very few white spots. Their sagacity is sometimes so extraordinary, as on many occasions to show that they only want the faculty of speech to make themselves fully understood.

The Rev. L. Anspach, in his history of the Island of Newfoundland, mentions some instances of this intelligence. One of the Magistrates of Harbour-Grace, the late Mr. Garland, had an old dog, which was in the habit of carrying a lantern before his master at night, as steadily as the most attentive servant could do; stopping short when his master made a stop, and proceeding when he saw him disposed to follow him. If his master was absent from home, on the lantern being fixed to his mouth, and the command given, "Go, fetch your master," he would immediately set off and proceed directly to the town, which lay at the distance of more than a mile from the place of his master's residence. He would then stop at the door of every house which he knew his master was in the habit of frequenting, and, laying down his lantern, would growl and strike the door, making all the noise in his power until it was opened. If his master was not there, he would proceed further until he had found him. If he accompanied him only once into a house, it was sufficient to induce him to take that house in his round. The principal use of this animal in Newfoundland, in addition to his qualities as a good watch-dog and a faithful companion, is to assist in fetching from the woods the lumber intended either for repairing the fish stages, or for fuel; and this is done by dragging it on the snow or ice, or else on sledges, the dog being tackled to it.

These animals bark only when strongly provoked. They are not quarrelsome, but treat the smaller species with a great degree of patience and forbearance. They will defend their masters on seeing the least appearance of an attack on his person. The well-known partiality of these dogs for water, in which they appear as if in their proper element, diving and keeping their heads under the surface for a considerable time, seems to give them some connexion with the class of amphibious animals. At the same time, the several instances of their superior sagacity, and the essential services which they have been frequently known to render to humanity, give them a distinguished rank in the scale of the brute creation. I will mention another instance of this. The Durham packet of Sunderland was, in 1815, wrecked near Clay, in Norfolk. A faithful dog was employed to use his efforts to carry the lead-line on shore from the vessel; but there being a very heavy sea, and a deep beach, it appeared that the drawback of the surf was too powerful for the animal to contend with. Mr. Parker, ship-builder, of Wells, and Mr. Jackson, jun., of Clay, who were on the spot, observing this, instantly rushed into the sea, which was running very high, and gallantly succeeded, though at a great risk, in catching hold of the dog, which was much exhausted, but which had all this time kept the line in his mouth. The line being thus obtained, a communication with the vessel was established; and a warp being passed from the ship to the shore, the lives of all on board, nine in number, including two children, were saved.

Newfoundland dogs may readily be taught to rescue drowning persons. In France, this forms a part of their education, and they are now kept in readiness on the banks of the Seine, where they form a sort of Humane Society Corps. By throwing the stuffed figure of a man into a river, and requiring the dog to fetch it out, he is soon taught to do so when necessary, and thus he is able to rescue drowning persons. This hint might not be thrown away on our own excellent Humane Society.

A gentleman who had a country house near London, discovered on arriving at it one day that he had brought away a key, which would be wanted by his family in town. Having an intelligent Newfoundland dog, which had been accustomed to carry things, he sent him back with it. While passing with the key, the animal was attacked by a butcher's dog, against which he made no resistance, but got away from him. After safely delivering the key, he returned to rejoin his master, but stopped in the way at he butcher's shop, whose dog again sallied forth. The Newfoundland this time attacked him with a fury, which nothing but revenge could have inspired, nor did he quit the aggressor till he had killed him.

The following interesting fact affords another instance of the sagacity and good feeling of the Newfoundland dog: — In the year 1841, as a labourer, named Rake, in the parish of Botley, near Southampton, was at work in a gravel-pit, the top stratum gave way, and he was buried up to his neck by the great quantity of gravel which fell upon him. He was at the same time so much hurt, two of his ribs being broken, that he found it impossible to make any attempt to extricate himself from his perilous situation. Indeed, nothing could be more fearful than the prospect before him. No one was within hearing of his cries, nor was any one likely to come near the spot. He must almost inevitably have perished, had it not been for a Newfoundland dog belonging to his employer. This animal had been watching the man at his work for some days, as if he had been aware that his assistance would be required; for no particular attachment to each other had been exhibited on either side. As soon, however, as the accident occurred, the dog jumped into the pit, and commenced removing the gravel with his paws; and this he did in so vigorous and expeditious a manner, that the poor man was at length able to liberate himself, though with extreme difficulty. What an example of kindness, sensibility, and I may add reason, does this instance afford us!

There was a Newfoundland dog on board *H.M.S. Bellona*, which kept the deck during the battle of Copenhagen, running backward and forward with so brave an anger, that he became a greater favourite with the men than ever. When the ship was paid off, after the peace of Amiens, the sailors had a parting dinner on shore. Victor was placed in the chair, and fed with roast beef and plum-pudding, and the bill was made out in Victor's name.

CHAPTER 7.
CARLO THE ACTING NEWFOUNDLAND DOG

> Now Attic wit's o'ercome by Gothic rage,
> And authors *throw cold water* on the stage;
> While, honest *Carlo*, envying even you,
> They make their very dramas *Dog*-grel too.
>
> *Times* Dec 6 1803.

In late 1803, the playwright Frederick Reynolds presented his latest script to the manager of the Drury Lane Theatre. In a Hispanic setting, the tyrant Don Gomez Muneral, Governor of Barcelona, falls in love with the beautiful Marchioness of Calatrava. He has the Marquis arrested on a trumped-up charge, and conveyed to prison in a caravan, guarded by the driver Blabbo and his large dog Carlo. Although the Governor successively threatens the Marchioness that unless she succumbs to his advances, her husband would be transported to Mexico, or even starved to death on his journey in the caravan, the virtuous lady is obdurate. When she and her young son Julio catches up with the caravan, she is relieved to find out that although Blabbo had orders to starve the Marquis on his journey, he has actually allowed the hungry nobleman to share the dog's food.[1]

Blabbo turns out to be a good friend, and he helps the Marquis escape, using a rope-ladder. But the luckless nobleman is again seized by the tyrant's henchmen and taken on board a fire-ship. The evil governor also turns up, as obnoxious as ever: unless the Marchioness proves more accommodating, he will blow her husband up in the ship. When the lady again rejects him, he orders a soldier to throw her son into the sea. Little Julio is torn from her, and flung into the sea from a precipice. But the dog Carlo plunges into the water and saves the child. In the end, Don Gomez is deposed, the Marquis liberated, and Blabbo and his dog rewarded.

"I have never heard such nonsense in my life!" you would have expected the manager to exclaim after he was made to listen to this absurd plot, but instead his response seems to have been more in the line of "This will surely be a huge hit!" Actors were recruited, suitable music written, and carpenters set to work constructing a precipice and an artificial lake on stage for the play's most dramatic scene. A large butcher's dog was purchased, renamed 'Carlo', and given a crash course in acting. Carlo was a black and white Newfoundland, and probably three or four years old when he made his stage debut.

When 'The Caravan, or the Driver and his Dog', opened on December 5 1803, reviews were very favourable. It was considered novel and praiseworthy to have a dog actor as one of the principal

Carlo makes his leap, from the *Sporting Magazine* of 1804.

performers, and little less than a masterstroke of modern scenography to have a precipice and artificial lake onstage. In particular, Carlo's intrepid leap was much admired. The *Morning Chronicle* found the play extremely attractive, in spite of the plot hardly being intelligible:

> "No one accustomed to go to the Theatre will be satisfied till he or she has seen the drowning Julio in the mouth of the daring Carlo – 'the dog will have his day'"

The *Spirit of Public Journals* described how the audience stood flabbergasted when the massive Newfoundland splashed into the water, exclaiming

> "An't he a fine dog? Did you see the dog? How excellently he did it!"

A reviewer in the *Theatrical Journal* liked the principal scene:

> "At this crisis, when every bosom sympathizes with the pangs of maternal agony, the voice of the Caravan Driver is heard vociferating 'Carlo! Carlo! A fine Newfoundland dog rushes forward, leaps from the rock, seizes the infant, and brings it safely to land!"[2]

Another article in the *Morning Chronicle* struck a more ribald note, since the journalist thought that the acting dog's onstage behaviour had been rowdy indeed: "We are extremely unwilling to touch upon the private foibles of the theatrical *corps*, when they do not interfere with their professional engagements, but we are compelled to observe, that on Monday night's performance Mr. *Carlo* was evidently *in liquor*!" It was no coincidence that the artificial lake was so very full, he continued, since Mr. Carlo had also given the stage hands a *lift* filling it up![3] The *Hampshire Telegraph* was somewhat more respectful, commenting that if the largest of all *bipeds* was Bonaparte, who fills all the prisons in *France*, the surely the greatest of all *quadrupeds* had to be the Dog Carlo, who fills the largest theatre in *England*.[4]

Carlo also joined the current political debate, in a satire inspired by the scare-mongering about a French invasion across the English Channel, and describing the reactions of a Tory and a Whig spectator:

> Mr. Dent was in the front row of the Stage Box at Drury-Lane to witness the third representation of the *Driver and his Dog*. It is said that he was so pleased with the exploits of *Carlo*, that he declared that he would himself, notwithstanding his general enmity to the species, bring a bid into Parliament, to *exempt* Carlo and his posterity, to the end of time, from all existing and future taxes on the canine race.
>
> Mr. Wyndham, however, who sat in the opposite box, expressed, if we are rightly informed, his entire disapprobation of the whole performance. contending, that a water dog saving a child in the presence of its frantic mother, is a scene wholly unsuited to the

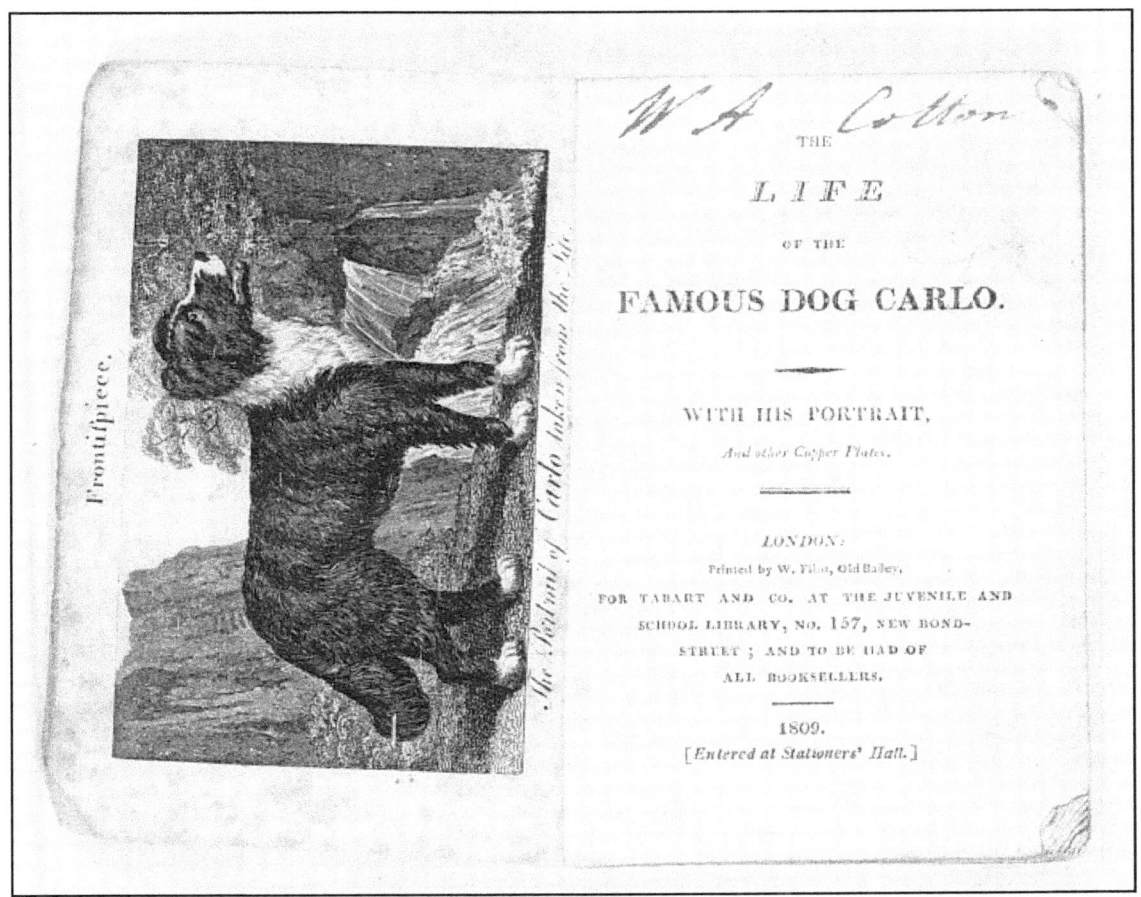

The frontispiece of Carlo's biography

Another image of Carlo on stage, with a suitable poem.

Carlo performing some further heroics, from his biography.

times, and calculated only to promote the weaker affections, which ought at the present crisis, even in the fair sex, to give way to a resolute defiance of the horrors which, no doubt, our invaders would soon familiarize to our eyes.

His idea is, that instead of the humane Carlo, a bull-dog should be loosed upon the infant; and he is as good a swimmer, Mr. W. asserts, as the Newfoundlander, who instead of bringing the child safe to shore, should fairly eat him up in the sight of the audience. Thus, at the slight expense of one single little child killed off per night, during the run of the piece, British mothers would be accustomed, without womanish panic, to brave the keenest miseries which French cruelty could indict.[5]

'The Caravan' was a great success, constantly playing to full houses, many of whom came to see the acting dog. A *Morning Post* journalist wrote that he would have believed that Carlo had bitten all of London, sending them into a canine rage, had it not been for the absence of the principal symptom, the *hydrophobia*.[6] When the acting dog made his bow (wow) on stage, there was a great roar of 'Carlo! Carlo! Carlo!' from the rowdy audience. When a trumpet sounded, to mark the arrival of the tyrant Muneral, Carlo responded with an equally sonorous howl. In March 1804, the mother of the child actor demanded that Carlo was replaced, since her son had been "terribly bruised" from the acting dog's powerful jaws when surreptitiously pulled out of the artificial lake. The manager got hold of a less squeamish child actor instead, however, and Carlo's career was saved. After two more kids had backed out, a dummy was substituted for the child just before it was thrown into the artificial lake.

The acting dog remained a controversial member of the cast, however, since he frequently improvised on stage. Once, he pushed the Marquis over and reclaimed the dog food he was supposed to share; another time, he prevented the throwing of the child by obstructing the soldier. Sometimes, the audience distracted him with their shouts of 'Carlo! Carlo! Carlo!' and made him jump about and bark excitedly; at other times, when the acting dog was bored, he lay down on stage and did not move a muscle. But Frederick Reynolds and the manager of the theatre were sufficiently astute to realize that Carlo's unpredictable behaviour was one of the prime attractions of the play; in fact, not two performances were identical. The audience were delighted when the acting dog was up to mischief, and some people came to see the play again and again to see what rowdy behaviour Carlo would be up to next. There were several unfounded rumours that Carlo had died, and been replaced with another dog, or that the theatre management had had enough of the rowdy acting dog, substituting a very docile mastiff in a Newfoundland dog's costume for Carlo, and only allowing the original star to appear in the final scene when he took his great leap.

The *Times* published an amusing review of Carlo's latest performance, which deserves to be given in full:

In the 'Caravan' *Carlo* gave signs of much confidence and improvement. He seems familiarized to the audience, and as proof of it, he lay down on the stage during the greatest part of *his* principal scene. In the *finale*, at the end of the first act, he made atonement; for, instead of *modestly* confining himself, as formerly, to a timely and occasional *howl*, he assumed the principal part of the chorus, and *barked away* highly to the entertainment of the audience, and not a little to the amusement of the performers, who were convulsed with laughter. We cannot with-hold him the justice due to his merit, in saying that he took the *leap* with gallant and desperate resolution.[7]

Children's author Eliza Fenwick was one of the many Londoners to see 'The Caravan'. By this time, Carlo's onstage exploits had made him a favourite among the children, and Eliza Fenwick was amazed to see many little boys and girls sitting in the front row of the boxes, applauding Carlo with the greatest enthusiasm. She was clever enough to exploit the situation: later in 1804, her little book *The Life of the Famous Dog Carlo* was published for a juvenile audience. Carlo had been so impressed with the "rapturous exclamations" of the hundreds of young gentlemen and young ladies who had come to see him act, she explained, that the dog had seen fit to compose his autobiography. Carlo's fictional life story was dramatic indeed: he saved people from drowning, dropped an angry little dog into the water after it had annoyed him, and dragged a young boy who had stolen half a roast goose in front of the Lord Mayor of London to make him confess the theft. According to Eliza Fenwick, Carlo's master, who kept a tavern, offered to have his dog play in 'The Caravan'. Since the acting dog had shown both zeal and sagacity, his reputation as a good actor was universally established. This version throws some doubt on the original story of Carlo being a butcher's dog purchased by the theatre. Both Eliza Fenwick and a writer in the *Sporting Magazine* depicted and described Carlo as large, handsome, purebred white and black Newfoundland, a fashionable and expensive breed of dog that the average butcher could ill afford at the time.[8]

Largely thanks to Carlo, 'The Caravan' was still going strong in 1805. After one performance, the wit Richard Brinsley Sheridan called out 'Author!' When informed that Mr Reynolds had retired, Sheridan replied 'Pooh! – I mean the Dog-actor, the *Author* and *Preserver* of Drury-lane Theatre!" A laborious satire in the *Morning Chronicle* instead presented a 'Comparison between a Certain Great Statesman and a Certain Great Actor; or, Lord Castlereagh and the Dog Carlo.' To gain his dinner, Carlo had to plunge into the water in an illuminated theatre, surrounded by applauding spectators; the Prime Minister made similar exhortations to save sinking cause, and a falling government. In another, more amusing joke of the time, one of the actors in 'The Caravan' had suddenly been taken ill. The prompter rushed off to see the manager, who initially seemed a good deal put out, before exclaiming "How you alarm me, the tragedian unwell! I was afraid it was the dog!"[9]

A number of satirical caricature prints were inspired by Carlo's onstage exploits. In *The Manager and his Dog*, Carlo swims in the artificial lake on stage, holding Sheridan's head above water by the hair, saying

> "------methinks it were an easy Leap
> To dive into the bottom of the Deep
> And pluck up drowned honour by ye Locks."
> [Henry IV, I. iii.]

The capital of the Corinthian pilaster that flanks the stage is formed of dogs' heads. At its foot is a figure of Thalia covering her face with her hands. At the base of her pedestal is an open book: 'The Caravan or the Driver and his Dog a Farce.' Other prints depicted Carlo bringing Sheridan a basket of new 'Growlo Dramas' for him to act in, or guarding a padlocked 'Drury Lane Strong Box', to symbolize his importance for the theatre's survival. In 1808, after the latest of several false rumours that Carlo had died, the print *A New Drop Scene for Drury Lane Theatre* depicted a man painting black spots onto a white dog with a collar marked 'Carlo'![10]

In 1806, Carlo went on tour, but the next year he was back in London, acting in another play. In 1808, an actor named Munden tried to recruit Carlo to play the role of the dog Crab in Mr Kemble's revision of *Two Gentlemen of Verona*, but the acting dog had other engagements at the time. Instead, Munden brought with him on stage another Newfoundland dog, named 'Caesar', but this dog misbehaved himself throughout, even by the low standards set by Carlo. In the scene where the dog was roughly handled, the large Newfoundland, "not understanding *making belief* in such matters, seized his assailant by the leg."[11] Nothing more was heard of Caesar after this short but violent acting career, but Carlo himself is said to have been alive and well, and still acting, when his biography was reissued in 1809. The last notice of this extraordinary dog is that he appeared in 'The Forty Thieves' at the Theatre Royal, Covent-garden, in May 1811.[12]

The caricature of Carlo helping Sheridan to keep his head above water in the artificial lake on stage

A fine caricature of Carlo the Acting Dog helping Sheridan select his next 'Growley Drama'

CHAPTER 8.
SOME OTHER ACTING NEWFOUNDLAND DOGS

> No actor great a histrionic name
> Than Carlo boasts a prouder, nobler name;
> E'en Garrick, Nature's favourite child, must yield
> Nature HERSELF with Carlo takes the field.
>
> Another poem on Carlo the Acting Newfoundland dog.

The great success of Carlo the Acting Dog set playwrights and theatrical managers thinking. In spite of possessing neither discipline nor any discernable acting skills, Carlo had established himself as a canine superstar. Newfoundland dogs were highly thought of at the time, and admired for their great strength and handsome looks. These fashionable dogs were also intelligent and easy to train, and large enough to fight villains, dive into lakes, and rescue people. Now what if a clever young Newfoundland dog was given acting lessons from an early age, and was made accustomed to the clamouring of the audience? And what if a play was deliberately written for the dog?

Not long after Carlo had retired from the theatre, an actor named Bush trained another Newfoundland dog to become his successor. In early 1817, the Dog Bruin acted in 'The Viceroy, or the Spanish Gypsey and the Assassin', saving a child from a burning castle. According to the *Morning Chronicle*, "the actions of the Dog Bruin almost exceed credibility". Advertisements for this play, or for its successor 'The Terrible Peak, or a Mother's Sorrows', never failed to point out that the Dog Bruin was part of the cast.

The first, archetypical dog drama 'The Dog of Montargis, or the Forest of Bondy', which originally premiered in Paris in 1814, was staged at the King's Theatre in London a few years later. It was to remain the staple item for canine thespians for many years. It is roughly based on an old French legend. In a forest outside Montargis, the officer Aubri is murderously attacked by two enemies, Macaire and Landri. He is valiantly defended by his large dog Dragon, but when the faithful animal is kept occupied by Landri, the second villain gives Aubri the fatal wound. Later, an innocent deaf-mute simpleton is 'framed' for the murder, but Dragon saves him by producing a sash he has torn off Macaire's uniform. Each time Dragon sees the murderers, he growls and tries to attack them. The King gives the brave dog the right to trial by battle, and after a long and gory fight, the defeated Macaire confesses the murder.

This scene introduced the trick of 'taking the seize', in which the acting dog leaps up onto the villain

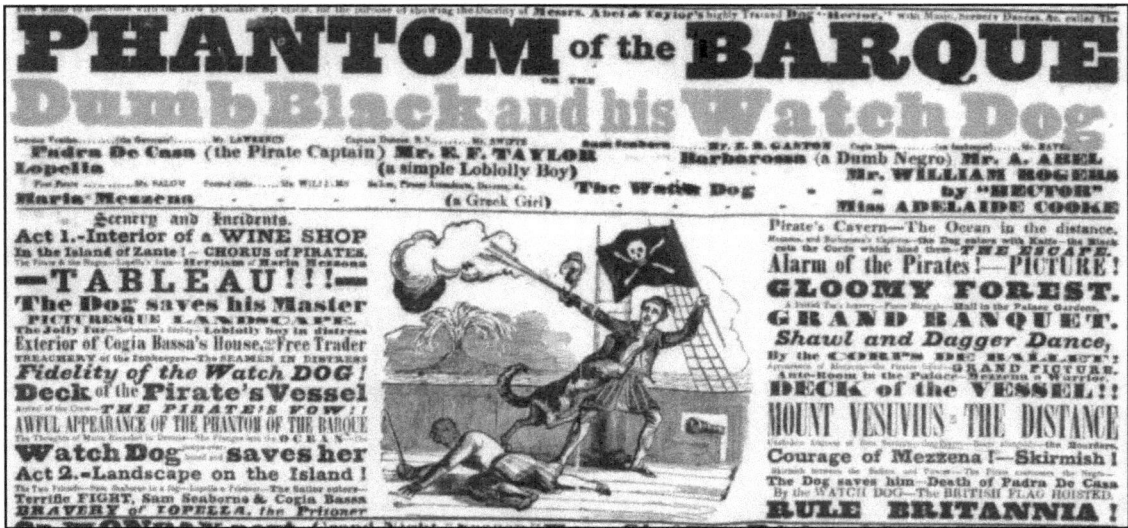

A poster for that astonishingly titled dog drama 'Phantom of the Barque, or, The Dumb Black and his Watch Dog'

and seizes him by the throat. The actor playing the villain had to wear protective padding round his neck, and yell 'Take off the dog!' once he was brought down. With its racy plot and exciting fight scenes, the 'Dog of Montargis' would remain a staple item of dog drama for decades to come. In spite of this, the play did not always come off as planned; it is recorded that once, the friendly acting dog stood watching the audience and wagging his tail, instead of 'taking the seize'. The infuriated villain desperately tried to induce him to attack; in the end, he had to fly at the placid dog himself and lift the animal up to his throat.

In 1819, the Dog Bruin acted in a piece entitled 'The Gipsy', which concluded with the hunting of a wild boar. It was an ambitious production, with guns being fired, horses ridden across the stage, and the appearance of a pack of hunting dogs, led by Bruin. After several successful performances, disaster struck one evening, when the powerful Bruin decided to improve on the plot. Breaking free from the huntsmen, he darted after the actor representing the wild boar. The fearful actor jumped into the orchestra pit, but Bruin leapt after him and seized hold of the wild boar costume. According to a newspaper review, "The terrified musicians fled, leaving the two champions in possession of the field. The most indescribable confusion prevailed throughout the theatre. The other dogs on stage encouraged their comrade with all the power of their lungs. The uproar was terrible, and the intrepid dog was separated from his prey with no little difficulty."[1]

In April 1820, the Dog Bruin starred in 'The Cottage of the Lake'. In this play, a child is thrown into an artificial lake, to be saved by the dog. The advertisement for the play also tells that the Misses Cawse, musical prodigies aged eight and eleven, also took part, hopefully in some more dignified position than being unceremoniously thrown into the lake, to be retrieved by Bruin's powerful jaws. The next year, Bruin again demanded trial by battle in 'The Smuggler's Dog', but this is the last we hear of this particular acting dog.[2]

THOSE AMAZING NEWFOUNDLAND DOGS

The Victorian theatregoers loved to see animals on stage. Hippodrama, with horses playing leading roles, was established already before Carlo's success, and these equine actors continued to hoof the boards for several decades. The Covent Garden theatre hired horses from Astley's circus to act in melodramas written particularly to suit these performers. If 'The Dog of Montargis' was the ultimate dog drama, the hippodrama 'Mazeppa', where a naked Tartar boy is strapped to the back of an apparently wild horse, had equal success, particularly if the leading role (the boy, not the horse) was played by the scandalous American star Adah Isaacs Menken.[3] In Victorian theatre, bulls and dragons were played by horses, and wolves and hyaenas by dogs; in some low budget productions, tigers were played by large black dogs painted with yellow stripes. In a play entitled 'The Hindoo Robber', two acting dogs played the part of leopards. When one of them was 'shot' it pretended to stagger and expire on a rock, amidst such tumultous applause that the other 'leopard' became jealous backstage. He rushed on the stage and simulated all the agonies of death "to show that he could die better". There was great amusement at this ludicrous scene, particularly when the spotted costume burst so that *two* tails were exhibited.[4]

A few years after the original Dog Bruin had retired from the stage, he was succeeded by a namesake, another Newfoundland. Along with his master, an impecunious young actor named Wood, Bruin II acted in 'The Dog of Montargis' and other plays, at the Warwick and Drury Lane theatres. In October 1826, a certain Philip Vincent summoned Wood before the Union Hall magistrate's court, claiming that he had reared Bruin from a puppy, and that the handsome and expensive dog had disappeared two years ago, without trace, until it had been found in the possession of the defendant. Things did not look particularly good for the actor Wood, who did not contest these facts. Fortunately he had consulted the solicitor Mr Harmer. It turned out that Vincent, who represented himself in court, had made a serious mistake. The statute under which the summons was granted expressly mentioned that there had to be a charge of theft, and in the present case no such charge had been made. On this technicality, the case was dismissed by the magistrate, since there was no charge of felony.[5]

The acting Newfoundland dogs Hector and Wallace attacking some Bad Indians in 'Dogs of the Forlorn Log House'

THOSE AMAZING NEWFOUNDLAND DOGS

'Take that, Pattaparo!' A Treacherous Indian receives his comeuppance at the paws of two sturdy acting dogs

Sometimes, it was useful to have an acting dog around. In March 1828, a poor woman, who made a precarious living selling watercress, walked along the floating timbers near Searle's boathouse in Lambeth, and plunged headlong into Thames. Fortunately, at the *Times* expressed it, "Wood, the owner of the famous dog of Montargis, was close at hand bathing his favourite". Regarding the situation as an unscheduled rehearsal, Bruin jumped in after the woman and dragged her to shore. When she stood up and threatened to jump back into the river, the acting dog practiced 'taking the seize'. When this suicidal woman was taken to a public house nearby, the servant girl fainted dead away. She was later reproached for her 'hysteria', but it turned out that "she had a more afflicting cause – the watercress woman was her own mother."[6]

In 1829, Wood and Bruin acted in 'Androcles and the Lion' at the Coburg Theatre, with the dog 'contrieved and fitted' in leonine guise. In 1830, Sir Walter Scott's *The Talisman* was adapted for the stage as the amazingly titled dog drama 'Knights of the Cross, or the Dog of the Blood-Stained Banner', with major parts for Wood and Bruin. Going through his entire acting repertoire, Bruin saves Edith Plantagenet from drowning, brings food and drink to a chained prisoner, discovers a thief, and kills a wicked Emir of the Desert. When the dog is ordered to guard the English Standard, a French traitor, played by Wood himself, sneaks up to steal it. The noble Bruin 'takes the seize' and pulls him to the ground, but only to be stabbed by the Frenchman's vassals. There was not a dry eye in the house when the brave dog fell lifeless to the ground, but much cheering and applause when Bruin leapt up a after 'playing dead' to join his fellow thespians in taking the applause.

Wood appears to have been the first person to realise that there was one thing better than keeping an acting dog, namely to possess *two* of these animals. Later in 1830, he procured, hopefully by more honest means this time, another Newfoundland, named Hector. The two acting dogs got on well together, and had several plays written for them, like 'The Foul Anchor' and 'The Cherokee Chief'. The last mention of Wood and his dogs dates from October 1831 when Hector played in 'The Dog of Montargis' at the Royal Pavilion Theatre.[7]

* * *

Old actors, and acting dogs, do not die; they merely fade away. Although we will hear no more from the impecunious, dog-stealing Wood, it must be suspected that his two acting dogs started another career, under new management. In May 1833, a performance of 'The Cherokee Chief, or the Dogs of the Wreck', featured the young actor Barkham Cony and his two dogs Hector and Bruin. Although a newspaper review praises Cony "for the very extraordinary degree of docility and intelligence to which he has brought his favourite animals" there is good reason to suspect that Cony had purchased Wood's dogs, particularly since the drama was one the dogs were already adept at acting in.

Barkham Cony was born in 1802, and became an actor when he was still a young man. In 1828, he was one of the leading performers at the Cobourg Theatre in London. A strong, muscular fellow, he was a useful boxer and athlete. The success of 'The Cherokee Chief' made him take up dog drama in a big way, and he would remain a major exponent of this form of theatre for decades. He soon joined forces with the young American actor Edwin Blanchard. This amusing character specialized in low comedy, sometimes playing the role of an orang-outang dressed in a specially manufactured suit. Cony's success with Hector and Bruin convinced Blanchard that dogs paid better than apes, however, and the two actors would remain inseparable for many years. By this time, there were several other actors specializing in training acting dogs; they were known as 'dog-men' and travelled from theatre to theatre, performing with their beasts.[8]

For decades, Cony and Blanchard kept their position as London's leading dog-men. In 1836, they even crossed the Atlantic with their acting dogs. Whether Hector and Bruin were still the original performers is anybody's guess, but their performance in 'The Dog of Montargis' at the Bowery Theatre in New York was a huge success. The Americans had never seen acting dogs like these two massive but sagacious Newfoundlands, and Cony soon became known as 'The Dog Star'. He usually played the villain, and was particularly adept in finding novel ways for the dogs to put an end to his career, by drowning or suffocating him, pushing him down a precipice, shooting him with a pistol held in the dog's mouth, or discharging a hidden explosive device. In 'The Dog of Montargis', Cony played the

'Get the key, Emile!' A dramatic scene from 'The Dog of the Pyrenees' with a heroic Newfoundland dog liberating his imprisoned master, from the *Illustrated London News*, February 10 1846

role of the villain Landri, introducing a new high point in dog drama when the agile Hector made a great leap to knock him from the saddle of his horse. He used protective padding underneath his clothes to lessen the bruising when the dogs grasped him with their powerful jaws. Blanchard sometimes played the hero, although the American's new-found wealth had caused him to put on much weight, rendering him quite unfit to be jumping about on stage.

Cony and Blanchard dominated the dog drama throughout the 1830s and 1840s. They were equally successful in Britain and in the United States. In 1840, they were back in London, acting with their dogs in 'Napoleon, or the Deserter'. One day, when Blanchard was taking Bruin to the theatre, a large dog came rushing out from a carpenter's shop and attacked the celebrated acting dog. When the massive Newfoundland fought back, driving his opponent into the shop, the carpenter emerged with a stick, which he used to belabour the acting dog. Blanchard, a useful boxer just like his fellow 'Dog Star', ended the fracas by knocking the carpenter out cold.

Later, when prosecuted for assault and battery, Blanchard calmly asserted that both he and his dog had acted in self defence. They were engaged at the Victoria Theatre, playing for full houses, and would he risk an injury to his star performer by setting the acting dog on some disreputable street mongrel,

THOSE AMAZING NEWFOUNDLAND DOGS

risking injury to his own valuable animal? It turned out that the carpenter had a bad reputation, and that his dog had been a nuisance to the local residents, once even biting a policeman on duty. When the case was dismissed, the carpenter with the black eye swore an angry oath at the spectators.[9]

* * *

Not all acting Newfoundland dogs were high-profile London performers. A sterling canine actor up north was Mr Samuel Wild's Newfoundland 'Nelson', who made his debut in the Huddersfield Theatre in 1848, aged three years. An incident the following year helped to make him something of a local hero. On June 6 1849, a young man travelling in a rowing boat on the river Ribble, near Preston, fell into the water. Probably due to insobriety, he was unable to keep afloat, but at that moment a powerful Newfoundland dog leapt into the river. As expressed by a breathless newspaper reporter: "On the cap of the man presenting itself to view, it was seized by the dog, but being loosely tied it gave way, and the body sunk a second time. The dog, however, finding that he had missed his object, abandoned the cap, and barking furiously returned in time to seize the drowning man by the arm as he again rose to the surface.

This hold he cautiously relinquished, and the collar of the young man's coat was firmly grasped in the dog's powerful jaws, who swam with him, keeping his head above water till he reached the shore."[10]

The half-drowned youth, named as Richard Craiston, a native of Kendal, was taken to the nearest public house, where he later recovered completely. There was sensation when it was revealed that this life-saving Newfoundland had a second career as a small-time actor. Giving an interview to the local newspaper, Mr Wild said that he had purchased Nelson in Wales, since he had seen some dog dramas in London, and

'Quick, Bruin, carry that burning torch away from the gunpowder store! 'Woof!'

A faded old print of Mr Cony as Landri, being attacked by his acting Newfoundland dog

wanted a canine actor of his own. The newspaper publicity did Mr Wild's struggling troupe of actors much good. Reviews of his performances seldom failed to point out that "the Newfoundland dog, Nelson, as usual, gave great satisfaction. In November 1850 the Huddersfield Theatre "brought out a new nautical drama, written expressly for the peculiar and extraordinary sagacity of Mr Wild's Newfoundland dog, Nelson, called *The Pirate Ship; or, the Dog of the Main*." In 1852, Nelson starred in *The Dog of the Wave*, at the New Theatre, Keighley. In 1856, Nelson starred in another play, in Halifax, along with the French Dog Lion, and the War Camels from the Crimea. In 1858, when Mr Wild's troupe was in Dewbury, the two dogs were still active on stage, but the camels proved a short-lived attraction.[11]

In November 1860, the Era newspaper, which had noticed Nelson more than once during his long career, had sad tidings for all northern fanciers of dog drama:

DEATH OF A THEATRICAL PERFORMER
We have this week to record the demise of a well-known stage favourite, who, in his time, played many parts, for which even our greatest histrionic artists would find themselves but incompetent representatives. The famous Newfoundland dog 'Nelson' (the property of Mr S. Wild, the theatrical manager), died on Sunday, November 3, in his seventeenth year. Among the good actions of his life must be recorded the fact, that he saved a man from drowning in the River Ribble, at Preston, on the 6th of June, 1849, and for which a silver medal was bestowed. The deceased Nelson was considered one of the best performing dogs in England, and he had the honour of being written for by several minor authors, who developed his sagacity in pieces suited to his canine talents. His death, which occurred at Blackburn, will be much regretted by those to whom his good qualities had rendered him greatly attached.[12]

* * *

Victorian dog drama was entirely unhindered by political correctness. A blind or deaf-mute character was considered quite hilarious, as was a clownish black servant, or a simpleton labouring under some unfortunate speech impediment. In the dog drama 'The Dumb Black and his Watch Dog', the intrepid dog is not only stronger, but also more intelligent than his pathetic, speechless human sidekick. The Dumb Black gets into trouble again and again, only to be saved by the noble, patient Watch Dog. When the hapless Black is framed for theft, the faithful dog turns detective, discovering evidence that exonerates him.

In 'The Smuggler's Dog, or the Blind Boy's Murder', the forceful Smuggler's Dog saves the life of the Blind Boy a number of times, but the sightless lad still keeps bumbling about in a dangerous manner. If there is a fire, a waterfall or an open trapdoor on stage, he heads straight for it. Having been rescued from drowning, fire and a cutlass-wielding pirate, the Blind Boy is finally pushed down a precipice when the dog is busy biting another villain. Still, the Smuggler's Dog witnesses the murder and demands trial by battle, with the inevitable result.

There was a good deal of interest in Native Americans in England at this time. Eschewing the Wild West adage that the only Good Indian is a Dead Indian, the London playwrights instead took the cue from the books of Fenimore Cooper: there were Good Indians, and then there were Bad Indians. The Good Indians were noble savages with names like 'Wonga' or 'Eagle-Eye', usually the last of their tribe, and accompanied by a 'funny' blind or dumb simpleton - and by a large dog. The Bad Indians had names like 'Rattlesnake' or 'Black Vulture', lurid designs on white women, a firm dislike for dogs, and a propensity to throw disabled simpletons into the water from high precipices.

THOSE AMAZING NEWFOUNDLAND DOGS

There were no canine actresses bitching about at this time: the dogs were all male, with martial-sounding names like Hector, Victor, Lion or Neptune. The majority of them were either purebred Newfoundlands or Newfoundland crosses: large, imposing animals capable of holding their own in the frequent fight scenes. One would have thought it a useful ploy to pit the acting dogs against each other: both the hero and the villain should be accompanied by Newfoundland dogs, one a noble and upright animal, the other a veritable Cujo. The drama would of course end with both the human and canine actors settling their various scores in a grand fight scene. This idea was never put into effect, however; in Victorian melodrama, the acting dogs were uniformly good, loyal and faithful, and more heroic than the play's hero himself.

* * *

Cony and Blanchard remained in London until 1844, acting in 'The Knights of the Cross', 'The Smuggler's Dog' and 'The Dumb Slave'. Blanchard made a burlesque contribution in 'The Orang Outang and his Double, or the Runaway Monkey'. In 1845 and 1846, they were back at the Bowery in New York. This was the time when dog drama was at its most famous. The New Yorkers' delight in seeing canine actors on stage led to some old plays being revised: 'Jack Sheppard, and His Dog', 'Dick Turpin, and His Dog' or even 'Caspar Hauser, the Blind Boy of Germany, and His Dog' were all more successful than the dog-less original versions.

When performing in New York in 1851, Cony and Blanchard had an angry quarrel, leading to the two 'Dog Stars' parting company, for good. Still, they remained in town, doing their best to put each other out of business. Blanchard was acting at the National with the dogs Hector and Bruin, whereas Cony was at the Bowery with his son Eugene Cony and the Dog Yankee. They acted in the same plays: 'The Dog of Montargis', 'The Butcher's Dog of Ghent' and 'The Dogs of Mount St. Bernard'. When Blanchard once more squeezed his bulky frame into the monkey-suit in 'The Orang Outang', Cony retaliated by having 'The Cross of Death; or, The Dog Witness' written expressly for himself and the Dog Yankee. Although some purists complained that two of New York's major theatres had been made into kennels, there was enough interest from the dog-loving theatregoers to make both outfits prosper.

Cony and Blanchard were to remain enemies and competitors until Cony's premature death in 1858. Young Eugene Cony tried to carry on his father's life work, but without much success. Blanchard, a more established name, remained a force to be reckoned with in New York show business until the 1870s. By this time, his main rival was the actress Fanny Herring, who performed with her dogs Lafayette and Thunder, in plays like 'The Rag Woman and Her Dogs'. Although classics like 'The Dog of Montargis' and 'The Smuggler's Dog' received an occasional airing as late as the 1880s, the enthusiasm for dog drama had all but ended by that time. It was considered old-fashioned and downmarket to have animals on stage, and the traditional Victorian melodramas continued without the canine actors

* * *

In September 1918, the American Corporal Lee Duncan was serving in Lorraine, France. One day, when he and his troop were checking out a bombed war dog kennel, they found a mother German Shepherd dog and her litter as the only survivors. Duncan made sure all the dogs were saved and himself took care of two of the puppies. He named them Rin Tin Tin and Nannette after some small puppets the French had given to the American soldiers for good luck. Rin Tin Tin survived the journey back to the United States, but poor Nannette soon died of disease. 'Rinty' as he was nicknamed, grew up to become a large, strapping German Shepherd dog, dark sable in colour and with very dark eyes. At

Dog drama at the Bower Theatre

a dog show in 1922, he amazed everyone with his extraordinary agility; the dog was able to clear a fence of eleven feet, nine inches. The canny Lee Duncan soon realized that such a handsome, well-trained dog could be an asset in the film industry. After Rinty had got his great break in the film industry by stepping in for a recalcitrant wolf in 'The Man from Hell's River', there was no stopping the acting dog. He successfully competed against Strongheart, Hollywood's resident acting German Shepherd, and made not less than 26 pictures for Warner Brothers, allegedly saving the company from bankruptcy, just like Carlo the Acting Dog rescued the Drury Lane theatre more than a century earlier. Just like the acting Newfoundlands of Victorian times, Rinty was always the 'good guy', saving people from drowning, carrying children out from burning houses, and fighting outlaws or Bad Indians with enthusiasm. A worthy successor to Carlo and Bruin, this agile and super-intelligent dog opened and shut doors and windows with the greatest of ease, boarded trains or stagecoaches when he thought he needed faster transportation, and understood the workings of firearms and explosives.[13]

In 1943, the sentimental story 'Lassie Come Home' about a collie making a long and heroic journey to rejoin her master after his family is forced to sell her for money, was made into a major film by Metro-Goldwyn-Mayer. Starring Roddy McDowall and Elizabeth Taylor, the film was a huge hit. It also launched the career of the handsome collie Pal, handled by the American brothers Frank and Rudd Weatherwax. Pal starred in seven films and two TV shows between 1943 and 1954. Like all other collies to play Lassie over the years, Pal was a male; not only are male collies larger than the females, they also retain a thicker summer coat which looks better on film. Although Lassie was a male in drag, her onstage character differed from that of Rin Tin Tin. As we know, Rinty was a masculine, gung-ho dog who never backed out of a fight, dispatching various outlaws, pirates and tomahawk-wielding Bad Indians with gusto. Lassie was more feminine, and her adventures more sentimental, although she sometimes made use of her fangs to defend small children against various mean-spirited characters. With her superior intelligence, Lassie was very adept at looking after foolish and imprudent children getting into trouble. If they fell into the water, she dragged them ashore; if they got struck by an avalanche, she dug them out; if they got caught by Bad Indians, she braved arrows and tomahawks to liberate them. If there was a landfall across the railway line, Lassie understood the danger, grabbed a red flag and stopped the train.

On Hollywood's Walk of Fame, there are stars for Strongheart, Rin Tin Tin and Lassie, the only three dogs represented. In contrast, the acting Newfoundland dogs of Victorian times are a forgotten part of canine history; their story is told here for the first time. It is clear that Carlo was the great forerunner, and that the concept of dog drama started with him. Although later acting dogs, like those managed by Cony and Blanchard, were more proficient and had more tricks in their repertoire, it was the great Carlo plunging into the artificial lake on stage who started it all.

It is also clear that there are some important parallels between Victorian dog drama and today's concept of the onstage canine. Carlo, Bruin and Hector were all superlatively brave and heroic, just like Rin Tin Tin and Lassie. They save their pathetic human sidekicks when they get into trouble: the child of the Marchioness of Calatrava, the Dumb Black, and the thoughtless and accident-prone children protected by Lassie. The mongrel dog Benji in the 1974 film with the same name also uses his superior intellect to find and rescue some kidnapped children.

Another long-lived concept is that of the dog as 'silent witness' to a murder, like the Dog of Montargis and the Smuggler's Dog. In the amusing and popular 1989 film *Turner & Hooch*, a large junkyard dog is taken care of by a detective after witnessing the murder of its owner. And indeed, the dog spots the killer and tries to attack him. In the end, Hooch is shot dead, giving his life to save that of his master, like many a Victorian acting dog before him.

In *Turner & Hooch*, the og is supposed to be a junkyard mongrel, but he is in fact a pedigree Dogue de

THOSE AMAZING NEWFOUNDLAND DOGS

Bordeaux, an uncommon breed notable for their large heads, powerful jaws and prodigious slobber-cheeks. Unlike the well-trained Rin Tin Tin and the spotlessly clean Lassie, Hooch is a very mischievous and destructive dog, in spite of his heroic qualities. The same is true for the disgraced police dog Jerry Lee in the 1989 film *K-9*: the intelligent but lazy dog works only when he wants to, and is up to all kinds of mischief. The detective masters of these two dogs, played by Tom Hanks and James Belushi, respectively, are depicted as equal partners to their heroic dogs, rather like the stalwart Knights of the Cross and courageous Good Indians in Victorian dog drama.

It is also rewarding to look for traces of Victorian dog drama in the very popular 1992 film *Beethoven*. In this hit comedy, a St. Bernard puppy escapes from dog thieves and is taken care of by an American family. Although Beethoven is full of mischief, and constantly filling his digestive cavity, they soon

A poster for dog drama at the Bower Saloon

become fond of him. He grows up to become a massive St. Bernard male. When the son of the family is annoyed by bullies, Beethoven frightens them off, and when the careless little girl falls into a swimming pool, the brave dog does a 'Carlo' to perfection and retrieves her. The dog thieves are not far away, however; together with an evil veterinarian, who wants to use Beethoven for an ammunition test, they imprison the great dog in a research facility. In the final fight scene, the acting dog 'takes the seize' like a champion to dispose of one of the villains.

CHAPTER 9.
NEWFOUNDLAND DOGS IN THE NEWS 1800-1850

>Thus when a little fearful puppy meets
A noble Newfoundland dog in the streets,
He creeps, and whines, and licks the lofty brute;
Curls round him, falls upon his back, and then
Springs up and gambols---frisks it back agen,
And crawls in dread submission to his foot;
Looks up, and hugs his neck, and seems t'intreat him,
With ev'ry mark of terror, not to eat him.

>The Newfoundland dog, conscious of his might,
Cocks high his tail and ears, his state to show;
Then lifts his leg (a little unpolite)
And almost drowns the supplicant below;
Then seems, in full-blown majesty, to say,
'Great is my power---but, lo! I'll not abuse it;
I'm Cæsar! paltry creature, go thy way;
But mind, I can *devour* thee, if I choose it.'

>Peter Pindar, *Ode upon Ode*.

As Mr. James Seaman, of Rupert-street, Haymarket, was, on Friday last, going to Bond-street, to pay a large sum of money into the hands of his banker, he fell down in a fit in the street, which bringing a crowd about him, a Newfoundland dog, much attached to him, would not suffer any person to approach his master, who continued in that state for about ten minutes, when he recovered. It is remarkable that this faithful animal saved his master from drowning, about two years since, when he fell overboard in this harbour. [*Portsmouth Telegraph*, June 23, 1800]

A few days since, a waterman's boy cleaning his boat at Cherry Garden Stairs, and playing with a Newfoundland dog, both fell overboard: the boy sunk in deep water; the dog playing in the water for its own diversion, stones were thrown where the lad sunk, by people from the bank, when the sagacious animal dived in his sportive manner, and instead of the stones brought up the nearly perished lad by the arm, who was happily restored to his friends. [*Morning Post*, May 7, 1801]

A remarkable instance in the sagacity of dogs occurred yesterday about eleven o'clock; as a gentleman was going along the path that leads from Kennington Common to Camberwell, and which stands between two ditches, he observed several children playing at a distance, and almost at the same instance

A sagacious Newfoundland dog giving a spaniel a ducking, from the *Sporting Magazine* of 1819

perceived one of them fall into the ditch – he hastened to the spot, accompanied by a very large Newfoundland dog he had with him – the sagacious animal no sooner perceived the child struggling in the water, than he plunged in, and seizing her by the hair of the head, brought her with some difficulty to the side of the footpath, when, with the assistance of his master, she was hoisted up on terra firma, without sustaining any other injury than a violent vomiting, occasioned by the stagnant water she had swallowed, and which is of so foul a nature that it would have caused immediate suffocation. [*Jackson's Oxford Journal*, December 31, 1803]

An extraordinary instance of the sagacity and utility of that useful animal the dog, occurred one day last week: - A gentleman of Newcastle, crossing the Ford, near Netherwitton, was thrown from his horse in the midst of the current, which was then running rapidly; and he would inevitably have suffered (not being able to swim, and having a great coat, boots, &c. on) had not a fine young Newfoundland dog, which had followed him from town, leapt into the water, and dragged him safely to shore. [*Lancaster Gazette*, June 9, 1804].

On Monday night a gang of thieves broke into the house of J. Asthall, Esq. at Harehatch, and stole from thence a quantity of plate, &c. They were seen by a man who resides in a neighbouring cottage, who did not suspect a robbery, until half an hour afterwards, when he heard a Newfoundland dog barking, and on running to the spot, the dog had seized one of the villains, who was secured, with a quantity of the stolen property. *[Times*, October 11, 1804]

SUICIDE - Yesterday morning the body of a very genteel dressed female, with two wedding rings on, money in her pockets, apparently about 30 years of age, handsome and fair, and with every appearance of a Lady that had walked out to take the air in her morning dress, was found in the New River in the following manner: - Two young lads having taken out a Newfoundland dog for exercise, threw in a stone for him to dive after, he brought up the body of the person we have described ... [*Morning Post*, August 22, 1805]

Saturday, at the Marlborough-street Office, Mary Johnson was charged with conducting a private distillery, in Gloucester-place, New Road. It appeared that the officers of Excise repaired to the defendant by information of her transactions. On entering the yard, one of them was seized by a Newfoundland dog, and was much injured by him. [*Times*, June 9, 1806]

On Friday afternoon as a young woman was going on board a collier, lying off Hill Wall, Limehouse, she fell over the gunnel of the boat, when a Newfoundland dog on the main deck leaped into the water, seized her by the clothes, and kept her afloat till she received assistance. The same valuable dog lately saved one of the crew, who fell overboard at Gravesend. Fifty guineas were offered for him by a West India Captain, and refused. [*Bury and Norwich Post,* August 6, 1806]

A singular instance of the sagacity of the Newfoundland dog occurred a few days since on the River: - As Mr Cock, who keeps a tavern, in Cleveland-street, and a party of friends, were returning from Richmond, where they had been spending the day, the boat upset a little below Kew bridge, in consequence of Mr C. (who is a very corpulent man) shifting from his side too suddenly. Having a Newfoundland dog on board, the faithful animal immediately laid hold of his master, and took him on shore, and returned again with an astonishing speed to the boat, and continued to go backwards and forwards until he had rescued six men from their perilous situation in less than a quarter of an hour, to the admiration of a multitude of spectators, who had assembled on the bridge. [*Jackson's Oxford Journal,* July 9, 1808]

On Wednesday, as a boy was reaching from one vessel to another, lying in the river Thames, near

Greenwich, he fell into the water; but a Newfoundland dog jumped in, and taking hold of his arm, dragged him to some timber that was floating near the place, by which means the boy was saved. [*Morning Chronicle*, September 30, 1808]

A CANINE MENDICANT - A venerable sailor, with white locks, has lately made his appearance in the Metropolis, attended by a large Newfoundland dog. The veteran tar, is an eccentric character, but the sagacity of his canine associate excites admiration. The dog takes the hat of his master in his mouth, and he implores charity, in the shops of the inhabitants by the most expressive signs. He bows his head, scrapes his foot on the ground, and looks steadfastly in the face of the person from whom he expects a donation. If he procures a halfpenny from one friend, he immediately walks to another, and returns to his master with the contribution he raised. It frequently happens that this honest servant meets with harsh treatment and a denial of aid; but his humility on such occasions is truly astonishing. Without waiting to trouble the uncharitable, he immediately returns to his master, and walks into another house, where he has a greater chance of success. The docility and discriminating faculty of this dog are the support of the old tar, who drinks, eats, and converses with him as a friend. Their intimacy is of long standing, and the sailor often gratefully declares, that the animal has rendered him more services than he ever received from his fellow men. [*Aberdeen Journal*, November 9, 1808]

One of the men would inevitably have been lost had it not been for a Newfoundland Dog, which saw him at a distance from all human aid, swam to him, seized him by the hair, and never left his hold till the man was safe, tho' both the dog and the man were frequently buried under the waves. This is the second instance in which the same dog has preserved the life of a rational being. He belongs to Mr Reed, of Lowestoft. [*Bury and Norwich Post*, December 20, 1809][1]

A Newfoundland dog was on Thursday last brought to the hammer in the neighbourhood of Wapping, among other effects of a Naval Officer, and knocked down for eighteen guineas! A competition was excited among the bidders by the auctioneer stating that the animal had at different times saved three persons from being drowned. [*Morning Chronicle*, December 5, 1810]

A vessel was lost on the Manacle Rocks, near Falmouth, on Tuesday, with all the crew; she had a vane, blue and white, vertical as the fore. A large Newfoundland dog swam ashore from her. [*Caledonian Mercury*, March 9, 1811]

A large Newfoundland dog was found by the side of his deceased master, (another officer of the Royals) three days after the engagement. On the approach of the French party, employed to bury the dead, the faithful animal showed considerable ferocity; but, being pacified at length, he permitted the corpse to be removed, and followed it to the grave. The impressive fact was communicated to General Rey, who instantly adopted the noble animal, and has brought him to England. [*Royal Cornwall Gazette*, October 2, 1813]

Sometime ago, a young woman was amusing herself with an infant at Aston's Quay, near Carlisle Bridge, Dublin. Whilst she was sportively toying with the child, it made a sudden spring from her arms, and in an instant fell into the Liffey. The screaming nurse and anxious spectators saw the water close over the child, and conceived that it had sunk to rise no more. A Newfoundland dog, which had been accidentally passing with its master, sprang forward to the wall, and gazing wistfully at the ripple in the water, made by the child's descent. In the same instant the child reappeared on the surface of the Liffey, and the dog sprang forward towards the water. Whilst the animal was descending, the child again sunk, and the faithful creature was seen anxiously swimming round and round the spot where it had disappeared. Once more the child rose to the surface – the dog seized him, and, with a firm but gentle pressure, bore him to land without injury. Meanwhile a gentleman arrived, who, on inquiry into the circumstances of the transaction, exhibited strong marks of sensibility and feeling towards the child, and of admiration for the dog that had rescued him from a premature death. The person who had removed the babe from the dog turned round to shew the infant to this sympathizing gentleman, whose arms were stretched out to embrace the little innocent; when lo! it presented to his view the well known features of his own son. A mixed sensation of terror, joy and surprise, struck him mute. When he had recovered the use of his faculties, and fondly kissed his little darling, he lavished a thousand embraces on the dog, and offered to his master a very large sum (500 guineas) if he would transfer the valuable to him; but the owner of the dog (Colonel Wynne) felt too much affection for the useful creature to part with him for any pecuniary consideration whatever. *[Caledonian Mercury,* May 15, 1815]

DROWNED BODIES FOUND BY A DOG - A few days back as a Gentleman with a Newfoundland dog was crossing in Air-street-fields, Bethnal-green, where there are two ponds, the dog plunged into one of them, and appeared to grapple with something, which his master perceived to be a human body; on examination it proved to be the body of a boy about 14 years of age. The dog instantly plunged into the other pond also, and brought out a woman's cap: this second circumstance created more alarm, and the pond was dragged, when the body of a woman genteelly dressed was brought up; both bodies appeared to have been for some time in the water; they were carried to the bone-house to be owned. [*Times*, August 4, 1815]

On Wednesday week, T. Smith, a young man of Sunderland, after an absence of nine years and a half, unexpectedly arrived at home, to the great joy and wonder of his family. He had formed one of the crew of a ship, supposed to have foundered, and the crew perished; and they were mourned for accordingly by their relations. The ship was cast on shore on some distant island, and by means of a Newfoundland dog a rope was conveyed on shore, and being made fast by the natives, the crew was saved. [*York Herald*, December 30, 1815]

REMARKABLE INSTANCE OF THE SAGACITY OF THE NEWFOUNDLAND DOG - A Gentleman returning from Hackney to London on Monday last with his dog, on their arrival near Hare-street-fields, Bethnal-green, the dog left him to go to a pond in the fields, whilst his master proceeded on his journey. A very short time afterwards the dog ran with the utmost fury after him, and was labouring under an anxiety that his master could not account for; on his paying little attention to him, the dog laid hold of his coat, and ran as of he bid him follow him; he followed the poor animal to the pond in the field, when the dog instantly plunged in, swam to the opposite side, and after staying under water some time, he rose with something apparently very heavy, but which proved to be a bonnet; the master of the animal supposing there was somebody in the water, encouraged him to go in a second time; he did, but his efforts proved fruitless; the next attempt the poor dog was quite exhausted; he was under water for some minutes, but at length rose with the body of a young woman, having a firm hold of her by the hair of the back of her head; the dog arrived safe with the object of his pursuit, which was taken from him, and he laid himself down on the bank almost dead, but by his master's and other assistance he was soon restored, and appeared highly delighted. The body was taken to the parish work-house, where it lies for the Coroner's inquest. It is supposed that in the first instance the bonnet string broke by the weight of the body. [*Trewman's Exeter Flying Post*, November 27, 1817]

CURIOUS RECOVERY OF STOLEN PROPERTY - On Saturday some boys playing in Hare-street-fields, Bethnal-green, with a Newfoundland dog, who was swimming across a large pond; suddenly they observed the dog dive under that water, and soon after rise with a large bundle of cloth, which he made many attempts to carry to the side, but from its weight did not succeed. The boys undressed themselves, and got out the bundle, and several others, which consisted of linen and shirting, which had been subsequently owned by a Lady residing at Bethnal-green, who was robbed of the property four months ago, and for which robbery two persons were tried last Old Bailey Sessions, and acquitted. [*Jackson's Oxford Journal*, May 9, 1818]

THOSE AMAZING NEWFOUNDLAND DOGS

A NEWFOUNDLAND DOG'S SAGACITY - At the Ferry-house, at Worcester, was some time ago kept a Newfoundland dog, famous for having saved the lives of several people from drowning; and so fond was he of the water himself, that he seemed to consider any disinclination to it in other dogs as insult to the species – at least if a dog was left on the bank by its master, with intent to oblige it to follow the boat across the river (which is narrow there), and stood yelping at the bottom of the steps unwilling to take to the water, the old dog would go down to him, and with a gasping noise as if in mockery, take him by the back of the neck, and throw him in, in the manner endeavoured to be described by the accompanying plate. [*Sporting Magazine* NS 3 [1819], 80]

PROVIDENTIAL ESCAPE FROM DROWNING - On Saturday, the wife of a Gentleman named Simmonds, residing in Battersea Fields, was going to visit a friend in the King's Road, Chelsea, and taking her child, which was about two years old, with her, she took a boat at Chelsea Reach; but when she got into the middle of the stream, the child suddenly, as it were, leaped out of her lap into the water. She, in attempting to save him in a moment of frenzy, overbalanced herself, and fell also into the water. A Newfoundland dog, which followed her from home, and which had been put into the boat, leaped out after the child, and kept it above the water, but the mother sunk. Another waterman, who witnessed the accident, was coming up, against tide, to their assistance, when he saw her rise to the surface, and fortunately he succeeded, at the first effort, in getting sufficient hold of her to keep her up till the other waterman, who, by the assistance of the dog, by this time had saved the child, came to his assistance, and they took her up. Both were taken, in a state of exhaustion, to the public-house upon the Bank, where prompt assistance was humanely rendered, and they were both restored. [*Morning Post*, December 23, 1819]

Apprehension of the Notorious and Daring Offender, JOHN WILLIAMS – The public will recollect, that some time ago this man succeeded in finding his way on board the Venus, Captain Martin, lying in the River, where he effected a robbery, by stealing the watch and some other articles belonging to the master. He then attempted to make his escape, and on perceiving that he was discovered, and that alarm had been given, jumped overboard. A Newfoundland dog, excited to the pursuit, jumped after him, and having seized him, held him until several persons who came to the assistance of the animal apprehended the robber. [*Exeter Flying Post*, January 20, 1820]

Accidents – During the gale of the 14th ult. Which proved fatal to the Thomas and Mary, and her crew, in Chiswell Cove, three boats were in imminent danger from the fury of the waves; when a Newfoundland dog plunged into the water, and reached the nearest boat. The crew immediately put a line into his mouth, and the sagacious animal returned with it to the shore! This line was eagerly grasped by the sailors on the beach, a rope was fastened to it, and all three boats were safely pulled to the shore. [*Liverpool Mercury*, May 25, 1821]

Last week an interesting young woman was observed wandering about the common near the Regent's Canal, singing hymns and clasping her arms across her bosom. She at length approached the bank, and after some loud ejaculations sprang into the middle of the water. The beholders were intimidated from venturing in; a foreigner with a Newfoundland dog came up, and the sagacious animal jumped in and brought her on shore by the collar of her pelisse. She recovered some hours after, and stated in answer to some questions, that she had attempted the rash act in consequence of seduction. [*Liverpool Mercury*, September 14, 1821]

On being overtaken, the delinquent drew a knife and stabbed his pursuer in the side, but the coachman calling aloud for assistance, the gamekeeper of Charleton, who was within hearing, came to his assistance, accompanied by a large Newfoundland dog. The dog being set on the miscreant, threw him down and so terrified him, that he was fain to be quiet, and was secured and carried to Montrose jail. [*Caledonian Mercury*, April 6, 1822][2]

THOSE AMAZING NEWFOUNDLAND DOGS

'Disputing the Prize': two young Newfoundland dogs are having a friendly scrap. A print by J. Scott Jr. after the original painting by J.M. Ward, from the *Annals of Sporting and Fancy Gazette*, 1825

The Earl of Mount Edgecumbe is occupying Mount Ararat House, in the Vineyard, Richmond. We are sorry to find that when his Lordship was getting better of his broken thigh and walking on his crutches in the garden, he was run against and thrown down by a Newfoundland dog; this had impeded his recovery. [*Morning Post*, October 30, 1823]

On Friday last, as a child, about 14 months old, was playing near the edge of the quay, at the upper drawbridge, Leith, a very large Newfoundland dog, belonging to the Captain of a vessel lying there, was running furiously along, when it came in contact with the child, which it precipitated with some violence to a considerable distance in the harbour; the dog ran on, when a sailor on board the vessel to which the dog belonged, called the dog back, and pointed to the child which was floating. – It immediately returned, plunged into the water, and seized the child by the back. One of the spectators, fearing that the child's head might still remain under the water, and thus occasion its death, although supported by the dog, plunged in, and endeavoured to take hold of it to bring it on shore; the dog, however, would not allow him to touch it, in consequence of which a battle took place, in which, however, the dog ultimately prevailed, and brought the little innocent, whose life it had unconsciously endangered, safe to the shore, amidst the greetings of hundreds who had witnessed the scene. [*Morning Post*, August 20, 1825]

Remarkable sagacity – Some time ago, a child was walking out with the maid-servant in George's-square, Edinburgh, where it would appear, the dogs are remarkable for their wisdom and benevolence; the child was throwing a ball before it, which happened to run into the middle of the street, and the child followed it. The servant happened to meet some one with whom she stopped to converse, and at the same moment a carriage came quickly round the corner of the square towards the child. A large Newfoundland dog, which was lying upon the pavement, darted forward, seized the child by the clothes, and laid it safely down at the feet of the servant. No wonder we have epitaphs on Newfoundland dog. [*York Herald*, September 10, 1825]

SINGULAR INCIDENT - A valuable Newfoundland dog, belonging to Mr John Rose, of Olton-end, in the parish of Solihull, was missing from the house of its owner, the week before last, and continued absent for seven days. On the morning of the eighth day, one of Mr Rose's servants, whilst walking round his master's grounds, passed by a rabbit-burrow, from which proceeded a sound similar to the whimpering of a dog, and by which he recognized the voice of the one so long missing. Having used various endeavours to get the animal out, without success, he commenced digging up the earth, and after two hours' labour, succeeded in penetrating to the prison of the poor dog, eight feet deep, and releasing him from durance-vile, after being in close and solitary confinement seven days and eight nights, without obtaining any food. The animal was much reduced, and unable to stand, but proper aliment being administered, it has ever since gradually recovered from its long abstinence. *[Times*, December 25, 1826]

On Sunday morning a man apparently drunk took off his clothes and went into the dam, on the Molendinar, opposite to the High Church, Glasgow, to bathe. Being unable to swim, he was just sinking, when a large Newfoundland dog rushed in and caught him by the back part of the head, and drew him ashore. When the votary of cheap whiskey recovered, the first thing he did was to give his faithful dog a severe kicking. Which was the brute? [*Lancaster Gazette,* April 21, 1827]

On Sunday last, a young woman from Kilmarnock, of the name of Charlotte Mackenzie, on stepping from a boat to the banks of the Canal, between the two bridges first from Port Hopetoun, fell into the Canal. She sunk to the bottom, and was ten minutes in the water, when a Newfoundland dog plunged in and brought her to the shore! Medical aid having been had resource to, she is now in a fair way of recovery. [*Caledonian Mercury*, July 26, 1827]

A remarkably fine Newfoundland dog (named Carron) belonging to Mr Henry Bell, of the Baths, Helensburgh, in the month of August last, was seen watching like a cat on the banks of the Clyde, behind the baths. A person observed at the same time a cod fish about 18 inches long, in sportive mood jumping repeatedly out of the water. The sagacious dog had noticed the unwary fish, and at a favourable moment plunged into the Clyde, and disappeared for a short time. He then made his appearance with the fish in his mouth, and delivered it to one of Mr Bell's servants, with very few marks of violence on it. *[Times*, November 2, 1827]

On the cross-examination of the witnesses by Mr Bligh, it came out that the game-keeping party had a huge Newfoundland dog with them; one of them had a bill-hook, others guns, and others pistols. 'Some saucy words passed from the prisoners, but not from us.' One of the keepers said that 'he would let the Newfoundland dog go to pitch into them', but the dog attacked one of his own species instead of attaching himself to a biped. [*Times,* March 11, 1829][3]

During the gale on Thursday last, a vessel was driven on the beach at Lydd; no boats could get off to the assistance of the crew, who were, however, all saved and brought ashore, through the activity of a

Newfoundland dog. The surf was rolling furiously, and eight poor fellows were crying out for aid which the spectators could not afford them, when one man directed the attention of his dog to the vessel, and the intelligent animal at once swum towards it, and the crew joyfully made fast a rope on a piece of wood, which the dog seized and swam with to his master on shore; a line of communication was thus formed, and the eight mariners rescued from a watery grave. [*Morning Chronicle*, June 9, 1829]

CANINE SAGACITY - On the occasion of opening the family vault of the Bosvilles, at Ravenfield, a short time ago, for the interment of Mrs. Bosville, a large Newfoundland dog belonging to Colonel Bosville, who was interred eleven weeks previous, found its way to its master's coffin, and placed himself upon it, and remained there until the funeral of Mrs. Bosville took place, from whence it could only be removed with force. It is worthy of remark, that though there were several coffins in the vault, the dog instantly proceeded to that of his master. [*John Bull*, August 31, 1829]

EXTRAORDINARY CIRCUMSTANCE - A party of Gentlemen in returning to their residences about one o'clock on Monday morning, were passing the end of Broad-street, when a large Newfoundland dog, which followed and belonged to one of them, sprang suddenly in pursuit of something which had caught his notice in the said street, and was not to be called back. Shrieks were soon after heard, which caused surprise, but which were presently explained by the return of the dog, with a bouncing hare in his jaws, that he had just deprived of life. The defunct animal is supposed to have deserted the adjoining grounds to avoid the streaming floods which the rains had left and were increasing. [*Morning Post*, September 17, 1829]

SAGACITY OF THE DOG - Mr. Smith, master of the William and Ann whaler, has a very bold and docile Newfoundland dog, to which he is particularly attached. When at Greenland, during the summer, his son observed a large seal, which he fired at and wounded slightly; the dog instinctively leaped into the water, and pushed directly for the spot where the seal dived when it was hurt, and on re-appearing the dog seized it by the fore foot, and a desperate combat ensued. During the struggle the combatants were frequently under water, but the dog resolutely kept his hold till a boat was launched to his assistance, and, when seized by one of the hands, he fairly pulled the seal aboard with him. On another occasion, when seven men were on an iceberg, it gave way; six of them got hold of the bow rope, but the seventh sunk – the waters closed over him, and his comrades concluded that he was lost. Mr. Smith was in bed at the time, but hearing the noise he promptly sprang on deck, and, in obedience to his signal, boats from the other vessels immediately came to his assistance. His faithful dog was at his foot, and while gazing intently he observed the head of his sailor appear above the water. He pointed it out, gave the word, the dog leaped from the bow of the vessel, and while swimming towards the man he barked, either with anxiety, or with a view to cheer the perishing sailor with the prospect of assistance. When within a few feet the man was picked up in a state of utter insensibility, by a boat from the Rambler of Kirkaldy. Observing the rescue of the man, the dog returned to his own ship, and when taken on board, his gambols, frisking, and his fawning on his master, indicated that though he had not saved the man, he was aware that he had done his duty. [*Morning Post*, November 7, 1829]

CLEVER DOG! - Admiral Maling of the Elms, Stockton, has a Newfoundland dog, which attends the Ludlow mail as it passes a short distance from his master's house, to retrieve the letter-bag; this is delivered to him by the guard, and the quadruped letter-carrier is as punctual in delivering the letters as any biped. [*Royal Cornwall Gazette*, November 27, 1830]

THE SALE OF A WIFE IN CARLISLE - After an hour or two, she was purchased by Henry Mears, a pensioner, for the sum of 20s. and a Newfoundland dog. The happy couple immediately left town together, amidst the shouts and huzzas of the multitude, in which they were joined by Thompson, who,

THOSE AMAZING NEWFOUNDLAND DOGS

Some Swedish courtiers try to give a Newfoundland dog a ducking, but the powerful dog has other ideas. The gentleman on the left, Crown Prince Charles himself, warns them that 'Han murrar' (He is growling). A drawing by the Swedish nobleman Fritz von Dardel, dated 1848, probably depicting one of the earliest Newfoundland dogs in Sweden

with the greatest humour imaginable, proceeded to put the halter, which his wife had taken off, round the neck of his Newfoundland dog, and then proceeded to the first public-house, where he spent the remainder of the day. [*Morning Chronicle*, April 25, 1832]

Yesterday afternoon, between two and three o'clock, a number of lads, from ten to twelve years of age, were amusing themselves bathing in the Regent's Canal, when one of them, the son of Capt. Griffith, a Gentleman residing in Seymour-street, Somers-town, got out of his depth. The poor little fellow called to his companions for assistance, but none of them being able to swim, they could not render him any. Capt. Burton, a Gentleman residing in the Alpha Cottages, regent's Park, fortunately was swimming a large Newfoundland dog about 100 yards off where the lads were bathing, and hearing a cry of 'Help me, help me, I shall be drowned,' called his dog out of the water and ran to the spot, where he directed the attention of the animal to the drowning youth, who instantly sprang into the Canal, and, seizing him by the hair of the head, succeeded in bringing him safe on shore just as he was on the point of sinking. After a short time he recovered, and proceeded home with some of his companions. [*Morning Post*, August 24, 1832]

A REGULAR POACHER - A short time since, a Newfoundland dog, not above 18 months old, belonging to P. Titley, Esq., of Penrhys, near Llanrwst, while accompanying Mr. Titley, Jr., and one of the Misses Titley, made a sudden plunge into the river Conwy. The unexpectedness of the move surprised Mr. Titley, who called and whistled, but to no purpose, and the dog pursued his course. After much swimming and many dives, 'Neptune' came ashore, and laid at their feet a fine salmon, weighing upwards of 17 lbs. [*Trewman's Exeter Flying Post*, Thursday, May 16, 1833]

The match between the Newfoundland dog and a pony under 13 hands, a distance of seven miles, each drawing a light cart with a person in it came off on Wednesday, in the neighbourhood of Shooters-hill. After going several miles, and the dog leading the pony about a mile, the Newfoundlander lay down and would not proceed any further. It was said that if the dog had been properly trained he would have been the victor. [*Bell's Life in London*, October 12, 1834]

COURT OF KING'S BENCH
BAKER v. OLIVER – This was an action brought by the plaintiff against the defendant, who lived in Fenchurch-street, to recover compensation in damages for an injury he had sustained in consequence of the defendant's dog having bitten him. The plaintiff's evidence went to show that he went to work at the defendant's in January last; that the defendant had a very fierce Newfoundland dog on the premises; that he had refused to work there unless the dog was tied up, as he had bitten him some time before; that on the day in question, as he was going up a ladder about his work in the defendant's yard, some person let the dog loose, which then ran and attacked him, in consequence of which he was prevented from attending to business for 12 days, and had paid a surgeon 1l. 12s. for attending him. The defendant's witnesses stated that the plaintiff had been in the habit of teasing the dog, which was extremely docile, and that he did so on this occasion. Lord Denman said it was a mere question – was the dog fierce or not? The Jury having retired for some time, returned a verdict for the defendant. [*Times*, July 6, 1836]

Thursday a hand cart was borrowed by the neighbour of a baker in this town to convey some luggage to a steam-boat, when a Newfoundland dog, the property of the baker, seeing a stranger in possession of his master's cart, went up, compelled him to stop, and very soon to quit his hold. The dog placed himself between the shafts, and threatened vengeance upon any one who dared to interfere with him. After some time fruitlessly spent in endeavouring to beat away the unlooked-for usurper, the effect of a piece of beef was tried by an obliging butcher, but the dog would neither be threatened, menaced, cajoled, nor bribed to quit his master's vehicle. The porter, finding ineffectual all attempts to regain possession of the cart, was proceeding to take out the baggage, but in this he was as furiously resisted as in his former encounters with the dog, who, having fairly baffled all attempts to conquer him, couched himself between the wheels until his master could be brought, who was of necessity procured from a distance of two or three streets, and to him the faithful animal delivered up possession with evident satisfaction. [*Times*, August 2, 1836][4]

As a gentleman was, last week, bathing in Carmarthen Bay, near Tenby, he got into a current of which he was not aware, and was driven out, unable to make head against it. He gave the alarm, and a servant standing by let loose a large Newfoundland dog, who plunged into the waves, and, mastering every obstacle, came up to the gentleman, who, nearly exhausted, threw his arm over the neck of the dog, which succeeded in bringing him to land. He was then conducted to the master of the servant, who rendered him every assistance. [*Bristol Mercury*, August 20, 1836]

The power of dogs to mark distinct periods of time cannot be denied; there are many instances on record in proof of it, but the following is detailed as having fallen under my own knowledge – A fine Newfoundland dog, which was kept at an inn in Dorsetshire, was accustomed every morning as the clock struck eight to take in his mouth a certain basket, placed for the purpose, containing a few pence, and to carry it across the street to a baker's, who took out the money and replaced it by a certain number of rolls. With these Neptune hastened back to the kitchen, and safely deposited his trust; but, what was well worthy of remark, he never attempted to take the basket, or even approach it on Sunday mornings. On one occasion, when returning with the rolls, another dog made an attack on the basket for the purpose of stealing its contents; when the trusty fellow placed the basket on the ground, severely punished the intruder, and then bore off his charge in triumph. [*Manchester Times and Gazette*, December 24, 1836]

Providentially Mr James Allan of the Hope happened to be among the anxious crowd on shore. Mr Allan bethought himself of his fine Newfoundland dog, and immediately had him at the beach, and pointed out the floating wood to him. In an instance, the noble animal plunged into the raging element, and succeeded (amidst the applause of the spectators), in bringing to land the end of the line. A stronger rope was then sent on shore by it, and the vessel was ultimately safely secured. [*Caledonian Mercury*, December 4, 1837][5]

A Newfoundland dog, which crossed the Atlantic in the Sirius, was advertised in the New York papers to be sold, and his claim on public attention was stated to be, that he was the first animal of his species which had traversed the great ocean in a steam ship. This interesting dog was instantly in demand, and was ultimately purchased for the sum of three hundred dollars, which some enthusiastic New Yorkers considered 'dog cheap'. [*Essex Standard,* June 01, 1838]

Last Friday evening, about eight o'clock, a large Newfoundland dog attacked a groom as he was walking up Ludgate-hill. The dog jumped at the groom's throat and knocked him down. The groom put up his arm to guard his throat, and was severely bitten by the dog. A butcher's boy who had charge of the dog, and had instigated him to attack the groom, immediately ran off without offering the slightest assistance, and, whistling to the dog, they both escaped in a moment. [*Morning Chronicle*, July 26, 1838]

We saw the seventeen who survived, with the captain, also a fine Newfoundland dog, which was on board, and by whom all the eighteen were saved! As soon as the vessel struck, a rope was fastened about his neck and he was sent ashore. It was then made fast, and the sailors got ashore along it, but the two men who perished fell from exhaustion, and were drowned. [*Liverpool Mercury*, December 7, 1838][6]

SAGACITY AND GREAT VALUE OF THE NEWFOUNDLAND DOG - On Friday last, a man named Bartlett was coming in a cart on the road from Thornford to Bradford, where the road was flooded with water to a considerable depth, and running with such violence that the cart was completely overturned, and Bartlett under it. The dog, which had been swimming directly at the head of the horse, missed the man and the cart, and turning back, dived and seized Bartlett by the collar of his coat, drew him from under the cart, and swam with him to the bank, when he got over into a field; as soon as the dog saw the man safe, he immediately plunged into the water again, swam after, and seized the horse by the ear, kept his head above water, and brought him to the bank. *[Northern Star and Leeds General* Advertiser, November 2, 1839]

On Wednesday week, as Miss Susan Shipley, a maiden lady, was walking in Regent's Park, a Newfoundland dog playing, put his paws upon her, which so terrified her, that she died in the course of a few hours afterwards. [*Blackburn Standard*, March 11, 1840]

POACHING EXTRAORDINARY IN THE TWEED - On the 30th ult. a Newfoundland dog, belonging to Mr Cameron, Peebles, captured a fine salmon in the river Tweed in the following singular manner: - Hector (for such is the dog's name) is exceedingly fond of the water; so much so, that whenever he gets loose from his chain he is off to the river, and with the greatest industry brings to land all the drift-wood, &c., he can find floating down the stream. On Wednesday, the 30th ult., while thus employed, he was observed by some boys to dive suddenly under the water, where he remained entirely out of sight for about half a minute. When he arose again to the surface he had a salmon in his mouth, which was struggling violently to escape, but he held it fast in his capacious jaws, and brought it safe to land, and would on no account quit his prize until he carried it safe home to his master. The fish was of the real salmon tribe, and weighed about four pounds. [*Morning Post*, January 23, 1841]

On Wednesday morning, much to the surprise of the people on the pier at Tarbert, a very large Newfoundland dog sprung into the sea, and in an instant appeared with a little boy attired in petticoats suspended from his mouth. It appeared that the little fellow had wandered from the side of his nurse, and fallen into the sea, where, no doubt, he would have perished, had it not been for the sagacious animal, as no one perceived the accident but Caesar, which apprised the bystanders of what had occurred, by carefully placing the boy safe and sound at the feet of his nurse on terra firma. [*Standard*, August 14, 1843]

THE UTILITY OF A PINCH OF SNUFF - A few days ago, as a gentleman was proceeding through Taunton, with a large Newfoundland dog, another animal of the same species came in contact with it, and a severe fight took place. No one could stop them; policemen, spectators, not even the owner himself could part them. At last a sober old gentleman took out his snuff box, and, watching his opportunity, administered to both dogs freely. The effect was instantaneous, both animals quitted their hold, and ran off as fast as possible. [*Lancaster Gazette and General Advertiser*, June 15, 1844]

A CANINE FISHERMAN - a fine Newfoundland dog may be seen in the Derwent, at Matlock Bath, at almost all hours of the day, in front of the Museum Parade, apparently luxuriating in the refreshing coolness of the stream. It was, however, remarked by some visitors who were watching Carlo's aquatic pranks from the balconies of the Devonshire Arms, that his chief employment was turning over with his paws the loose stones in shoal water near the bank, and it was at length distinctly seen that he was in search of crawfish which are plentiful there. He has since been seen to snap up and devour several with great apparent relish. [*Derby Mercury*, June 18, 1845]

STRANGE CONFLICT - A few days ago, as two gentlemen were near the Meikle Rock between Avoch and Portrose, with a Newfoundland dog, a fish was seen about 20 yards in the sea, its fins topping the water. The fish was fired at, and the dog immediately swum in pursuit. He caught the fish by the tail, when the fish elevated itself out of the water, and got clear of the dog. The dog again caught it by the mouth, and they both dived under the water, when a violent struggle took place. The dog, however, succeeded in vanquishing the fish, and dragged it ashore. The fish is, we understand, a fox-shark, and measured 5 feet in length. [*Times*, December 11, 1846]

The *Ayr Advertiser* tells a story of canine murder, which is very remarkable, if true. It is to the effect that a large Newfoundland dog enticed a small spaniel, of the opposite sex, into the river for a swim, and when in the middle of the stream, seized his helpless and too confiding companion by the neck, and held her under water until she was drowned. [*Leeds Mercury*, July 15, 1848]

An engraving by J. Greenaway, for the *Illustrated London News*, of J.W. Bottomley's remarkable painting 'Erebus and Terror'. The original Erebus and Terror were the two ships that perished in the ice during Sir John Franklin's ill-fated polar expedition. Clearly, the two dogs symbolize the stricken ships, but will the sturdy Newfoundland Erebus rescue the terrified dog surrounded by blocks of ice?

CHAPTER 10.
THE CULT OF THE NEWFOUNDLAND DOG

> Though kings may sway at will an empire's fate,
> And sages sit and guide the helm of state,
> Or warriors boast their deeds of valour done,
> Of heroes vanquish'd, and of battles won; -
> E'en yet a simple lesson we may learn
> From this unknown – unconsecrated urn:
> For trusty Lion 'neath this sod is laid
> Who fawned like man, - but ne'er like man betray'd:
> And tho' nor Elves their moonlit vigils keep,
> Nor Fairies here in silence softly weep,
> Yet Truth and Worth call forth that generous tear
> For Truth and Worth are both sepulch'red here.
>
> Epitaph on the Newfoundland dog Lion',
> *Nottinghamshire Guardian*
> November 28, 1862.

Throughout Victorian times, Newfoundland dogs were very highly regarded, mainly due to their ability to save human lives during shipwrecks or bathing accidents. The struggle between life and death, with the helpless human in the hands of the hostile elements, when a compassionate brute creature takes his side and brings him to safety, was a subject that fascinated the Victorians. Heroic Newfoundland dogs were depicted in schoolbooks, on popular engravings, and in books on natural history. These dogs were considered not just brave and altruistic, but also extremely intelligent. A large proportion of the anecdotes of dogs told and re-told by the early Victorian dog-fanciers were related to the extraordinary sagacity of the Newfoundland.[1] To the sentimental Victorian naturalist, these dogs were not just superior to all other members of the canine tribe, but also more admirable than non-human primates. Apes and monkeys were viewed with suspicion at this time: did these filthy monkeys not hide their nuts in an unmentionable place, and did the great apes not have lurid designs on white women?

In Victorian collections of dog stories, and children's books and magazines, wise and altruistic Newfoundland dogs make use of their superior intellects to protect children, catch thieves, and rescue people from various calamities. If an imprudent child is in danger from drowning, fire, or falling down a precipice, a sagacious Newfoundland dog is never far away. If burglars or robbers are up to mischief, the watchful Newfoundland drives them away. The Cult of the Newfoundland dog in popular culture reigned supreme throughout the nineteenth century, not just in Britain but in most European countries,

THOSE AMAZING NEWFOUNDLAND DOGS

A sagacious Newfoundland saves a child from drowning, from the *Illustrated Police News*, July 4 1868. Note the swooning Mrs Titherleigh in the background

even those where Newfoundland dogs were extremely scarce, like Sweden.[2] Some authors have suspected that this cult rest on far from solid foundations. Some of the unreferenced old yarns about super-intelligent Newfoundland dogs, told and re-told by Edward Jesse and his contemporaries, read more or less like fairy tales; were they equally devoid of factual foundation?

* * *

So, how many *true* stories of sagacious and lifesaving Newfoundlands are there? The answer has to be certainly very many! These dogs have a powerful instinct to retrieve objects from the water, and to save people struggling to swim. In November 1812, after the *Fantome* sloop of war had anchored in Hamoaze, eleven sailors, a woman, and a waterman rowed out to this sloop in a shore-boat. Unfortunately, this heavily loaded boat capsized and all its crew were struggling in the water. A Newfoundland dog on the quarter-deck of the sloop instantly leapt into the sea, and seized one of the men by the collar of his coat. Another boat was lowered, and all the sailors were saved except the waterman. Amazingly, the dog seemed to know that this individual was still missing, since he swam a wide circuit around the ship, although finding nothing but an oar, which he retrieved.[3]

On March 8 1834, two little boys aged six and nine, the sons of a Mr Horncroft, were amusing themselves by climbing a crane at the old Grosvenor Canal, Pimlico. When the youngest boy lost his footing and plunged into the water, the elder boy jumped after him, but since they were both indifferent swimmers, they soon went under. Fortunately for them, the comedian Mr Ryan came past, accompanied by his acting Newfoundland dog 'Nero', the favourite of Astley's Theatre. After a man who had seen the children sink threw a pebble to the spot, Nero plunged in and dived. He soon retrieved the boys, who both recovered completely. As a result, Nero became quite a newspaper celebrity, something that

THOSE AMAZING NEWFOUNDLAND DOGS

is likely to have done his acting career no harm at all.[4]

Sometimes, the powerful lifesaving instinct of the Newfoundland dog led to unfortunate mishaps. Once, in 1839, a friend of the Pall Mall tailor Mr Ashton went to have a swim in the Serpentine, accompanied by the tailor's large Newfoundland dog. But when the dog saw the man swimming about, it presumed he was drowning, and seized him hard by the hair, elevating his head above the water. The poor man struggled with the dog for several minutes, before men from the Humane Society could save him from his over-zealous canine companion, very much injured from the incisions on his scalp made by the dog's teeth.[5] Just weeks later, another Newfoundland was in the news, for a better reason this time. When the Hon. Mr Westenra M.P. was returning to his residence at Bishopsgate, he was attacked by a ferocious mastiff. He defended himself with his stick, until it was broken in pieces. Fortunately, a Newfoundland dog rushed up and attacked the mastiff. After a desperate struggle, the sagacious Newfoundland killed its opponent by dragging it to a ditch and keeping it below water until it was drowned.[6]

In 1829, there was a newspaper appeal that rivers and lakes used for bathing, like the Serpentine, should be patrolled by Newfoundland dogs. The dogs should work in pairs, joined by 'connecting rods' of bamboo, that the drowning person was supposed to seize hold of. Due to its obvious impracticality, this idea was never acted upon.[7] In the 1840s, several newspapers announced that ten Newfoundland dogs were to be imported into Paris, for use as life-savers. They were to live in handsome kennels erected on the bridges across the Seine, and experienced trainers were to teach them to "draw from the water stuffed figures of men and children". The newspaper writers gave no explanation why the dogs should be trained to ignore the female inhabitants of Paris, and leave them to drown! In fact, the whole thing may well have been a newspaper *canard*, since contemporary French sources mention nothing about these alleged life-savers.[8]

The clever Newfoundland saving Mrs Fletcher and her daughter, from *Illustrated Police News*, March 30 1872

THOSE AMAZING NEWFOUNDLAND DOGS

A Newfoundland dog saves a child from drowning in the Thames, from the *Illustrated Police News*, September 8 1883.

In July 1868, Mrs Jane Titherleigh, the wife of a Hull ironmaster, was taking a cruise with her little son in a small sailing boat, when the son suddenly fell overboard. Consternation ruled among the humans on board, since they were all indifferent swimmers, but a Newfoundland dog leapt overboard without being prompted in any way, swum up to the young lad, and dragged him back to the vessel. The boy was none the worse for his ducking, but poor Mrs Titherleigh fell into hysterics.[9]

In February 1872, some watchmen on duty at Sable Island, off Nova Scotia, saw a large Newfoundland dog come walking up to them. Although the dog seemed quite exhausted, it whined like if it wanted them to follow it. The Newfoundland dog led the men to the shore, but it was becoming very dark. One of the watchmen got the idea to let the dog hold a lantern in its mouth to guide them, and the dog willingly obliged. The Newfoundland dog led them to a woman and a child, both half dead from privations. It was the wife and daughter of Captain Fletcher, of the Liverpool barque 'Lilly Parker', which had been shipwrecked nearby. When the ship had sunk, Mrs Fletcher had hung on to her little daughter with one hand, and to the Newfoundland dog's collar with the other. After the powerful dog had dragged them ashore, the sagacious animal had spontaneously gone to look for help.[10]

In June 1875, some children were sitting on the Thames embankment near Waterloo. A gust of wind suddenly blew a little girl into the river, where she could be seen to be struggling. A gentleman passing by unleashed his Newfoundland dog, appropriately named 'Ready', and made the dog aware of the girl's situation. Without further prompting, the dog leapt into Thames, seized the girl by the collar of her cape, and swam to the stairs nearby.[11] In August 1892, a youth bathing in the river Towy near Carmarthen was seen to be struggling. The local dog fancier Mr T. Davies immediately ordered his celebrated Newfoundland dog

A Newfoundland dog saves the boy James Alford from falling down a precipice, from the *Illustrated Police News*, November 18, 1876

'Picton' into the water, and the young Welsh lad seized the dog round the neck and was towed to safety.[12]

Australia did not have many Newfoundland dogs in Victorian times, but when the Yarra river flooded Melbourne in 1881, one of these sagacious animals was ready for some proper heroics. A cab driver named Thomas Brown fell out of his vehicle and was swept along the flooded street by the torrent. The local hairdresser Mr W. Higginbottom, and his Newfoundland dog Nelson, heard the cabman's cries and dashed into action. Nelson leapt into the water and twice caught hold of Brown's clothes, only to lose his grip as both man and dog sped along the flooded street. Brown's lifeless body disappeared into a covered rainwater channel under the street, but the sagacious dog stood ready to dive again as it emerged on the other side of the channel. In the end, Brown was saved, and the *Illustrated Australian News* praised Nelson for his heroics, suggesting that the sagacious animal ought to receive the Humane Society's medal. But there is no evidence that the ungrateful Australians gave Nelson anything more valuable than a bone or a sausage. The dog's collar has found its way into the collections of the National Museum of Australia, and it has been speculated that it might well have been given as a reward for the saving of Brown in the floods. This is clearly not the case, however, since the collar is an ordinary cast metal one, with the inscription 'Dog Nelson, W. Higginbottom, 122 Swanston St' clearly intended to facilitate the dog's return if he was lost or stolen. Presentation collars given to heroic or useful dogs normally have an inscription to celebrate the animal's praiseworthy actions. There is no information how Nelson came to Australia (possibly as a ship's dog walking ashore), nor what happened to the dog after his sole newsworthy exploit.[13]

In June 1913, when little Willie Frampton, aged just two, fell into a river, a certain Miss Hewett appeared with her white and black Newfoundland dog 'Donovan Dondo'. 'Save him, Donnie!' she cried, and the dog plunged into the water and pulled little Willie to safety. For his heroism, Donovan Dondo was inducted into Spratt's Canine Heroes League, a short-lived order of merit for dogs sponsored by the Spratts dog biscuit factory. The following year, the sturdy Newfoundland paraded round the ring at the Crufts dog show, along with nine other Canine Heroes.[14]

* * *

The life-saving dog 'Princess May', from *Lloyd's Weekly Newspaper*, November 15 1896

In this book, I have collected twelve primary newspaper accounts of Newfoundland dogs being ordered by their masters to leap into the water and rescue a drowning person.[15] Furthermore, there are not less than eighteen newspaper stories of these dogs spontaneously plunging into the water to go to the rescue, without any command.[16] The majority of these accounts provide the place, the name of the person rescued, and sometimes even the name of the dog and its owner. Most of these accounts were

John Climpson and 'Help', a drawing from *Young England*, March 1 1884

published in good-quality newspapers, and published by more than one version, by different journalists, providing additional credibility.

As we have seen, there are also four primary newspaper accounts of Newfoundland dogs either swimming to shore from a ship carrying a rope, or swimming from shore with a rope to a stricken vessel.[17] The following is a fifth example:

A gentleman connected with the Newfoundland fishery was once possessed of a dog of singular fidelity and sagacity. On one occasion a boat and crew in his employ were in circumstances of considerable peril, just outside a line of breakers, which, owing to some change in wind or weather, had, since the departure of the boat, rendered the return passage through them most hazardous. The spectators on shore were quite unable to render an assistance to their friends afloat. Much time had been spent, and the danger seemed to increase rather than diminish. Our friend, the dog, looked on for a length of time, evidently aware of there being great cause for anxiety in those around. Presently, however, he took to the water, and made his way through to the boat. The crew supposed he wished to join them, and made various attempts to induce him to come on board, but, no! he would not go within their reach, but continued swimming about a short distance from them. After a while, and several comments on the peculiar conduct of the dog, one of the hands suddenly divined his apparent meaning. 'Give him the end of a rope,' he said, 'that is what he wants.' The rope was thrown – the dog seized the end in an instant, turned round, and made straight for the shore, where, a few minutes later, boat and crew – thanks to the intelligence of their four-footed friend – were placed safe and unharmed. Was there reasoning here? No acting with a view to an end or for a given motive? Or was it nothing but ordinary instinct?[18]

If the reader still doubts that a Newfoundland dog has the sagacity to swim with a rope to a stricken vessel, or to retrieve a rope from the wreck and take it back, the story of the brave Newfoundlanders George and Ann Harvey, and their dog Hairy Man, needs to be retold. When out fishing on July 12 1828, George and his eldest daughter Ann saw wreckage in the water. Realizing that some ship must have perished nearby, they went home for reinforcements in the form of George's 12-year-old son Tom, and Hairy Man the Newfoundland. It turned out that the brig Despatch, taking Irish immigrants to Quebec, had been wrecked, and that nearly 200 people had taken refuge on a small island. George could not get close to the island due to the heavy sea, so he threw a billet of wood, to which the survivors attached a rope, and then Hairy Man swam for it. In the course of three days, 180 people were saved. The Harveys lived on a desolate small island named Isle aux Morts, and the hungry immigrants ate their entire winter store. After the shipwrecked immigrants had been evacuated to Halifax, the Harveys were given a reward of £100, and their winter store was replenished.

Instinct to seize an object in the water may well have played a part in many of these incidents, as may the good training the ship's dogs received, to be useful in dragging the nets ashore. Still, the Newfoundland dog's ability to sense danger, and take appropriate action, is truly astonishing. This remarkable ability also worked on dry land, as judged by Edward Jesse's anecdote of a Newfoundland dog in Worcester dragging a child that had fallen down in the street out of the way of a horse and cart, and the equally sagacious Edinburgh Newfoundland dog seizing a child by the clothes to drag it out of the way of a carriage, as attested by the *York Herald* of September 10, 1825. Edward Jesse was a credulous author, however, and it attracts suspicion that he names neither the child nor the dog; the sceptic will also be aware that Edinburgh, the hometown of Greyfriars Bobby, is not highly rated for truthfulness when it comes to canine lore. But although these two stories of Newfoundland sagacity and altruism on dry land rest on relatively feeble foundations, the following one is even more remarkable, and also has the advantage of being very well attested.

Photo and Career.

I am **Bruce** of **Swindon**, the famous Collecting Dog of £**450** for **Charity**. I have travelled over **10,000** miles by rail. A Solid **Silver Collar, 15 Gold and Silver Medals** have been **Presented** to me for my noble work. I am also a member of the **Brotherhood** of **Hero Dogs London**. My age is eight years, and for each coin I say **Thank You**.

THIS LITTLE DOG HAS COLLECTED OVER 10,000 PENNIES FOR SOLDIERS' AND SAILORS' COMFORTS.

Bruce, a member of the Brotherhood of Hero Dogs, along with the tiny Southville Beau, who was active throughout the Great War, collecting **10,000** pennies for the Soldiers & Sailors Wool Fund

THOSE AMAZING NEWFOUNDLAND DOGS

In June 1896, some children were playing on the tram lines near Daubhill Mill, Bolton. They were watched by a Newfoundland bitch named 'Princess May', lying down in front of the door of her master's house. But when the tram-car approached at a brisk pace, one of the children fell down in front of it. The driver desperately tried to rein in the horses, and people shouted with alarm, but Princess May dashed across the road, grabbed the three-year-old boy by his frock, and pulled him to safety. When some journalists were incredulous of this novel instance of Newfoundland dog sagacity, they were taken to task by Mr Fred. Lomax, the secretary of the Bolton and District Humane Society, who had carefully collected witness testimony of the rescue. He, too, had initially doubted this extraordinary story, but four witnesses unanimously stated that Princess May had acted independently, and that she had been clearly seen to drag the boy to safety before any human rescuer could reach him. The boy himself, the three-year-old son of Mr T. Hurst, of No. 10 Stainsbury Street, Daubhill, was tracked down by Mr Lomax, as was Mr T. Baxendale, of No. 18 Oak Street, who had run to pick up the child when the dog came bounding up to carry it out of danger. Princess May herself was a sturdy black Newfoundland bitch, the property of Mr J.H. Edge, of Daubhill. He told a journalist that his dog had once won a prize at a dog show in Dublin; she was very fond of children, and a good swimmer and plunger. The Newfoundland dog which used to walk in front of the local Artillery Band was the brother of this splendid animal. In November, Princess May appeared at a Humane Society presentation ceremony at Bolton Town Hall, along with eleven humans who had performed various heroics. Lord Stanley M.P. and the Mayor of Bolton presented them a silver medal each; the dog also received a silver collar to be able to wear hers in a becoming manner. The next month, Princess May was the guest of honour at a grand dog show in London, walking round the ring to show off her collar and medal.[19]

* * *

In Victorian and Edwardian Britain, collecting dogs were not an infrequent sight.[20] These animals were trained to collect money for various charities, and equipped with collecting boxes strapped onto their harnesses, or piggy-banks fastened to their collars. There were collecting dogs already in the 1860s, but the great forerunner was the collie 'Help', trained by the veteran railway guard John Climpson to collect money for the Railway Servants' Orphan Fund. Help was active from 1880 until 1890, travelling on the London to Brighton train. Later, as Help proved quite successful, the dog travelled widely on the trains, with other railway guards. It was said that Help had 'worked' every railway line in the country, and visited every principal town in England and Wales. After Help's death in 1891, his body was stuffed and put in a glass case on the platform at Brighton Station. By that time, there were collecting dogs based at every major railway station in England and Wales. Some of them travelled on the trains, but the majority worked the station platforms. Often, these railway dogs were stuffed after death, and put on the platforms to continue collecting for their charities. Another troop of collecting dogs were owned by the Red Cross, the RSPCA, and various other charities or humanitarian organizations.

Considering the popularity of Newfoundland dogs in Victorian Britain, it is not surprising to find that quite a few Newfoundlands were recruited as collecting dogs. The dogs were docile, intelligent and easy to train, and they liked to interact with people. At Waterloo Station, a famous dynasty of collecting dogs were active from 1894 until 1931: the five London Jacks. After he had been stolen by dog-thieves and held ransom by them for several weeks, the black Labrador Jack I had to retire, but he was succeeded by his son Jack II, a Labrador-Newfoundland cross. In 1910, the Euston porter R.E. Edwards purchased a very attractive Newfoundland cross named 'Brum'. This clever dog knew how to put out a fire, balance a penny on his nose, and bark by the tap until he was given a drink of fresh water. Brum appears to have been a great friend of royalty. In 1912, the Queen and Princess Mary went from Euston to join the King at Balmoral. As they were to enter the train, "the Railway Benevolent Fund collecting dog 'Brum' approached, and her Majesty patted the handsome creature. The Princess insisted on 'Brum's' following her into the carriage and put some

Collecting Jack, a handsome black Newfoundland dog collecting for charity. The money he collected was for the SWR orphanage

coins in his box." In 1913, when King George V and Queen Mary were going to Crewe, the King put a sovereign into Brum's collecting box and patted his head, the dog showing his appreciation by barking loudly.[21]

A magnificent Newfoundland dog named Nelson, who collected for various Bournemouth charities, used to carefully pick up every coin thrown to him and put them into a collecting box standing nearby. Several collecting Newfoundland dogs were depicted on picture postcards, including the Red Cross collecting dog Carlo and Southampton Jack, collecting for the railway orphanage. The Waif and Strays Society's home for crippled children in Byfleet had its own collecting Newfoundland dog 'Rover', but his exertions could not prevent the closure of the home in 1908.

During the Boer War, the Ladies Brigade of Collecting Dogs collected for the families of dead soldiers, with 35 dogs employed. In early 1900, not less than 400 collecting dogs, ranging in size from massive St Bernards and Newfoundlands to the most diminutive breeds, took part in a large

THOSE AMAZING NEWFOUNDLAND DOGS

military-style parade. The Brigade of Collecting Dogs was divided into ten companies: the Die Hards, the Dare Devils, Loyal Dutchmen, Cavalry, Artillery, British Bulldogs, Ladies' Own, Sportsmen's Own, Friendly Foreigners and British Watch Dogs. Field Marshal Lord Wolseley's dog Rover oversaw proceedings, and a reporter from *Animal World* magazine noted that he grunted and nodded when he spotted some dog with proper military bearing. Basingstoke Jack, one of the railway collecting dogs, received mention in dispatches for his attitude of military sternness.[22] In the Great War, this army of patriotic collecting dogs was once more mobilized. One postcard shows the black and white Newfoundland 'Doone' doing his best to collect money to support the wounded. Another, better-looking Newfoundland had his collecting box marked with the flag of St George, and a black Newfoundland managed to collect £2 11s. 11d. for Kentish Prisoners of War in Germany.

The black Labrador 'Sandy' was collecting at Exeter as late as 1952, and the Airedale terrier 'Laddie' was active at Waterloo until 1956, but after that time, no further collecting dogs were recruited. Some of the stuffed dogs were sold or given to collectors of curiosities, but the vast majority were simply destroyed. Complaints from the public, who liked the collecting dogs, and from the railway orphanage superintendents, who lost much funding as a result of the dogs being 'phased out', went unheeded. But in spite of this wholesale vandalism, a few stuffed collecting dogs have been saved for posterity, although unfortunately none of the Newfoundlands. The celebrated 'Station Jim', who amused the railway passengers by climbing ladders and growling at lighted matches back in the 1890s, is still there, in his glass case on Platform 5 at Slough Station. The stuffed Laddie was donated to the National Railway Museum in York, where he has become quite a favourite, collecting for the Friends of the Museum on Platform 3 in the Station Hall. Two

The Dog Carlo, collecting for the Red Cross

Miss Ellen Terry photographed on board the *Philadelphia*, on her way to tour America; she is holding the lead of the Newfoundland dog collecting for the Seamen's Orphanage. A postcard from a photograph originally published in the *Daily Mirror*, January 14 1907

of the stuffed London Jacks have also survived. One of them is likely to be Jack V who expired in 1931. A burly Golden Labrador wearing his collecting box and a number of gold and silver medals, he now collects in the waiting room of the Bluebell Railway in Sussex. The original London Jack has ended up at the Natural History Museum, where he has been restored to his former glory, wearing his heavy brass collar and collection box on leather mounting.

* * *

In Victorian London, well-organized gangs of dog-thieves preyed on the valuable dogs of the wealthy. Those who had lost a dog could contact a 'dog-finder', or 'dog-restorer': criminals who negotiated with the thieves to secure the stolen dog's safe return, for a fee. The kingpins of the dog-stealing racket made a good living, earning as much as £150 per year. Their methods were very cunning indeed. After locating a valuable dog to steal, they tempted the animal with cooked liver, or even with specially prepared dog biscuits made from fried or pulverized liver, often with some added opium! The drowsy and stupefied dog was bundled into a bag and carried away. Another trick was to use a bitch in heat to entice the dog away from its owner. The poetess Elizabeth Barrett had her cocker spaniel Flush stolen three times, costing her a total of £20 paid to the dog-finder. The third time, she had to travel to Whitechapel in person to negotiate with the objectionable gang leader Mr Taylor, eventually securing Flush's release for £6, after the poor animal had spent five days in the hands of the thieves.[23]

THOSE AMAZING NEWFOUNDLAND DOGS

In the mid-1800s, small dogs belonging to wealthy people were at constant risk of being stolen and held at ransom. Even a Newfoundland was not safe from the dog-thieves. Although these sagacious dogs were usually wary of strangers, and attached to their owners, they were not immune to the lure of the thieves' tasty liver snacks. In 1858, a Newfoundland dog belonging to a certain Mr Pierre was observed to be missing from a yard near his premises. A witness had just seen two thieves trying "to entice it away by throwing pieces of liver which it caught and devoured". But the dog became wary of its two new 'friends' and would not go with them; there was a scene in the street, and one of Mr Pierre's servants pointed the thieves out to a police constable. One of the men was caught, and later sentenced to three months in prison for attempting to steal a Newfoundland dog, valued at £10.[24]

In 1856, a gang of dog-thieves stole a valuable Newfoundland dog belonging to Mr Latty, a gentleman residing in Gloucester Gardens, near Hyde Park. He advertised a reward of £2 for information about the dog, and sure enough, a dog-finder named Roberson soon came to call, offering to return the dog, for a fee. But Mr Latty should not try any tricks, for he "could steal any dog he liked, and as often as he liked". Mr Latty coolly remarked "That is a poor inducement for me to give you two guineas for mine", opened the door and admitted his groom and a police constable, who had been listening to the conversation! The dog-finder offered to return the dog for £2, and to give the thief who had stolen the dog into the custody of the police, and those terms were accepted. Mr Latty got his Newfoundland back, but as the policeman waited for the thief in a public house, two ruffians burst into the pub and beat him until he was well-nigh dead, before ill-treating the groom in a similar manner. All three were

A Newfoundland dog representing the 'Rover League', collecting for the St. Nicholas Home for Crippled Children in Byfleet. The card is unposted, but the home was active between 1893 and 1903

'Prince Cornwallis', another collecting Newfoundland dog

eventually caught: the two thugs were fined £10 each, and Roberson had to serve six months in jail.[25]

In 1834, the German clockmaker Carl Wilhelm Naundorff claimed to be Louis Charles, Dauphin of France. This little prince, the son of Louis XVI and Marie Antoinette, was presumed to have been killed during the Terror, but Naundorff claimed to have been saved from the Temple Tower in Paris. Naundorff was the most persistent of a number of 'False Dauphins' who claimed the throne of France. After he had been expelled from France, Naundorff settled down in London and got himself a Newfoundland dog. In October 1842, the 'Duke of Normandy', as he called himself, lost his favourite 'Triumph', however. Six weeks later, the adventurer saw his Newfoundland dog being led along in the street by a well-dressed gentleman. The 'Duke' personally collared the suspected dog-thief, called him some very unpleasant things in French, tied his handkerchief to the dog's collar, and took the animal home. The man who had walked the Newfoundland dog, a certain Mr Fry, turned out to be a respectable gentleman, and he took the 'Duke' to court for unlawfully detaining his Newfoundland dog. A dog-seller in Leadenhall Market testified that he had sold the dog to Mr Fry in February 1842. But several witnesses had seen this very same dog with the 'Duke' and his entourage. In the end, the exasperated magistrate decided to let the Newfoundland decide for himself: "The dog was accordingly set free, and when called 'Lion' he immediately ran towards Mr Fry, and raising himself on his rear feet, put up his fore paws on that gentleman's shoulders. The 'Duke' said that even that exhibition was no criterion of Mr Fry being the owner, for he (the 'Duke') would show that 'Triumph' had not forgotten his old master. The 'Duke', who was sitting on the bench next to the magistrate, called 'Triumph,' and he readily came round to him and seemed to know him well." In the end, Mr Fry's summons was dismissed, and the 'Duke' kept the dog.[26]

Just a few weeks later, the dog-thieves infesting London struck again, this time against a real Duke rather than a bogus one. In December 1842, a police constable pursued a man who had stolen a terrier back to his lodgings in Stanhope Street. Having collared the man, a well-known miscreant named Michael Leary, his attention was attracted by loud barking from another room on the premises. When the constable opened the door, a large Newfoundland dog bounded out. It toppled him over, wrenched off his helmet, and tore the backside off his trousers. As the constable was staggering around, trying to avoid the dog's fangs, Leary hit him hard in the eye, knocking him down. The tough London Bobby still managed to capture the dog-thief, and restrain the angry Newfoundland dog. Four other dogs, all stolen, were also kept on the premises. The collar of the fierce Newfoundland the miscreant had set on the policeman turned out to have the crest of the Duke of Buccleugh, from whom the dog had been stolen. The nobleman made sure that Leary was prosecuted, but once more the sentence was a lenient one: this hardened wretch, with many previous convictions for dog theft, got off with having to pay the Duke £3 compensation, and a fine of £10.[27]

This was a sum a professional dog-thief could easily recoup through a few successful capers. In the 1840s, Sir Francis Burdett, the Duke of Cambridge and Sir Richard Peel all lost favourite dogs. The high value of certain breeds of dogs at this time, and the bond between them and their owners, have been quoted as contributing factors to the epidemic of dog-stealing in the mid-1800s, but another must surely be that the law was not equipped to give the professional thieves of dogs the lengthy prison sentences these scoundrels so richly deserved.

* * *

Henry Russell was a popular singer, active in Britain in the 1840s and 1850s. His hits included

'Life on the Ocean Wave', 'Cheer, Boys, Cheer!' and 'Woodman Spare that Tree!'[28] Although Russell was a landlubber, many of his songs had vaguely nautical themes, none more so than his 1843 hit 'The Newfoundland Dog', with breathless and overblown lyrics by F.W.N. Bailey. Russell claimed that once, when crossing the Atlantic as a passenger on board the packet ship *Montezuma*, he had seen a child fall overboard, only to be saved by the ship's Newfoundland dog Carlo:

> Hist! a flash and a motion
> Ha! Carlo, Ha! Carlo, again,
> Good dog, then, good dog, then
> Bear a hand, then, pull tight,
> A boat hook a boat hook,
> He's in and all right;
> Come, Carlo, quick, follow,
> Fine fellow hard strife!
> Wave stemmer! Deep diver!
> We owe you a life!

An odd-looking cove with a strong baritone voice, Henry Russell found unexpected fame and fortune. After being treated to a performance of 'The Newfoundland Dog', a north countryman exclaimed 'Was the child saved, mon?' After Russell had confirmed that this was really the case, the man earnestly asked 'Could ye get me a pup?'[29] It is curious that 'The Newfoundland Dog' has two different sets of lyrics: those quoted above, and another set (said to be by Eliza Cook), in the same style:

> Now, now he is lost in the trough of the sea,
> Where's the dog! The Newfoundland, quick bring him to me!
> Brave Carlo! go seek him, a____way! fetch him out!
> And the dog has leap'd off while the ship puts a____bout!
> A____way! hie on boy! dash o___ver the spray!
> Strong swimmer, bold diver, go deep as you may!

In March 1850, Henry Russell was at large at the Lyceum in London, filling it every day. A sneering newspaper reviewer was openly envious of his success: "But it is surprising to see a man with a very limited voice, singing always in one key, and mostly to one tune, a round of songs descriptive of horrors, and then telling cooked up anecdotes ... It is singular that so little intrinsic merit should go so far and be made so profitable. Mr. Russell talks like one who was never at school, commences every song with a *Hush!* or a *Hark!* sings in half-a-dozen bass notes at most, with a tricky accompaniment, aptly played, and made telling by the assurance of the performer; and yet he draws, while a whole company of actors play to empty benches."[30]

Having saved much money, Henry Russell retired in 1857, and lived in comfortable affluence until 1900. His obituary in the *New York Times* pointed out that 'Carlo, the Newfoundland Dog' was one of the most popular of his songs, and that he always prefaced it by telling the story of its origin."[31] Henry Russell's considerable success is quite hard to understand, and to say that his work has not stood the test of time would be an understatement. That includes 'The Newfoundland Dog', with its ludicrous ending:

> A moment, Hur___rah! they are safe in the bow!
> Good dog, where's the man that is nobler than thou?

Doone "Doing his bit" to comfort the wounded.

Two Newfoundland dogs collecting for patriotic purposes

> Thou shalt live in our hearts, for tho' soul___less and mute,
> Yet God's beau___ti___ful image was saved by the brute!

As we have seen, Britain had a healthy population of Newfoundland dogs already in late Georgian times. The importation of dogs from Newfoundland continued, and the wealthy people who owned fine specimens made sure they were bred from. In contrast, Newfoundland dogs were few and far between in continental Europe. One would have supposed that the French fishermen working the Newfoundland fisheries would have made sure to bring a dog or two with them to *La Belle France*, but although there is good evidence that the fishermen made use of Newfoundlands as ship's dogs, there are few accounts of these dogs setting paw on French soil on a permanent basis. According to Captain Sidney Smith RN, his father kept a Newfoundland dog at Caen in Normandy, where this fine animal attracted much notice. When the dog expired in the late 1810s, "His body was begged by the public museum as the first specimen of his variety the French had ever seen. He was stuffed, and is at this moment a conspicuous ornament in the Gallery of Natural History, Hotel-de-Ville, Caen."[32] The earliest certain Newfoundland dog in continental European art is a white and black bitch with puppies, painted in 1824 by Pierre François de Noter, of Gent. Perhaps it was his own dog, or perhaps the animal was owned by some local magnate, who wanted a likeness of his favourite dog and her offspring.[33]

Prince Leopold of Sachsen-Coburg-Saarfeld had married the Princess Charlotte, the only daughter of George Prince of Wales, in 1816. After her death the year after, Prince Leopold remained in Britain, where he was exposed to the Cult of the Newfoundland dog. In 1831, he was invited to become King Leopold I of the recently independent Belgium. Just like the British royals he had befriended in London, King Leopold kept quite a menagerie of dogs and other animals. In 1835, the court artist Eugène-Joseph Verboeckhoven painted 'The Dog of Leopold I', a sturdy white and brown Newfoundland. Ten years later, the same artist painted 'The Favourite Animals of Leopold I': a handsome white and black spotted Newfoundland dog, a whippet, two small spaniels, a monkey and a macaw.[34]

Even by the middle of the nineteenth century, when Britain had a very healthy population of Newfoundland dogs, and the dogs were no longer ruinously expensive, the Newfoundlands remained scarce in continental Europe. Although some wealthy magnates, like Leopold I, imported dogs from Britain, they were too few for any breeding to take place. The celebrated French artist Jean-Léon Gérôme's 1858 painting 'L'Attente' is one of the finest studies of a Newfoundland dog ever. Subtitled 'Etude de Chien de Terra-Nuova', it shows a large white and black spotted Newfoundland sitting in what looks like the reception hall of an ancient château, looking very dignified and superior. Zacharias Notermann's 1876 portrait of a Newfoundland dog is also quite felicitious. Several of the paintings of the Belgian artist Wouterus Verschuur involve Newfoundland dogs. Apart from 'A Landseer Newfoundland in a Landscape', there is the excellent 'Comforts of home' with a contented-looking Newfoundland stretched out in front of a fire.[35]

Already in 1793, the German naturalist Johann Friedrich Blumenbach kept a white and black Newfoundland dog. Some crowned heads, like King Friedrich Wilhelm of Prussia, King Maximilian Joseph of Bavaria, and the Margravine Amalie of Baden, also found it fashionable to have a Newfoundland.[36] Otherwise, Newfoundland dogs were few and far between in Germany until 1883, when the dog enthusiast Max Hartenstein imported four good-quality dogs from England, to breed from them at his kennel in Saxony. At a Berlin dog show, he once exhibited sixteen of his dogs, to great admiration.

The frontispiece of Henry Russell's sheet music for 'The Newfoundland Dog'

By the turn of the century, Germany had 144 Newfoundland dogs. Some of them belonged to Kaiser Wilhelm himself, and were depicted on postcards with his children. In Switzerland, the veteran cynologist Professor Albert Heim took an interest in Newfoundland dogs. His large male Türk successfully competed at the German dog shows. Wodan, the son of Türk, lived to an advanced age and had many offspring, in spite of his dangerous habit of chasing trams. The Scandinavian countries had very few, if any, Newfoundland dogs prior to 1840. At the first dog show in Sweden, in 1886, four Newfoundlands took part.[37]

CHAPTER 11.
SIR EDWIN LANDSEER AND THE NEWFOUNDLAND DOG

> She looks at the paintings so rare, Bloudie Jacke!
> That adorn every wall in your house;
> Your *impayable* pieces,
> Your Paul Veroneses,
> Your Rembrandts, your Guidos, and Dows,
> Morland's Cows,
> Claude's landscapes – and Landseer's Bow-wows.
>
> Richard Harris Barham,
> *The Ingoldsby Legends.*

Edwin Henry Landseer was born in 1802. He was something of a child prodigy, whose considerable artistic talents were recognised at an early stage. Landseer studied under several artists, including his father, the engraver John Landseer, and Benjamin Robert Haydon, who encouraged the young Landseer to perform dissections in order to fully understand animal musculature and skeletal structure. Already in 1815, he exhibited at the Royal Academy. He had an early interest in dog painting, exhibiting his 'Fighting Dogs Getting Wind' to considerable acclaim in 1818. Prints made from his portrait of the celebrated 'Alpine mastiff' 'Lion', said to have been the largest dog in Britain, sold well for several decades. Several litters were bred from Lion, with various imported bitches. His son 'Caesar' featured in yet another well-known early Landseer painting, 'Two Alpine Mastiffs reanimating a Stranded Traveller' from 1820.

When the rich and famous wanted portraits of their dogs, Landseer was always ready to oblige; as a result, his output was very considerable.[1] His earliest known portrait of a Newfoundland dog is 'The Champion', also known as 'Newfoundland Dog with Rabbit', but this thin, setter-like dog is certainly no pure-bred Newfoundland. In 1821, Landseer painted Mr Alsop's Newfoundland bitch 'Cora'; she has quite a pointed muzzle but otherwise looks reasonably Newfoundland-like. In 1822, Landseer was inspired by Robert Burns' poem 'Twa Dogs' to paint a Scottish collie and a white and black Newfoundland dog. Burns had originally intended to contrast the scrawny Scottish collie, a working dog found in every farmyard, with the expensive, valuable Newfoundland dog, the property of some visiting English aristocrat:

> The first I'll name, they ca'd him Caesar,
> Was keepit for His Honor's pleasure:
> His hair, his size, his mouth, his lugs,

> Shew'd he was nane o' Scotland's dogs;
> But whalpit some place far abroad,
> Whare sailors gang to fish for cod.
>
> His locked, letter'd, braw brass collar
> Shew'd him the gentleman an' scholar;
> But though he was o' high degree,
> The fient a pride, nae pride had he;
> But wad hae spent an hour caressin,
> Ev'n wi' al tinkler-gipsy's messin:
> At kirk or market, mill or smiddie,
> Nae tawted tyke, tho' e'er sae duddie,
> But he wad stan't, as glad to see him,
> An' stroan't on stanes an' hillocks wi' him.

In Landseer's painting, Luath the collie looks rather apprehensively at the hulking Newfoundland, but neither dog appears aggressive. In Burns' poem, they talk to each other: it is Caesar who opens the conversation, expressing curiosity as to how the poor man can endure his life. Luath owns that the cotter's lot is a hard one, but declares that in spite of poverty and hardships the poor are "maistly wonderfu' contented." The talk then drifts to the corruption of politics and the vices of the rich. Caesar at last brings it to an end by describing the wearisome monotony and emptiness of the fashionable life. By this time it was sundown, and the two friends separated, rejoicing "that they were na men, but dogs." The contrast between the two dogs is well brought out in Landseer's painting. The collie is sitting on his haunches, nervously alert, but the noble Newfoundland dog lies at his ease with one paw elegantly crossed over the other. Recognized as one of Landseer's masterpieces, 'Twa Dogs' was issued as a print more than once; there was even a pirated American version, erroneously entitled 'Newfoundland Dog and Terrier'!

In 1822, Landseer was invited to paint Mr Ellis Gosling's celebrated Newfoundland dog 'Neptune'. The first version of his painting was 'Canine Friends: Newfoundland Dog and Irish Terrier beside a Stream'. He then went on to repaint the dog in a slightly different pose, with the open sea in the background as 'Neptune' in 1824. Again, this painting deservedly became popular, and was engraved as a print more than once. A head study of Neptune was engraved by Thomas Landseer, the artist's brother, and issued as 'Neptune, the Property of W.E. Gosling Esq.' Both the original paintings of Neptune are in private hands. It has been alleged that the Newfoundland dog in 'Twa Dogs' was Neptune, but from the dog's distinctive colouring, this is clearly not the case.

In 1823, Landseer accepted a commission from another wealthy Newfoundland dog fancier, Mr William de Merle, to paint his favourite dog 'Lion'. This portrait is yet another masterpiece, showing this splendid white and black Newfoundland dog in a mountainous Scottish landscape. The painting of Lion was donated to the Victoria & Albert Museum by Mrs Ann de Merle in 1894; it is on permanent exhibition there, and a magnificent sight it is too. There are two other, lesser known Landseer paintings of Newfoundland dogs from the same period. Firstly there is 'A Newfoundland' showing a large white dog with a black face-mask turning its head away from the painter. Secondly, there is the more felicitous 'Dogs and a Frog' from 1825, showing a Newfoundland and a terrier examining a frog they have discovered. The terrier barks, and the Newfoundland puts its huge paw right next to the startled amphibian. The Newfoundland's head resembles that of Neptune, with the distinctive dark patch on the white forehead, but its fur appears darker.

Landseer's portraits of these handsome early Newfoundland dogs indicate that already in those days, there was some kind of inofficial 'breed standard': very large dogs, with luxuriant fur and elegant long

An 1865 print of Landseer's 'The Connoisseurs': a self-portrait with his dogs

A print of Landseer's 1822 painting 'Twa Dogs', inspired by famous poem by Robert Burns

tails, were preferred to the rather scrawny animal depicted by Reinagle, and the strange-looking Boatswain.

* * *

John William Ward, the first Earl of Dudley and a former Foreign Secretary, was extremely fond of his large and handsome white and black Newfoundland dog Bashaw. Since the wealthy bachelor nobleman wanted a portrait of his favourite dog, the ubiquitous Landseer was again called into action. In his portrait, entitled 'Bashaw, the Property of the Right Honourable Earl of Dudley', Landseer hinted at the dog's life-saving abilities by showing him at the seashore, on the verge of leaping into action. Lord Dudley was very pleased with the painting, and he wrote to Landseer that "I hear it may be numbered among your most successful performances." The painting is today in private ownership, but it was engraved by Thomas Landseer in 1858, with the title 'Off to the Rescue!' There is also an 1874 engraving by Alfred Lucas, and a pirated American version entitled 'He is ready!'

THOSE AMAZING NEWFOUNDLAND DOGS

After receiving Landseer's painting of Bashaw, the dog-loving Earl of Dudley was not done yet. In December 1831, he commissioned the artist Matthew Cotes Wyatt to make a statue of his favourite dog, since he thought Bashaw should "live to posterity in breathing marble".[3] The peer agreed to pay the prodigious sum of 5000 guineas for the statue. Since the perfectionist Wyatt kept beavering away for many months, the poor dog was sent from Lord Dudley's country seat, Himley Hall in Staffordshire, to Wyatt's study in London for not less than fifty modelling sessions. Blocks of black and white marble were carefully fitted together to build up the dog's body. Bashaw was a sturdy dog, and Wyatt became fearful that the heavy statue might collapse, since the legs would not hold it. He cleverly introduced a bronze boa constrictor, whose head is trodden on by the dog, into the image; it served as a much-needed support for the statue. Bashaw's eyes were made from precious gems, Persian topaz and sardonyx taken from Lord Dudley's family jewels, and the pupils were sculpted from black lava. In early 1833, when the statue of Bashaw was nearing completion, Lord Dudley came to London to see it. 'There you stand, Bash, *in propria persona* indeed!', the delighted nobleman exclaimed. He made plans to have the marble dog placed in the drawing-room of his Park Lane town house. The obscure poet James Bird, who was also allowed to see the marble Bashaw, wrote a poem 'On the Seeing of the Statue of the Earl of Dudley's Newfoundland Dog':

One of several prints of Landseer's 1822 painting of Neptune

Another version of the Neptune print

> Most noble creature of a noble race!
> Pugnacious Prince of Newfoundland breed!
> There dwells a surly grandeur in your face,
> Of which 'tis well to take especial heed –
> there starts a stern, and care-for-nothing grace
> From your keen eye like lightning in its speed.
> And, he who looks upon you, scarce can fail
> To fancy that he sees you wag your tail.

But Lord Dudley died later in 1833, and his heirs did not appreciate the logic of spending 5000 guineas on the statue of a dog. The old Earl had always been eccentric, and towards the end of his life, he had been far from sane. After much wrangling, the disgruntled Wyatt had to keep the statue. In February 1834, he exhibited it to some London journalists, hoping that the resulting publicity might persuade some other magnate to purchase the marble dog. The *Court Journal* declared that "the work must be regarded as a triumph of art" and the *Literary Gazette* judged it "the most elaborate representation of a quadruped ever produced by ancient or modern art...singularly effective, magnificent and unique". The *Morning Chronicle* wrote that "the union of objects so seldom seen in combination as a down cushion, a boa constrictor and a Newfoundland dog, all form large deductions from the enjoyment of the spectator". The *Morning Post* journalist struck a more ribald note, remarking that "If we were disposed to be critical we might demur to the propriety of our sagacious friend being represented so complacent and unconcerned under circumstances of such excitement, if not of danger."[4]

Later in 1834, Wyatt wrote to the *Morning Post*, to announce that in spite of "the extraordinary conduct of the Executors of the late Earl of Dudley in withholding the fulfilment of the act and wish of their principal", he felt very proud of the marble dog. He would be willing to offer it to the National Gallery, he announced, but they did not take him up on the offer, and the marble Bashaw had to remain in his studio.[5] The dog was exhibited as 'The Faithful Friend of Man trampling underfoot his Most Insidious Enemy' at the Great Exhibition of 1851, attracting considerable praise, but no good cash offers. At the time of Wyatt's death in 1862, he had still not earned a penny from the marble dog, and nobody wanted to buy it. In his will, Wyatt declared that the statue of Bashaw could be sold to some art-loving nobleman for any sum, or presented to the British Museum or some other repository; any member of the Dudley family would have to pay the full five thousand guineas, however, to be able to reclaim their heirloom. But the Dudleys took this snub with the greatest composure, and again there were no buyers, private or institutional, for the marble dog.

The celebrated aesthete John Ruskin saw the marble dog in a loan exhibition at the South Kensington Museum in 1870. He pronounced it "the most perfectly and roundly ill-done thing I ever saw produced in art". He went on, "the persons who produced it had seen everything, and practiced everything; and misunderstood everything they saw, and misapplied everything they did...and misunderstanding of everything had passed through them as mud does through earthworms, and here at last was their worm-cast of a Production."[6] A *Pall Mall Gazette* journalist who saw the marble Bashaw the same year agreed: "A fat black and white dog, expressionless and ill-modelled, stolidly pawing a huge snake on the top of a sofa cushion on top of a pedestal, is a thing not produced even by aristocratic patronage of British sculpture every day." The marble dog was a sign of the very worst taste in art, giving little credit to either the Earl of Dudley, Matthew Cotes Wyatt, or the South Kensington Museum.[7] But the thick-skinned museum officials did not mind this scathing criticism, since Bashaw was still at the Museum in 1882. The marble dog was seen there by another sneering art critic, who objected that the Museum was in danger of becoming a gratuitous pantechnicon for unwanted works of art: "Above all, would it not be possible to return to its distinguished owner the statue in coloured marble of a Newfoundland dog, which has for so many years been the solace and delight of the nursemaids and children who frequent the museum ..."[8]

But the aesthete's call for the expulsion of Bashaw again went unheeded. It was not until 1887 that the marble dog was removed from the South Kensington Museum, to be auctioned off at Christies after Wyatt's son had died. In spite of being advertised at "The Celebrated MARBLE FIGURE of the Newfoundland Dog Bashaw, executed by Matthew Cotes Wyatt for the late Lord Dudley and Ward, on pedestal, enriched with Florentine mosaics, recently exhibited at the South Kensington Museum", it went unsold, but was shortly after acquired by John Corbett of Impney Hall, Droitwitch, Worcestershire.[9] He sold to another country magnate, Edward Stevens of Prescott House, Stourbridge, in 1906. In 1957 the sculpture was sold again, wthis time to a firm of stonemasons, who began to dismantle it, removing the gemstones in the dog's eyes, and the hardstone decorations on the marble plinth. Just in the nick of time, the marble dog was bought by the Victoria and Albert Museum for £200 in 1960. Bashaw was put in the main entrance hall, where he dominated all the other works of art. Once more, he became a firm favourite of the children, who were delighted to find that they were allowed to stroke the marble dog.[10]

The marble Bashaw can still be met with at the Victoria and Albert Museum, albeit in a less prominent position. He is a majestic sight indeed, although the contrast between the sturdy, placid-looking dog and the coiling boa constrictor is an unhappy one. Ruskin certainly had a point when he lambasted its lack of artistic merit. On leaving this extraordinary marble Newfoundland dog, it is tempting to quote the end of James Bird's ludicrous poem:

> Farewell! Cold monument of art and skill!
> Thy living prototype will never die –
> While marble lasts his first existence still
> Thy form and lineaments will well supply –
> Struck into being by the sculptor's will
> And *he* has fame that on Time's wing will fly
> Till that fleet wing be stripped of every feather
> And *Time* and *Wyatt* quit this world together.

* * *

In 1837, there was hubbub in the newspapers about 'Bob', a dog presumed to have been shipwrecked off the coast of England. As a stray, he became well-known along the London waterfront saving people from drowning. He was declared a distinguished member of the Royal Humane Society, which not only entitled him to a medal, but also a free supply of food every day. When Landseer decided to paint Bob in 1837, the dog could not be located, and there is still debate whether he really existed, or if the whole thing had just been a newspaper hoax. But one day, Landseer saw a very handsome white and black Newfoundland dog walking down a street in London carrying a message for his mistress, Landseer's cousin Mrs Newman Smith. Although there is no evidence the elusive 'Bob' was really a Newfoundland, Landseer got a brilliant idea: he would cash in on Bob's fame by painting a substitute dog! The large Newfoundland dog, whose name was 'Paul Pry', was taken to the artist's studio to play the part of the heroic distinguished member of the Humane Society. Through bribing the great dog with various treats, Landseer persuaded him to lounge on a table, the table-top becoming the quayside. He painted the dog against a dull threatening heaven: the light falls beautifully on his white coat, and his dark head stands out against the brightest part of the sky.

A print of Landseer's 1824 portrait of 'Lion'

Landseer's 'Off to the rescue!'

Mr Newman Smith bought Landseer's painting of his Newfoundland dog for £80. When 'A Distinguished Member of the Humane Society' was exhibited at the Royal Academy in 1838, it was pronounced a masterpiece, and Landseer's popularity increased even further. The ubiquitous Thomas Landseer was of course at hand to produce prints of the painting: these would decorate many a parlour wall in Victorian houses great and small. One of the most iconic dog pictures ever, it came to symbolize the virtues of the Newfoundland dog. A Victorian cottage industry made the most of the image of the 'Distinguished Member': it adorned letter weights, plates, porcelain figures and table inlays.

Mr Newman Smith expired in 1866, leaving the 'Distinguished Member' to the National Gallery, stipulating that the immense painting must be hung in a prominent position, and remain on permanent display. The *Morning Post* praised Mr Smith for his generosity, since the painting might have fetched £1000 at auction; it was "one of which any national collection may well be proud".[11] But already in late Victorian times, Landseer's animal paintings were going out of favour among the snobbish aesthetes. Just after the turn of the century, the National Gallery gave the 'Distinguished Member' to the Tate Gallery, whose museum officials did not care for it much; it languished in the store-rooms for nearly a century, and was damaged in a flooding incident. At the 1982 exhibition of Landseer's work in Philadelphia and London, it was not in a fit state to be shown. Mr Ron Pemberton, an American Newfoundland dog fancier, thought this a great pity. He and other enthusiasts collected money to finance its restoration and subsequent exhibition at the Philadelphia Museum of Art. On its return to the Tate Gallery, its ungrateful custodians again consigned it to the vaults, but it has since been lent to the Kennel Club, where it is on prominent display in the Art Gallery, to considerable acclaim.

An engraving of the marble Bashaw being admired during the Great Exhibition, from the *Illustrated London News*

* * *

The great success of the 'Distinguished Member' provided Landseer with royal patronage. Queen Victoria was one of the many people impressed by his work. An avid dog fancier, she commissioned Landseer to paint portraits of several of the royal dogs. In 1835, he was asked to paint 'Prince George's Favourites': the pony, Newfoundland dog, spaniel and falcons of the elder son of the Duke of Cambridge. Just like our old friend kept by the Duchess of York, this royal Newfoundland was also called 'Nelson'. In 1839, Landseer painted the Princess Mary, Prince George's younger

THOSE AMAZING NEWFOUNDLAND DOGS

A print of Landseer's 'A Distinguished Member of the Humane Society'

sister, with her favourite Newfoundland dog, Nelson, balancing a biscuit on his broad nose. The original painting, kept in the Royal Collection, shows that this large and handsome dog is white and brown spotted, a fur colour variation more common at the time than it is today. Like many of Landseer's dog portraits, it was engraved by Thomas Landseer and sold in considerable quantities.

The Duke of Beaufort, who had a Newfoundland dog named 'Lion', summoned the ubiquitous Landseer to immortalize his favourite in 1840. The result is far from prepossessing, however: in one painting, 'Lion and Dash', the comatose, ill-looking Newfoundland dog lies outstretched in an unnatural position, as a little spaniel barks at him. In 'The Duke of Beaufort and his Children', the dog has at least managed to get up on his feet, to be caressed by one of the Duke's children.

After a lapse of 16 years, Sir Edwin Landseer returned to Newfoundland dog painting in 1856, when he exhibited 'Saved', dedicated to the Royal Humane Society, before the Royal Academy. Again, the bold and powerful image attracted considerable praise: a large white and black Newfoundland dog lies panting on the beach, having just rescued a little girl from drowning. Its obvious lack of realism made it a target for the critics, however: John Ruskin was not the only aesthete to remark that when a little girl is saved from drowning in the open sea, her clothes are usually *wet*. And how on earth could she still be wearing her hat? Nor does the dog's fur look wet in the slightest. In spite of these defects, several prints of 'Saved' were issued, with very considerable sales. It was particularly popular in the United States, where a pirated print was issued under the erroneous title 'He is saved!' prompting the obvious transatlantic jibe 'Gee, no wonder that little girl looks tired, having just dragged that huge lump of a dog out of the water!'

In 1859, Landseer painted a novel version of 'Twa Dogs', this time only with the heads of the Newfoundland and the collie; it is far inferior to the original, and has not been much noted. In 1866, Landseer added some details to an earlier painting by Henry Wallis, depicting the stairs in Shakespeare's house in Stratford-upon-Avon. One of these additions was a Newfoundland dog, with its rump towards the painter, and its tail between its legs; again, it is entirely unworthy of his talents. Furthermore, the notion that any Newfoundland dogs set paw in Stratford-upon-Avon in Shakespeare's time is an adventurous one indeed. Unfortunately, as these rather miserable paintings indicate, Sir Edwin Landseer ended his life in very unhappy circumstances. Already by the 1860s, he had become a wreck of a man, from alcoholism, general ill-health, and considerable mental derangement. His career, and the

A plate featuring the 'Distinguished Member', produced by The National China Co. of East Liverpool, Ohio, between 1899-1910

THOSE AMAZING NEWFOUNDLAND DOGS

Two mugs and a model featuring the 'Distinguished Member'. The model is possibly Continental, but lacks any markings. The very fine china (nearly translucent) mug to the left was produced by W.H. Goss, possibly 1890s to early 1900s. The mug to the right is by an unknown manufacturer

quality of his output, suffered badly as a result, as did his reputation as a leading animal painter.

* * *

As perceptive dog historians have noted, Landseer's portraits of fine Newfoundland dogs in the 1820s and 1830s prove that Britain had a healthy population of fine Newfoundland dogs, looking very much in line of today's breed standards, except that they were white and black (or white and brown) spotted. The paintings of Neptune, Lion and Bashaw are not just great works of art, but important snapshots of Newfoundland dog history.

Sir Edwin Landseer, the money-grubbing painter of the dogs and horses of the wealthy, had more than one string to his bow. In some of his paintings of dogs, he used elements of realism and satire to good effect, in silent but eloquent 'dog dramas'.[12] 'Dignity and Impudence' shows a sombre-looking bloodhound and a mischievous little terrier sharing a kennel. 'The Old Shepherd's Chief Mourner' shows a dark Scottish bothy, inside which a collie keeps vigil by the coffin of its master, an old shepherd. The mourning dog rests its head on the coffin, and one paw is slightly raised, like if it had been scraping the coffin wall. In 'A Jack in Office', a sturdy, well-fed dog belonging to a cat's meat seller guards his master's barrow against some half-starved, miserable-looking street dogs. The theme of 'Alexander and Diogenes' comes from the anecdote of Alexander the Great visiting the unworldly philosopher Diogenes of Sinope, asking if there was anything he could do for him. 'Yes', the philosopher responded, 'stand out of my light!' In Landseer's hilarious painting, a dapper, sturdy, white terrier-like dog stands outside the kennel of a scruffy-looking mongrel, blocking the light. The startled white dog looks like if it has just received an unexpected rebuke from the canine philosopher inside the kennel.

Landseer's 'Uncle Tom and his Wife for Sale' is a more disturbing image. Two bulldogs are chained together, advertised for sale. One of them, Uncle Tom. is grinning with his wide mouth, seemingly carefree of what lies ahead, but his 'wife' looks up at him apprehensively, like if she has a feeling their

A fold-down Victorian papier-maché table inlaid with mother of pearl, again featuring the 'Distinguished Member'

buyer is unlikely to treat them kindly. A large dog-whip is hanging on the wall nearby, a reminder of the slavery of the fictional Uncle Tom at the American plantation, and the unpleasant life of a dog with a cruel owner. 'The Otter Hunt', with the perforated otter dangling helplessly from the hunter's spear, as the baying otter hounds celebrate the kill, is a quite repellent image of pointless cruelty. Another of Landseer's lesser-known paintings, 'The Last Run of the Season', depicts a panting, exhausted fox turning to face its unseen enemies, the hounds; baring its teeth, it prepares for its final battle, which it is not going to win.

In contrast to Landseer's vibrant and innovative paintings of 'dog drama', in which the dogs think and feel essentially like humans, his portraits of Newfoundland dogs are more conventional. The theme of a noble Newfoundland interacting with a smaller dog, used to emphasize the animal's size, had been used already by Schwanfelder in 'Nelson with a Terrier'. The technique of showing the Newfoundland on the shore or quayside, ready to show its aquatic prowess, dated back to Morland and Stubbs. Still, the 'Distinguished Member', and the paintings of Neptune, Lion and Bashaw stand out as masterpieces of canine portraiture. In Landseer's mind, the Newfoundland dog had enough mystery and symbolism on its own; it did not require any elements of 'dog drama' to appeal.

A print of Landseer's 'Saved'

Princess Mary of Cambridge with a Newfoundland dog, an engraving after Landseer's 1839 portrait, published in the *Illustrated London News* of 1891

CHAPTER 12.
WILLIAM GORDON STABLES AND SOME OTHER VICTORIAN NEWFOUNDLAND DOG FANCIERS

> Thus, in confused and scattered monologue,
> Here, there, and everywhere, the Scholar's mind
> Bestirred itself, as a Newfoundland dog
> Doth in a shipwreck all about him find
> Something to do; tho' now and then a log,
> Or empty barrel, by mistake, the kind
> And zealous creature brings, with loving eyes
> And wagging tail, to shore as some great prize.
>
> Lord Lytton,
> *Glenaveril; or, the Metamorphoses*

William Gordon Stables was born in Scotland around 1837. He was educated at Aberdeen grammar school, and later studied art at Aberdeen University, remaining a member of the arts class until 1857. He then studied medicine and graduated in 1862. He became a naval surgeon and enjoyed many adventures in faraway lands. Once, his ship was sent in pursuit of slavers off the Mozambique coast; another time, he took part in an expedition to the Arctic. A jolly, carefree character, Dr Stables very much liked life on the ocean wave. He mostly served in small ships, where his medical knowledge was seldom called upon. His main challenge was venereal disease, contracted by the seamen on shore leave. But in 1871, the Doctor himself contracted severe rheumatic and jungle fever in Africa, and was invalided home on half-pay.[1]

A friend of the Doctor's asked him to take care of his young Newfoundland dog Nero, since the mischievous and powerful dog was quite out of control. Dr Stables was very much taken by the handsome black dog, whom he renamed 'Theodore Nero' because he thought the majestic animal needed a more dignified name. Initially, Theodore did not appear to think much of his new master. But after the great dog had fallen ill with a fever, the Doctor made use of his medicine-chest to cure him, and these two would remain the greatest of friends for many years to come. They travelled the country extensively, for the Doctor to recuperate from his illness. They shared the same cheap hotel room, and if the railway guard objected to the hulking Newfoundland travelling inside the carriage, the Doctor shared the van with his dog. Apart from filling his digestive cavity, Theodore's main pleasure in life was fighting other large dogs. The Doctor, whose ideas of canine discipline were of a similar standard to those of Lord Byron, did nothing to prevent him from such amusements.

Dr Stables was fond of teaching his dog various silly tricks, like imitating a circus elephant, or carrying a large sheep's head through the streets, with a placard saying 'I am starving!' He thought it great fun to teach Theodore to grab people's sticks, but this sentiment was probably not reciprocated by an old Irish sailor with a wooden leg, who was toppled over by the great dog. When Theodore grabbed an Admiral's bamboo cane, Dr Stables was severely reprimanded. It would also be quite hilarious, the Doctor thought, to teach Theodore to take people's hats off, but this time the fun was ended when the massive Newfoundland wrestled a police constable to the ground, and tried his best to wrench the constable's helmet off his head. It was capital fun to have Theodore shake himself on command, after the great dog had enjoyed a swim, particularly if there were some children nearby to give a proper soaking. And what could be more amusing than to set Theodore on a German marching band, scattering them like as many chickens? When the Doctor visited Brighton, an elderly misanthrope complimented him and his dog for their sterling efforts to subdue the German marching bands infesting that city.

After a year of travel, Dr Stables was ordered to report to the flagship at Sheerness, for it to be determined whether he was fit to return to his duties. He asked if he could bring a dog, and this was allowed; what the officers of the flagship thought when they saw the massive Theodore come on board has unfortunately not been recorded. There were two other dogs on board, both of them Labradors. The Doctor liked to watch the three ship's dogs leap overboard and race each other swimming for the shore; although the hulking Theodore was a slow starter, he gradually overtook the other two, and completely outclassed them. Theodore soon made his presence felt on board the flagship. The Marines were very fond of him, and used to feed him at table. Theodore knew their mealtimes like a walking clock. In contrast, he very much disliked the words 'eight o'clock', since they signified that the time-gun would be fired, and he always took refuge underneath a sofa at that time. When the sailors marched with their walking band, Theodore led the parade.[2]

When the Doctor bragged about Theodore's fighting prowess, the sailors pointed out that the *Great Eastern* had just come to Sheerness. This ship, the greatest in the world, had a Newfoundland dog named Sailor, famous for his ability to leap into the sea from the top of the paddle-box, a distance of seventy feet. Surely Theodore could not give *him* a drubbing? The Doctor and Theodore accepted the challenge. When they waylaid Sailor on the beach, the two massive dogs started a furious fight, until the sailors helped to separate them. But since from that day, Sailor would always run away when he saw Theodore, the Doctor thought he had proved his point. This was not the first time Theodore Nero had fought other dogs on the beach; interestingly, the Doctor noted that the great dog had twice deliberately tried to kill his opponents, by dragging them out into the water and drowning them, a behaviour that appears to be typical for the Newfoundland.[3] Even less creditably for the Doctor, he once took Theodore to a nearby village, where a large cur dog had killed several other dogs, and bitten a sailor as well. The two dogs fought fiercely, and Theodore was allowed to bite his opponent to death.

* * *

Unfortunately, Dr Stables was not passed fit for serving afloat, possibly because it was thought that the fever had affected his brain. He had to leave the flagship and retire on half-pay. All he possessed was a Cremona fiddle, his old sea chest, and his Newfoundland dog. The Doctor again went travelling, this time with plans to tour Britain and enter Theodore into various dog shows. This scheme worked a treat. The great dog won nineteen first prizes and cups in little over three months. Theodore was formally proclaimed a champion, and the doctor boasted that there was not a Newfoundland dog from Glasgow to Neath that would have cared to meet him in the show ring. In Edinburgh, an envious lady tried to poison the great dog, for her own animal to win the cup, but thanks to the Doctor's ministrations,

Dr William Gordon Stables, from *Penny Illustrated Paper*, March 19 1892

Theodore was soon up and about again. In August 1873, the Doctor was at the Keighley Agricultural Show, where he "took first with his champion dog 'Theodore Nero'. This dog has a long list of achievements, amongst which are first at Edinburgh, second at the Crystal Palace, first at Boston, Lincolnshire, Preston, Ormskirk, Paddock, Rochdale and Chorley, and three prizes in one day at Gainsborough."[4] Theodore Nero was much sought after as a stud dog and sired several litters of pups, some of whom went on to become champions themselves. The Doctor himself took care of at least three of Theodore's sons, the pick of the litters, he hoped, but he was an indifferent judge of dogs and neither of these animals went on to distinguish themselves in the show ring.

After serving in the merchant navy for a while, Dr Stables married Theresa McCormack in 1874 and settled down to become a general practitioner. Many years of cruising abroad and examining sailors for venereal disease had not done his general medical knowledge any good, however: he was quite a dangerous doctor, particularly after becoming addicted to alcohol and chloral hydrate. After nearly killing a child with a carelessly written prescription, he gave up medical practice, for good. After weaning himself off the chloral hydrate, Dr Stables settled down in Twyford with his family, in a house he called the Jungle, to become an author of juvenile literature. Unaffected by the miserable ends to his naval and medical careers, he was quite a jolly, eccentric character, with a great fondness for animals. He rose at 4.30 each morning, had a cold bath, looked after his various pets, had breakfast, and retired to a small garden bungalow called the Wigwam, to settle down with pen and paper and write all day. In the coming twenty years, he would write at least a hundred books, and countless articles for *The Boy's Own Paper* and other juvenile periodicals. He wrote a dangerous-sounding advice column for boys, recommending cold baths, early morning walks, and hot porridge as cures for a variety of ailments. His novels today appear very dated, with heroic young midshipmen, hearty Jack Tars and foolish black servants with names like 'Sambo' setting off for various adventures. But the Doctor knew the taste of his readers: in a 1899 poll of the readership of the *Boy's Own Paper*, he was voted their favourite author, outclassing Jules Verne who only managed fourth.

In a *Boy's Own Paper* article on dogs, Dr Stables pointed out the Newfoundland as the most sagacious of the canine tribe. Theodore Nero used to carry the Doctor's cane for him, and took great pride in doing so. When the Doctor went shopping, he indicated the parcel on the shop desk to his dog, saying 'I believe this is paid for, Master Nero!' The great dog immediately stood up on his rear legs and took the parcel, proudly carrying it home. The mischievous Theodore soon 'improved on' this particular game, however, taking parcels from other people and bringing them to the Doctor. It was important, the Doctor wrote, that the Newfoundland dog was spoken to like an adult, since the sagacious creature was greatly pained by being addressed in baby-language. Once, he had known a Newfoundland dog who had run off, never to be seen again, after its foolish owner had tested its endurance too far by speaking to it like if it had been a small child, rather than a rational being.[5]

Theodore Nero followed his master through all his vicissitudes. In December 1875, he was introduced to a Manchester journalist as "the champion Newfoundland dog of England; he carries on his collar the record of twenty-one victories." 'Such a splendid black fellow!' exclaimed the journalist.[6] At the Maidstone Dog Show of 1876, Theodore took part in the first water trials held for Newfoundlands and other dogs. But although Dr Stables had boasted that his dog would take to the water leaping from a steamer doing fifteen knots, poor Theodore stood howling at the water's edge, refusing to leap in, and ignoring his master's frantic entreaties. A sarcastic Scotsman said "Eh, Doctor, mon, be canny or ye'll get the dowg wat; 'Theodore Nero' will be drooned!"[7] The pair returned for the Portsmouth water trials later the same year, in which the dogs were supposed to swim out to a boat, fetch a large dummy, and bring it to shore. This time, the Newfoundlands outclassed all other entrants, the black dog 'Commodore' beating Theodore by just one second, although the Doctor complained that the boat had

THOSE AMAZING NEWFOUNDLAND DOGS

Sable I. and Champion Theodore Nero, Black or True Newfoundlands.

Theodore Nero and Aileen Aroon, from an article by W. Gordon Stables in *The Boy's Own Paper*, May 1 1880

drifted out to sea, so that the great Theodore had further to swim.[8]

In time, the Doctor thought Theodore should have a 'wife'. A friend gave him a black Newfoundland bitch, and he renamed her 'Aileen Aroon'. At first, Aileen did not at all like things at the Jungle, and she ran off at the first opportunity. The Doctor heard a frightened schoolboy say that he had seen a black bear rambling in the woods! He acted with his usual eccentricity, mobilizing all the schoolboys and appointing himself Captain of the search party, with Theodore Nero as First-Lieutenant and the schoolmasters as Drill-Sergeants. Aileen was duly recaptured and brought back to the Jungle, where she soon became accustomed to her surroundings. The Doctor was amused to see that she learnt by imitating Theodore: after he had made his master a courteous bow to obtain a treat, she soon followed suit. Both Aileen and Theodore were fond of chasing bicyclists, and the Doctor never did anything to dissuade them of this habit. After Aileen had died, he decided to write her biography. Since she had not done much interesting in her life, the book was bolstered with various tales of Theodore amusing himself and his master through doing various pranks. The great dog did not lie down on his 'wife's' grave, but the astute Doctor noticed that he visited it regularly. Once, when the Dr Stables went to dig a hole to plant a rose-bush on Aileen's grave, the overjoyed Theodore thought that he was about to dig her up, to bring her back to life and him, or so at least the Doctor claimed.

Theodore lived to become very old. In his last illness, the kind Doctor left his writing to sit by the side of the great dog, to comfort him. One bleak December evening, Theodore breathed his last. As the Doctor expressed it at the end of his *Aileen Aroon*:

> Down at the foot of our bird-haunted lawn, in a little grassy nook, where the nightingales are now singing at night, where the rhododendrons bloom, and the starry-petalled syringas perfume the air, is Nero's grave – a little grassy mound, where the children always put flowers, and near it a broken, rough, wooden pillar, on which hangs a life-buoy, with the words – 'Theodore Nero, Faithful to the end.'

A proper Victorian eccentric, William Gordon Stables had a large horse-drawn caravan constructed. In this 'Land Yacht', the 'Gentleman Gypsy', as he called himself, travelled all over England, Wales and Scotland, describing his adventures in a series of books. With him were his coachman and valet, the Newfoundland dog Hurricane Bob, and a favourite Cockatoo. A minor celebrity due to the impressive sales of his books, the Doctor milked his fame for all it was worth, even endorsing various products in advertisements: 'I am never without Bovril in my household.' Although he kept drinking hard, his constitution remained solid, and his literary output undiminished, in quantity at least.

A lover of animals and an active supporter of the Sea Birds Protection Society and the Humanitarian League, Dr Stables became known as an expert authority on dogs, cats, and rabbits, frequently acting as judge at shows. He wrote a number of books on animals, the most popular being *Our Friend the Dog*, which was issued in several editions Although having no academic education in either zoology or veterinary medicine, and possessing only an outdated medical degree, he fancied himself as a leading authority on all canine matters. For some reason or other (possibly that his great friend Theodore was solid black), he made up his mind that the solid black variety was the original breed of the Newfoundland dog. The white and black dogs had briefly been fashionable at the time of Landseer, the Doctor pontificated, but now they were again in decline. When interviewed in 1875, the Doctor told a journalist that the white and black Newfoundland dogs should be called the Landseer, because although the solid black dogs were the original breed, the white and blacks had been commonly met with in this artist's time. In an 1880 article, the Doctor proclaimed that "The black-and-white breed is now generally called the 'Landseer Newfoundland', a name the writer originated some few years ago, out of compliment to the great artist who loved so much to paint these dogs."[9] The denomination 'Landseer Newfoundland' thus did not originate with some Newfoundland breeding association, or knowledgeable expert on dogs, but with a Victorian eccentric who wrote silly children's books, and who liked to scatter German marching bands with his mischievous Newfoundland dog.

In his efforts to rewrite the history of the Newfoundland dog, the bold Doctor had support from two cronies of his: the clergyman Thomas Pearce, who wrote under the name of 'Idstone', and the dog fancier J.H. Walsh, who made use of the pen-name 'Stonehenge'. These two shared not only a predilection for silly pseudonyms, but also a strong wish to believe that the solid black Newfoundland was the superior breed. In his 1872 book *The Dog*, Idstone wrote that although white and black Newfoundlands had been fashionable in Landseer's time, the solid black dogs were the original breed. A few white hairs on the chest, or a white toe, showed no impurity of blood, he pontificated, but a white tip to the tail should be viewed with suspicion. In his 1882 book *Dogs of the British Islands*, Stonehenge boldly went on to claim that Landseer had been a faddist with a fanatical predilection for white and black dogs. Although these animals were not pure Newfoundlands, he had selected them for their contrasting colour, and thus corrupted the public mind what a proper Newfoundland dog should look like.

In late Victorian times, another leading breeder of Newfoundland dog was Mr Henry Richard Farquharson. Having made a fortune in the tea trade, he settled down at stately Eastbury House, Tarrant Gunville. Unlike some breeders of the time, he was not convinced by the 'pure black original breed' theory, and bred both solid black dogs and Landseers. Not content with having just a few Newfoundland dogs, he hoarded more and more of these animals, housing them in large, purpose-built kennels. He had an advantage over other Newfoundland fanciers, since he lived not far from Poole, so that he could send down carts to collect the

The Jungle, from W. Gordon Stables' *Aileen Aroon*

dogs when the timber ships arrived from Newfoundland. After several years of breeding and collecting dogs, Farquharson (who was apparently quite sane) possessed a total of 125 Newfoundland dogs, one pack of 50 bitches and another of 75 dogs. Two country lads were employed full time to look after the dogs. Twice a day, the two packs were taken for long walks, one towards Blandford Camp, the other in the opposite direction, towards Chettle. But one day, one of the lads took a wrong turning, and the packs met on Chettle Down. Since Newfoundlands have a strong pack mentality, the dogs started what must surely have been the biggest dog fight since the days of the Roman arena. Not less than 45 dogs were either bitten to death or had to be put down; in addition, the two careless kennel boys were thrashed within inches of their lives by the irascible Mr Farquharson.[10] In spite of the 'Battle of Chettle Down', as this epic fight became known among the locals, Farquharson continued breeding Newfoundlands: he had several champions, and his dogs were very highly regarded at the time. Later, he became a Member of Parliament and made efforts to expose the true identity of Jack the Ripper, but he was heavily fined for libelling another politician in 1892, and expired three years later.

* * *

It is important to recall that Dr Stables, Idstone and Stonehenge were active during the heyday of the Victorian dog fancy. These new dog fanciers picked out some of the most striking and attractive breeds, and proclaimed certain variants 'better' than others, at times only because they were unusual or difficult to produce. In the 1880s, the pedigree dog champion was not just a piece of canine perfection, but also a testimony to the breeder's power to purchase and to manipulate. The bulldog has been pointed out as an example of how the late Victorian dog fancy rewrote the history of the canine race, to suit their own ideas of what a dog should look like.[11] In olden times, these bulldogs had been large, formidable animals, bred to bait bulls or to fight other dogs.[12] But the late Victorian bulldog breeders produced a smaller, rather more benign-looking animal, with a large head, a squat muscular body, and short legs. The history of the bulldog breed was revised accordingly: they were friendly, good-natured dogs, and even endowed with a good deal of intelligence.[13] The fact that many fashionable ladies owned these ungainly beasts, and entered them into various dog shows, was further proof of their kindliness of disposition. As a result of this propaganda, and the obvious patriotic motives to want to own a breed of dog that was traditionally British, the bulldog became quite fashionable in late Victorian times. A breed that had long outlived its usefulness had been successfully rehabilitated.

The Newfoundland dog is another example of the historical revisionism of the Victorian dog fancy. The solid black Newfoundland, originally appreciated for its relative scarcity, was proclaimed the original breed, mainly for the reason that they were considered more desirable than the white and black dogs. When Landseer's paintings of white and black Newfoundland dogs became an embarrassment for the revisionists, they countered by declaring him a faddist with a fanatical liking for white and black spotted dogs. The sole voice objecting to the activities of Dr Stables and his two cohorts came from a veteran Newfoundland dog fancier, writing in the *Kennel Gazette* of 1881. He pointed out that in olden times, red, brown, bronze, white and red, white and brown, and white and black dogs were continually being landed on the long quays of Poole, the Mecca of the Newfoundland dog trade. He had even seen yellow dogs of undoubted purity. Selection and careful breeding had made the dogs more homogenous, and produced animals as beautifully marked as Landseer's 'Distinguished Member'. The exertions of certain Newfoundland dog fanciers to exclude all but solid black dogs from the dog shows had sordid and selfish motives that were known to the Kennel Club when it provided a class for 'other than black' dogs. The term 'Landseer Newfoundland' was a misnomer if there ever was one.

But still, in the 1884 edition of *Our Friend the Dog*, Dr Stables calmly asserted that "The true Newfoundland is a very large jet-black dog, with a long straight coat and bushy tail, and a face extremely expressive, and eyes that beam with intelligence".[14]

CHAPTER 13.
A HISTORICAL ANALYSIS OF NEWFOUNDLAND DOG FUR COLOUR GENETICS

> When featuring a dog review,
> Much laudatory praise is due,
> The Newfoundland – a dog world famed,
> That came from a small island named.
> A massive body, square-set thighs,
> A noble head and kindly eyes;
> A coast guard dog, it knows no fear,
> And oft saves lives when death is near.
>
> Althea Bonner,
> *Dictionary of Dogs.*

Today, the majority of Newfoundland dogs are solid black. Various monographs, some written by acknowledged experts on the breed, agree with Dr Stables and his two cohorts that the black Newfoundland is the 'pure' breed, whereas the white and black variety should be referred to as 'Landseer' since these dogs were so very often depicted by the Sir Edwin Landseer.[1] Thus, the 'black supremacy' hypothesis, first proposed by some late Victorian dog fanciers, has become the generally accepted version of Newfoundland dog history. Some fantasists have even asserted the existence of 'large black bear dogs' left behind by the Vikings, or alternatively a troop of Tibetan mastiffs crossing the Bering Straits by some unspecified stratagem, to interbreed with the friendly Newfoundland wolves. Again, these lucubrations have been taken seriously not only by 'tourist office historians' wanting to promote what they perceive as Newfoundland's great indigenous breed of dog, but also by authors of recent breed monographs.[2]

Professor Albert Heim, the veteran Swiss Newfoundland fancier, had some strange ideas of his own, namely that the white and black Newfoundland dog was in fact a development of the "large black and white English mongrel dog", also known as a butcher's dog. For some reason or other, dog fanciers had interbred these butcher's dogs with Newfoundland dogs and St Bernards, to create the Landseer.[3] This of course disregards that the first St Bernard set paw on English soil in 1815, when there had already been a healthy population of white and black spotted Newfoundland dogs in that country for half a century at least.[4] 'Butcher's dog' was an uncouth term used mainly in Georgian times to signify large mongrel dogs, the point being that these animals ate so much they could only be kept by a butcher with a plentiful supply of meat and bones. A butcher's dog was worth a few shillings at the most, whereas a

A solid black Newfoundland with a Landseer, from Rawdon Lee's *History and Description of the Modern Dogs of Great Britain and Ireland*

fine Newfoundland dog could be sold from the timber ships at Poole for twenty guineas; this makes it extremely unlikely that the early Newfoundland fanciers saw fit to interbreed their valuable animals with such low-quality mongrels. The normally reliable Margaret Booth Chern quoted Heim's theory with approval, adding the remarkable statement that had it not been for Landseer; the white and black Newfoundland dogs would have faced total extinction, since they were very few already in his time![5]

Over the years, a few dissenters to the 'black supremacy' hypothesis have made themselves known. Already the old dog author Rawdon B. Lee found it odd that although the Landseer Newfoundland was clearly more common then the black dogs in the early part of the nineteenth century, the late Victorian dog breeders and dog judges preferred the 'original' solid black dogs, considering even a white chest and white toes as 'disfigurement'.[6] The aforementioned Albert Heim pointed out that "the Newfoundland dogs in Britain from 1780 until 1850 were almost all Landseers, and exposed the falsehoods of Dr Stables.[7] Nor was the distinguished dog historian Edward C. Ash particularly impressed with the bluster of the Victorian Newfoundland dog fanciers, clearly recognizing that due to selective breeding, the dogs had changed very much in the last century.[8]

* * *

The first Newfoundland dog specialist to openly challenge the 'black supremacy' theory was the American art historian Dr Emma H. Mellencamp.[9] In 1976, she published an article in a leading specialist magazine, pointing out that not just Sir Edwin Landseer, but a multitude of other British or continental European painters from the first half of the nineteenth century, had depicted white and black spotted Newfoundland dogs. The bluster of our old 'friend' 'Idstone' was exposed, as was a remarkable statement from the old dog author Vero Shaw, namely that Landseer "corrupted the public mind upon the subject of the Newfoundland. A vast number of people, without troubling themselves to inquire into the matter, have associated the black & white dog with the correct type of Newfoundland, utterly regardless of the fact that Sir Edwin may have selected this colour as brighter and more suitable for the object he had in mind." But Landseer had portrayed many solid black dogs, of various breeds, nor was it conceivable that a painter of his immense talent would be unable to depict a black Newfoundland, had these dogs been commonly met with in his time. 'Idstone' had been writing at a time when Landseer was losing both his powers and his popularity. Ill-health, alcoholism and periodic insanity meant that he could no longer maintain his standards, and he lost his position as Britain's leading animal painter. This paved the way for characters like 'Idstone' and Dr Stables to attack the no longer fashionable Landseer, and accuse him of being a faddist with a fanatical liking for white and black Newfoundland dogs.

In 1978, Dr Mellencamp published another valuable article, this time pointing out that certain paintings of Newfoundland dogs alleged to portray solid black dogs were in fact portraits either of white and black Newfoundlands, or dogs belonging to other breeds.[10] For example, Landseer's 1852 drawing 'The Head of Caesar, a Newfoundland Dog', claimed to depict a solid black dog, is clearly a study of a white and black spotted specimen, with the characteristic black face-mask. It had also been claimed, by an authority on Newfoundlands, that a large solid black dog disappearing into a hedge in Emmanuel Gottlieb Leutze's painting of Washington crossing the Delaware might have been a Newfoundland, thus implying that such dogs existed in Washington's time. But it turned out that the painting was not contemporary: it had been finished in Düsseldorf in 1851; thus, all that could be concluded was that a large black dog of a retiring disposition might have been at large in that city in the early 1850s. Dr Mellencamp ended her article by pointing out that "I have found very few paintings of the all-black Newfoundland in the early half of the 1800s. None, at least, that I could certainly verify."

In two articles published in 1989, the English Newfoundland dog expert Denis Conlon and the German cynologist Christa Matenaar presented an impressive inventory of Newfoundland dog iconography. From the 1740s until the 1840s, there were many paintings and drawings of white and black spotted Newfoundlands, but no convincing illustrations to support the existence of solid black dogs at the time, in Britain or on the European continent.[11] In another valuable review of Newfoundland dogs in art, British cynologist Nick Waters reproduced many early paintings and drawings of white and black (or brown) spotted dogs. An important find was John E. Ferneley's 1829 painting 'Coachman with a Newfoundland Dog', showing a black dog with a white patch on its chest. In contrast, Mr Waters reproduced no images of solid black or solid brown Newfoundland dogs dated prior to 1850.[12]

* * *

The accepted facts of Newfoundland dog fur colour genetics are as follows. Firstly, the reason brown dogs were (and still are) in a minority is that the basic colour of a Newfoundland dog is determined by what is known as the B locus, with 'Black' colour being dominant over 'brown'. Thus, the BB homozygotes will be black, as will the Bb heterozygotes; only the bb homozygotes will be brown. Then there is the D locus, with 'Non Dilute' dominant over 'dilute'. The DD and Dd dogs will be black, whereas the dd homozygotes will be grey, or diluted black. There are a few grey Newfoundland dogs in the United States, but very few elsewhere. Many grey Newfoundlands experience hair loss and other symptoms of colour dilution alopecia, and it may be questioned whether they should be bred from.

It is another accepted fact that the regulation of solid colour versus spotting in Newfoundland dogs is

A brown and white Newfoundland dog, from Tuck's series of cards depicting dogs, posted in 1906

controlled by the S locus, where 'Solid' colouring is dominant over 'spotted'. Thus the SS homozygotes and the Ss heterozygotes will be solid black (or brown), whereas the ss homozygotes will be spotted. In Newfoundlands, there are several different patterns of spotting, ranging from dogs that are white with a few black spots, to dogs that are black with white feet, chest and tip of tail. The geneticist Dr Charles Little constructed a model with an allelic series where S is Solid, s^i is 'Irish spotting' with white head blaze, breast, paws and tail tip, s^p piebald spotting with coloured plates, separated or confluent, and s^w extreme-white piebald spotting. He discussed the possibility of plus and minus modifiers affecting the type of spotting, and also the putative existence of a 'pseudo-Irish' spotting pattern that might occur in Solid/spotted heterozygotes in some breeds of dogs.[13] His Norwegian contemporary Ojwind Winge preferred a simpler model with two alleles at the locus for white mottling: T for solid coloured or nearly so, and t for white mottling.[14]

In 1990, the German scientist H. Pape proposed a model of polygenic inheritance to be applied to the piebald spotting patterns in Landseer Newfoundland dogs and Holstein-Friesian cattle.[15] Not at all unreasonably, he divided the Landseers into three classes: the dark dogs with white legs, chest, tail and head blaze (Mantel), the white and black spotted dogs with and white legs and tail (Medium), and the nearly all white dogs with a black face-mask and a few black sports on the body (Light). Dr Pape postulated that the recessive major spotting gene worked with at least two modifiers, which he termed s_2 and s_3. Dogs that were S_3S_3 homozygotes, and either S_2S_2 homozygotes or S_2s_2 heterozygotes, were dark (Mantel). Dogs that were s_2s_2 homozygotes, and either s_3s_3 homozygotes or S_3s_3 heterozygotes, were nearly all white (Light). All other combinations resulted in the traditional white and black spotted dogs (Medium). This model was tested in large populations of cattle, and a much smaller population of dogs, and proved to work quite well. It would have been interesting to see it evaluated in a larger population of dogs.

Dr Pape also addressed the problem of the inheritance of small white marks in Newfoundland dogs. He was aware that most Solid/spotted heterozygotes were solid black or brown, but presumed that modifier genes might again be playing a part in the 'pseudo-Irish' spotting, as well as in the inheritance of other patterns of small white marking. Pape differed the solid-coloured dogs without white marks (Class I), the solid-coloured dogs with some white on the chest (Class IIa), the dogs with small white marks on the chest and one or more paws (Class IIb), and the 'Irish spotted' dogs with white on the head, chest, belly, paws and tail tip (Class III). Again, he constructed a model of two modifiers determining these spotting patterns, and tested it using a database of stud book material. His theory worked reasonably well, but with one exception: when dogs from Class I were mated with each other, the expected values of Class I, II and III pups was 1740, 250 and 9; the observed values were 1765, 234 and 0, quite possibly indicating that entirely solid-coloured dogs do not have 'Irish spotted' pups. In matings with dogs from Class I with dogs from Class II, the expected value of Class I, II and III pups was 641, 293 and 16; the observed values were 627, 320 and 3; again a considerable underestimation of the number of 'Irish spotted' pups, casting doubt on Dr Pape's hypothesis.

In 2007, the gene 'Microphtalmia associated transcription factor' (MITF) was recognized as causing one or more spotting patterns in dogs, including Landseer Newfoundlands. The insertion of a short interspersed nucleotide element (SINE) in the MITF start codon was linked with random spotting in many dog breeds.[16] A later population study indicated that dogs homozygous for the SINE had white markings comparative to those in Pape's three classes of Landseer Newfoundlands. In most breeds, dogs heterozygous to the SINE insertion were either solid coloured or had minimal white markings, but in certain breeds, the dogs had the kind of 'pseudo-Irish' pattern discussed by Little.[17] Experienced Newfoundland dog breeders have recognized the 'Irish spotting' pattern, which their observations have made them presume to be dominant over Landseer, although this hypothesis lacks experimental

The Landseer champion 'Dick', from an article by W. Gordon Stables in *The Boy's Own Paper*, May 1 1880

support, and is not accepted by the geneticists.

* * *

To investigate the historical variation of Newfoundland dog fur colour, I made use of the 'Times Digital Archive' database of the advertisements for lost or stolen dogs in the *Times* newspaper. For these advertisements to have the desired effect, they needed to contain a good description of the animal in question, thus hopefully eliminating the bias due to carelessness or journalistic license. Many of the descriptions of the dogs are very good, like this one from 1785:

LOST on Saturday last, May 28th, a large Black Newfoundland Dog, has White Feet, a little White in the Forehead, the end of his Tail White, answers to the Name of Lyon.[18]

Excluding the advertisements that did not describe the fur colour of the dogs in question, as well as those that concerned mongrels or were obviously confused, there were a total of 134 advertisements to recover lost or stolen Newfoundland dogs from 1785 until 1890. Excluding a grey Newfoundland advertised for in 1814, and a white and yellow dog advertised for in 1839, the remaining dogs belonged to the fur colour patterns seen today (Table I). It turned out that prior to the year 1840, there was not a single advertisement describing a solid black (or brown) Newfoundland, but numerous dogs that were obvious white and black spotted (Landseers). Most of these Landseers belonged to the 'Medium' and 'Light' subgroups. Between 1840 and 1850, solid black dogs begin appearing, and in the period 1850-1860 they caught up with the other fur colour variations. In the period 1860-1890, solid black dogs were in the majority. It is quite telling that during the latter part of this period, some of the advertisements emphasized the 'purity' of the solid black dogs. This investigation thus strongly supports the arguments from the art historians quoted above: it would appear as if solid black Newfoundland dogs were very scarce in Britain prior to 1840.

TABLE I
FUR COLOUR VARIATIONS IN NEWFOUNDLAND DOGS OVER TIME, FROM THE 'TIMES DIGITAL ARCHIVE' DATABASE

TIME PERIOD	LAND-SEER	WHITE/ BROWN	IIA	IIB	III	BLACK	BROWN
1785-1799	1	1	0	0	1	0	0
1800-1819	2	1	0	0	2	0	0
1820-1839	8	2	0	0	5	0	0
1840-1849	9	1	0	0	6	4	1
1850-1859	10	1	4	3	4	17	1
1860-1869	6	0	5	2	5	20	1
1870-1890	1	0	2	0	0	6	0

Making use of Dr Pape's system of classification, it was also obvious that the 'III' pattern of fur colour was represented in many early (pre-1840) dogs. The 'IIa' and 'IIb' dogs were all post-1850, however, and thus appeared after the 'Solid' gene had been introduced.

This would support the hypothesis that small white marks on the chest and paws is a random event rather than the result of a specific allele. Because the melanocytes migrate down from the spinal column during embryogenesis, not all the dogs complete this process by birth or thereafter. This results in a white toe or a white spot on the chest in an otherwise solid-coloured animal (Pape's 'IIb' and 'IIa' classes, respectively). Table I provides no support for the existence of a 'pseudo-Irish' spotting phenomenon in Newfoundland dogs, however, but instead supports Little's original hypothesis of an 'Irish spotting' allele, indicating that Pape's 'III' fur colour pattern occurs in spotted/spotted homozygotes. The role of modifiers in regulating this fur colour pattern remains unclear.

It was also possible to make use of another online newspaper database, the Nineteenth Century British Library Newspapers, although the descriptions of the dogs (for sale, for auction, lost or found) were of a much lower quality.

TABLE II
FUR COLOUR VARIATION IN NEWFOUNDLAND DOGS OVER TIME, FROM THE 'NINETEENTH-CENTURY BRITISH LIBRARY NEWSPAPERS' DATABASE

TIME PERIOD	LAND-SEER	WHITE/BROWN	IIA	IIB	III	BLACK	BROWN
1760-1769	1	2	0	0	0	1	0
1770-1779	20	2	0	0	9	2	0
1780-1789	10	4	0	0	3	3	0
1790-1799	12	2	0	0	1	0	1
1800-1809	14	1	0	0	4	0	1
1810-1819	12	0	0	0	4	1	0
1820-1829	14	1	0	0	1	1	0
1830-1839	16	0	0	0	0	0	0

Out of a total of 149 advertisements, there were two solid white dogs and one that was red and white; the remainder fitted into the present-day classification system (Table II). The result was much the same as for the Times Digital Archive, although the British Library database seemed to indicate that there were a few solid black dogs in Britain prior to 1840, although this might be a result of a lack of cynological sophistication in the provincial newspapers of the time. Not only was the definition of a Newfoundland dog somewhat vague in Georgian times, but a brief advertisement like 'For sale by auction, a black Newfoundland dog' does by no means rule out that the animal had some white markings. Still, a few of the advertisements for solid black Newfoundlands appear bona fide, and it seems likely that although the larger, white and black or white and brown spotted dogs were preferred by the dog fanciers, a few of the smaller, solid-coloured, retriever-like black dogs were also imported from Newfoundland, although they were not interbred with the spotted dogs to any extent prior to the 1840s when solid black dogs became fashionable.

In the light of the data described above, and the art history studies of fur colour variation in Newfoundlands, it is reasonable to suggest that the 'Solid' gene was introduced into the British population of Newfoundland dogs some time in the 1840s, quite possibly through importation of smaller, solid black dogs from parts of Newfoundland, and certain dog fanciers making breeding experiments to produce solid black Newfoundland dogs with the size and general phenotype of the finest white and black spotted specimens. Being dominant over 'spotted', the 'Solid' gene soon made an impact on the Newfoundland dog phenotype, particularly since the solid black dogs became highly fashionable in late Victorian times, with selective breeding playing a part. Interestingly, in some Victorian illustrations of Newfoundland dogs, the solid black dogs are smaller than the Landseers, with shorter fur and a less massive head. Even Dr Stables had to admit that "In size the Landseer should be, if anything, larger than the black".[19] The historical data presented here supports the hypothesis of small white marks on the chest and paws being a random event, rather than the result of a specific allele. In contrast, the historical data does not support the existence of a 'pseudo-Irish' spotting phenomenon in Solid/spotted heterozygote Newfoundland dogs. The 'Irish spotted' phenotype existed before the Solid gene was introduced, and it must be suspected to be the result of an 'Irish spotting' allele in spotted/spotted homozygotes, although a model of multiple modifiers, like that suggested by Dr Pape for the Landseer Newfoundlands, might also play a role.

Black, brown and Landseer Newfoundlands playing

CHAPTER 14.
NEWFOUNDLAND DOGS IN THE NEWS 1850-1900

> Alas, poor Dash! Thou wert no vulgar dog;
> Nor were thy merits of the common kind –
> Tho' underneath this undistinguish'd turf,
> All cold and lifeless, lie thy poor remains!
>
> Elegy on a Newfoundland dog,
> from G.H. Harley, *Poems* (London 1796).

PROVIDENTIAL ESCAPE – A very extraordinary and unprecedented occurrence took place on board the *Ayrshire*, of Houndsditch, in her homeward voyage from Calcutta in May last. Shortly after the ship had crossed the line, Captain Browne, the master, had occasion to pull at a rope passing through a block, which was badly secured with some rope yarn. While tugging at the rope the block gave way, and his own impetus suddenly carried him over the side. A noble Newfoundland dog, which was a great favourite on board, with the generous instinct natural to its species, jumped in to his master's rescue, and seizing him by the collar brought him in safety alongside when both were hoisted on board. It was only then that the danger to which the captain and his brave deliverer had been subjected became fully evident. A huge shark, which had been playing for some time about the ship waiting for windfalls, had marked the captain for its prey, and was making towards him just as his four-footed deliverer bounded to his assistance. They did not, however, escape altogether unscathed, for just as they were getting up the side their voracious assailant bit away half the dog's tail. The gratitude of the captain for his double escape will be better felt than described, effected as it was in so providential a manner. The poor dog, who was of course much caressed, suffered a good deal from the injury, but was ultimately cured. [*Era*, January 13, 1850]

We are sorry to find that Mr. Roebuck, M.P., has met with a somewhat serious accident. It appears that, some ten days ago, the honourable member was amusing himself with his Newfoundland dog, and was feigning to throw a stick, when the dog, eagerly springing to seize the stick, caught Mr. Roebuck's hand in his mouth, and severely lacerated the muscles of the thumb. [*Freeman's Journal,* July 22, 1851]

VORACITY OF A DOG - A Newfoundland dog, belonging to a regiment quartered in a town in the Nord, was lately found dead in the midst of a quantity of meat, which he had attacked with such voracity as to bring on a fit of indigestion, which carried him off. Having got into a well-stocked pantry, he devoured a large piece of beef, a leg of mutton, several fowls, and other things quite raw, weighing more than eight kilogrammes. [*Freeman's Journal,* December 29, 1854][1]

A rather sorry-looking Newfoundland dog, from the 1863 edition of Brehm's *Tierleben*

THOSE AMAZING NEWFOUNDLAND DOGS

SAGACITY OF A NEWFOUNDLAND DOG - A large Newfoundland dog, that may be seen any day at No. 9, Argyle-street, Glasgow, has added one more instance to the many on record of the extraordinary sagacity of dogs. It seems that being, like other juveniles, sometimes rather fond of fun, he required to receive occasional discipline, and for that purpose a whip shaft was kept beside him, which was occasionally applied to him. He evidently did not like this article, and was found occasionally with it in his teeth moving slily to the door with it. Being left at night on the premises, he found the hated article, and thrust the small end below the door, but the thick end refused to go. A few nights afterwards, the whip shaft was left beside him, and was never seen again. He had put the small end below the door, and someone had pulled it out. The same dog gets his provisions brought to him in a tin can. Taking a walk he saw a child carrying a can exceedingly like his. He quietly seized it by the handle and carried it to his quarters, the child holding on and screaming all the way. When shown his own he seemed quite ashamed of his mistake, and allowed the frightened child to go with the tin he had mistaken for his own. This sagacious dog is in the habit of begging money from his biped acquaintance, with which he marches to a baker's shop and buys bread, which he comes home with, and eats when hungry. [*Times*, October 26, 1858][2]

STORY OF A DOG - We have a good dog story for the commencement of the season. Mr. Tewes, who keeps a restaurant in William-street, has a large Newfoundland dog, a finer specimen of his kind that is ordinarily met with. Among his other wonderful marks of intelligence, we witnessed this a day or two ago. A gentleman entered the restaurant holding by a cord a dog which served as watch on board a ship. While in the place the gentleman supposed the dog was safe, and released his hold upon the string. The door was opened while the parties were in conversation and the dog made his escape. Mr. Tewes said to his Newfoundland, 'Go bring him back, sir.' The dog obeyed the mandate, and within a block or two overtook the fugitive. He first proceeded to give the object of his charge a slight reprimand for his delinquency by means of a smart shake or two, and then took the rope in his mouth to lead the dog back to his master. Some holding back was manifested, the string was dropped, and another shaking administered. Finally, by alternate chastisements and pullings at the cord, the runaway dog was brought into the restaurant, and Newfoundland, with a sly wink at his master, seemed to say, 'There he is.' The scene was witnessed by many, and caused no little excitement. Taken all in all, we think it is about as good a dog story as usually finds its way into the papers, and has the advantage of being true, too. [*Lloyd's Weekly Newspaper*, July 10, 1859][3]

A WONDERFUL DOG - On Sabbath last two local preachers, belonging to the Primitive Methodists at South Shields, went to preach at Usworth, a colliery village some eight or nine miles off. They finished the labours of the day a little after 8 o'clock, and soon after set their faces homeward. The evening had passed, and night, robed in her starry stillness, had approached, giving the two preachers an opportunity of conversing on the sublimities of the stellar regions. They had not proceeded far in their interesting conversation when they were overtaken by a large Newfoundland dog, and some time elapsed before they took any particular notice of the animal. They pursued their way and still the dog followed, when they thought it necessary to drive him back, as he appeared to be a valuable animal, and his owner might come to some loss should he stray away from home. Notwithstanding all the means employed, the dog followed, keeping the two preachers ahead at a respectful distance. They continued on their way, and came through some fields which lead to the main road. When coming through one of those fields, the dog passed them, making a whining noise as he came by, which, by their interpretation, sounded like a mark of disapprobation at their driving him back. Before they came to the hedge at the bottom of the field they heard the dog growling and barking, and upon advancing a few steps further, they were terror stricken at beholding three men in the hedge ready to pounce upon them. Two leaned back in the hedge, and the other slunk down, as the dog snarled and the two preachers passed by. The preachers went on quickly, leaving the dog in front of the rascals. After they had got about a mile further the dog came up to them again, and appeared pleased, as if he had found his master. They determined that he should follow, and that, when they separated, the one he followed should take him home, give him his supper and a night's lodging, and take him back the next day. They went on and down the railway, and as soon as they turned off the line to come into a lane leading into the town, the dog turned round and took his departure home, leaving the two preachers in safety, and thankful for his sagacity and protection. *[Times*, October 1, 1859]

A DOG'S REWARD - The crew of one of the steamers which ply between Havre and Rio de Janeiro relate the following incident: In the last voyage out one of the sailors fell overboard not far from the coast of Brazil; and a large Newfoundland dog named Pollux, belonging to the vessel, immediately jumped into the sea, and seizing him by the cravat maintained his head above water until a boat could be put off and pick him up. The sailors state that they were so delighted with the exploit that they unanimously resolved that on the voyage home the dog should be formally rated as one of their mess and share their meals. [*Lloyd's Weekly Newspaper*, April 1, 1860]

A DOG-COLLAR FOR THE PRINCE - The inhabitants of St John's, Newfoundland, intend presenting the Prince of Wales a very appropriate specimen of their native production. A fine large Newfoundland dog has been selected for his royal highness, and to have this noble animal appear to the best advantage, a silver collar was necessary the collar is of solid silver, and is formed of a wide heavy chain, with an ornamental centre piece, and weighs forty five ounces. Some idea of its size may be formed from the fact that the dog's neck is twenty-four inches in circumference. The centre piece, which is surrounded by a wreath of oak leaves, and surmounted by the prince's crest, bears this inscription: Presented to his Royal Highness the Prince of Wales by the inhabitants of Newfoundland. [*Lloyd's Weekly Newspaper*, August 5, 1860][4]

THE NEWFOUNDLAND DOG - It will be remembered that the Hindoo was destroyed by fire on Friday, the 24th ult., off Formby, near Liverpool, and that five of the crew perished. On board there was a large Newfoundland dog, but it was generally believed by those rescued from the wreck that the dog was lost. Such is not the case, however, for on Saturday morning he was found by some fishermen rambling about the shore at Hoylake, Cheshire. Although the poor animal must have borne the full force of the terrific gale of Friday, and swam an immense distance through a fearfully heavy sea, he seemed none the worse. *[Times*, November 1, 1862]

SHIPWRECK, AND SINGULAR INCIDENT - A correspondent of the Dublin Express reports the total loss of the Culloden, a large ship of 1300 tons. Captain Ness and his wife, 33 seamen, and Mr. White, passenger, took to the boats, but with such haste that only a small quantity of provisions could be taken, and a large and beautiful Newfoundland dog was forgotten. He appeared on the bulwarks soon after, but of course he had to be left to his fate. Half an hour later the tall masts of the ship disappeared beneath the waves ... [*Liverpool Mercury*, October 29, 1863; for the happy ending, see below]

A LIVING WAIF - The English schooner *Theodore*, which arrived at Havre the day before yesterday from Newcastle, picked up at sea, a fine Newfoundland dog, which was standing on a piece of timber about two yards long, forming part of the wreck of some vessel, other portions of which were seen floating near. When the dog, which is a very fine animal, saw the schooner's boat approaching, it jumped into the water and swum to meet its deliverers. It has since evinced the greatest attachment to the captain. *[Times*, October 28, 1863]

Hausfreundschaft, a German engraving from 1872

LIFE SAVED BY A DOG - At the late wreck at Sanday, a Newfoundland dog belonging to the vessel, seeing a poor fellow struggling among the breakers, leaped into the sea, and having seized in his mouth the upper part of the man's jacket bore his head up, and swam ashore with him. [*Times*, May 23, 1864]

NOVEL STYLE OF SKATING - On Wednesday thousands enjoyed the healthy and exhilarating exercise of skating on Lochburnie. Among those on the ice a young lady skater attracted much attention. She had with her a large Newfoundland dog, and attached to the collar round the animal's neck was a pair of reins; these she held in her hand, and, directing his course on the ice, she in this way glided along in very swift and graceful style. [*Standard*, January 4, 1867]

One incident is worth recording. A large black Newfoundland dog, who accompanied its master on the ice, and managed to get back on the shore, has since Tuesday afternoon never quitted the ground, not have the police been able to drive it away. Sergeant Neal, 9D, has on three occasions brought food for it, but the poor dog has refused it. [*Morning Post*, January 18, 1867][5]

In Minnesota, recently, two men were kept all night flat on their back and motionless, feigning death, by a ferocious animal which they supposed to be a bear, but which the morning light showed to be a Newfoundland dog. [*Dundee Courier & Argus*, October 18, 1867]

A New York paper says: A Newfoundland dog was seen carrying a bundle in its mouth down Second Avenue, on Thursday night. Arriving at No. 451, occupied by Mr. Van Winkle, he walked up the steps, and having deposited the bundle on the topmost step, ran off. The package contained a female infant about one week old. [*Nottinghamshire Guardian*, February 21, 1868]

RESCUE BY A DOG - A few days ago, a young lad, a son of Mr. Dunlop, of Aughanloo, near Newtownlimavady, went to the river Roe to bathe. He got carried beyond his depth, and, being unable to swim, he sank to the bottom. There were only a number of little boys present, who were unable to render him any assistance. He would have drowned but for a Newfoundland dog, who, seeing the little fellow sink, jumped into the water, dived, and, catching him by the hair of the head, succeeded in bringing him to the bank, and thus saved him from drowning. [*Daily News*, July 14, 1868]

A hen belonging to a gentleman at Chapeltown has selected the dog kennel in which to rear her young. A Newfoundland dog is the joint occupant of the kennel with her, and they live on the most amicable terms. [*Liverpool Mercury*, August 8, 1868]

At Dieppe, in France, the following notice has been issued by the police: 'The bathing police are requested, when a lady is in danger of drowning, to seize her by the dress, and not by the hair, which oftentimes remains in their grasp. Newfoundland dogs will regulate themselves accordingly. [*Hampshire Advertiser* (Southampton, England), Saturday, December 19, 1868]

A large Newfoundland dog is not a bad pioneer, if you can only persuade him to venture on the ice; but these animals, though ready to plunge boldly into any depth of water, have a strong objection to appearing ridiculous, and they are aware that they do look ridiculous when they are floundering about with their legs wide apart, and a helpless expression on their sagacious countenances. [*Graphic*, January 14, 1871][6]

EXTRAORDINARY REQUESTS - Captain Annesley, of the 2nd Battalion 6th regiment, stationed at Drogheda, who died a few days ago, requested that after his decease a splendid grey charger, value £150, should be shot, and a phaeton of great value should be destroyed. Yesterday these requests were carried out, the charger being shot and the phaeton broken up. The deceased officer has bequeathed 5s. per week to

THOSE AMAZING NEWFOUNDLAND DOGS

support a Newfoundland dog. [*Morning Post,* April 15, 1873]

A DOG CALLED AS WITNESS - Mr. Alexander John Baylis, of Heathfield Lodge, Acton, was summoned at the Hammersmith Police Court yesterday for detaining a dog claimed by Mr. John Doris to be his property. The defendant said it was his dog. At the request of the complainant, who disputed that the defendant's description of his dog corresponded with the one in question, it was fetched and brought into court. It was a large black Newfoundland dog. Mr. Mullenger, who received the dog which was sold to the complainant, from Sevenoaks, called 'Pluto', but the dog turned its head away from him. Mr. Baylis called 'Lion,' and the dog immediately answered to the name. Mr. Bridge thought it was not the dog which the complainant lost, and dismissed the summons. [*Huddersfield Daily Chronicle*, July 10, 1873]

RESCUING A NEWFOUNDLAND DOG FROM DROWNING - A curious incident occurred in Kensington gardens a day or two since. The ice on the Long Pond was not thick enough to bear the weight of skaters, but a Newfoundland dog was, through thoughtlessness or love of mischief, induced to rush across the ice after a stick. It gave way beneath him, and the poor animal was hemmed in by the ice. His swimming powers served to keep him afloat, but there was no chance of his escape, for the ice broke beneath him, whenever he tried to climb up it. Crowds of spectators gathered on the banks and the bridge, watching the dog's frantic struggles and listening to his pitiful howls, but not knowing how to help him. At last a private soldier volunteered his services, and by means of a life-boy from the Humane Society's hut, he contrived to reach the poor dog, who was almost exhausted, and succeeded in dragging him out amid the cheers of the

A NEWFOUNDLAND DOG AND HER FAMILY.

A Newfoundland bitch and her seven pups, from *Harper's Young People*. June 19 1886.

lookers on, who gladly sent the hat round and made a liberal collection for the brave fellow. It is something like carrying coals to Newcastle for a man to save a Newfoundland dog from drowning, and the achievement pays off one item from the long list of debts for similar services rendered by Newfoundland's kinsfolk to man. [*Sheffield & Rotherham Independent*, December 23, 1874]

At St. Gaudens a Newfoundland dog saved in succession twelve people, dashing into the raging torrent bravely, but making the attempt the thirteenth time the poor animal was drowned. [The Star, July 03, 1875][7]

THE BEST DOG STORY YET - The *Portland* (Me.) *Press* of Thursday tells it thus: Yesterday, as the morning train over the Rochester Road was nearing Alfred, the engineer discovered a large Newfoundland dog on the track. He blew the whistle, but the dog stood his ground, and thinking something was wrong, the engineer whistled down brakes, and the engine stopped within a few feet of the dog. It seems that a four-ox load of logs had attempted to cross the track, but the sled caught on the rails. The driver heard the train approaching round a curve, and rushed down the track to stop it. His dog took in the situation, and dashed around the curve and stopped the train. It would have been impossible to stop the train after seeing the man. [*Cheshire Observer,* April 22, 1876]

Under the pressure of hard times the keeper of a Paris café has hit upon an ingenious device for reducing the

**A nasty French soldier turned rapist on the prowl? You are safe if you have a Newfoundland dog!
From *La Nature* 16(1) [1888], 397-8**

cost of his establishment. He keeps a fine Newfoundland dog, which is a great pet with frequenters of the house, and from every consumer of coffee contrives to extract one lump of sugar per diem, insomuch that men have marvelled how a dog could eat so much sugar without being very sick. The secret is this. The dog has been taught to take the sugar back to the store-room, and there deposits it in a large basin, whence it is again taken for the supply of other customers, the dog himself receiving a commission of 10 per cent. [*Hampshire Telegraph,* November 11, 1876]

On the second night, in the lecture 'Has a Man a Soul?' Mr Bradlaugh said: 'I stand on the river's bank. A child is playing there. An idiot is passing. He pushes the child into the stream. A Newfoundland dog rescues the child; and yet theologians tell us that the idiot has a soul and the Newfoundland dog has not one. [*Daily News*, May 25, 1880][8]

Ernest and Richard Weedon, of Rotherfield-street, Essex-road, would assuredly have lost their lives but for the promptitude of a servant girl in one of the gardens, who unchained a Newfoundland dog. And sent it into the water, whence it emerged a minute afterwards holding the arm of Richard Weedon in its mouth. The boy was fast locked in the embrace of his brother Ernest, and after a great deal of difficulty both were pulled out, and taken home in a cab. The occurrence was witnessed by a large number of persons, who had congregated in the gardens and roadway on either side of the river, and when the boys were brought out of the water a hearty cheer was given for the dog who had saved the lives of the children. [*Reynolds's Newspaper*, August 20, 1882]

SAVING OF LIFE BY DOGS – TO THE EDITOR OF THE MORNING POST - Sir – Two lives were the other day saved by a Newfoundland dog. It has occurred to me to inquire whether trained dogs are employed by the Royal Humane Society; if not, whether they might not advantageously be so employed. Yours faithfully, F.J. Crosland Fenton, The Dens, Caterham [Morning Post, August 25, 1882]

It is interesting, but melancholy, to hear that there are few fine specimens of the Newfoundland dog in the island. For several reasons the race has degenerated to that few traits of the original remain. These dogs, in fact, thrive better elsewhere. The origin of this fine race of animals is obscure. [*Morning Post*, August 2, 1883][9]

At the Hammersmith Police-court two men were charged with endeavouring to steal a valuable Newfoundland dog by throwing pieces of highly-seasoned meat to it in the street. The owner of the animal had been watching their proceedings, and when the dog returned to him the collar which it had worn was missing. Both Prisoners were remanded for inquiry. [*Standard,* July 23, 1884][10]

A REMARKABLE SHOW OF STRENGTH BY A NEWFOUNDLAND DOG - The American journal *Kennel Gazette* tells that during a winter storm off Long Island, a dredging-ship sank, and the entire crew was lost. At the time of the shipwreck, a black Newfoundland dog was also on board, and after swimming for 18 hours, this animal managed to reach land. The dog had swum 15 miles against a very strong wind. [Translated from the Finnish newspaper *Nya Pressen,* January 16, 1888]

REMARKABLE CASE OF CANINE SAGACITY - Last night a child about eighteen months old was left in charge of a Newfoundland dog in a house in Portrack, Stockton, while its parents were both from home. In the course of its gambols the child fell into the fire, and its clothes were at once in flames. The dog, seeing its predicament, seized the child and carried it into the back-yard, where by barking it attracted the attention of the neighbours. A man rushed into the yard, and foolishly put the child under the tap, effectively subduing the fire, but adding very seriously to the child's injuries. The child is still alive, but is suffering acutely. [*North-Eastern Daily Gazette*, May 11, 1888]

Forgotten to lock the brakes on the pram? No danger, if there is a Newfoundland dog nearby. From the *Illustrated Police News*, June 8 1907

THOSE AMAZING NEWFOUNDLAND DOGS

ONE DOG DROWNS ANOTHER - Two dogs. a Newfoundland belonging to John Holland of Winstead and a foxhound owned by a man named Mason, fought at the shore of Highland Lake Thursday afternoon. The fight ended by the big Newfoundland dragging the hound into the lake and holding his head under water until he was dead. The foxhound was worth $50, and Mason will sue the owner of the Newfoundland dog, which was the aggressor, for the value of the drowned hound. [*New York Times,* April 30, 1889]

A DOG CAUGHT ROBBING A HOUSE - A big Newfoundland dog, trained at thieving, was captured, says the New York Tribune, by a police-sergeant in the act of robbing a house in Pennsylvania Avenue. The officer saw the dog trotting out of an alley separating two houses. It carried in its mouth a bundle, which the sergeant thought to be a baby. He pursued the dog, and the animal dropped the bundle, which turned out to be a fancy sofa-cushion. Wondering where the dog could have secured it, the sergeant returned to the alley and secreted himself. In a few minutes the dog came back, entered the alley, and soon re-appeared with a big white bundle in its mouth. The officer followed the animal, which deposited its prize in another alley some distance away. After some time the dog returned for more booty, but was captured. The police think the animal was trained by thieves, who were in waiting to receive the booty when frightened off by the sergeant. [*Berrow's Worcester Journal*, October 19, 1889]

During Mr Charles Arnold's forthcoming tour with Carl's Folly he will give public exhibitions of life saving with his Newfoundland dog 'Earl of Highgate'. This dog took third prize in his class (fifteen months old) at the Agricultural Hall dog show recently. [*Era,* February 28, 1891]

The next night another comical thing happened. To give more effect to distant drums and trumpets, the musicians were sent into Kean's dressing-rooms. Now, he was the proprietor of a magnificent Newfoundland dog that usually remained in his room. When the musicians left the apartment at the end of the scene they forgot to close the door. As the last scene commenced the dog heard his master shout 'For one or both the time has come,' and rushing on to the stage, furiously faced Richmond, who was obliged to flash his sword in front of the dog to keep him off. To complete the picture, the theatre valet, after in vain trying to call the dog off, ran onto the stage in full livery, and, chasing the animal around, finally pulled him off by the collar and conveyed him from the public gaze. [*Star,* January 5, 1893][11]

WHEN ANIMALS MOURN - Last year, an English barque loaded timber at the Svartvik timber yard outside the town of Sundsvall. The captain's young wife died at that time, and she was buried in the local cemetery. This summer, the ship returned, and the captain's Newfoundland dog, which had been on board the ship also when the captain's wife died, was again on board. As soon as the ship was at the docks, the dog ran off to the cemetery, where it has since kept vigil on the grave of its former mistress. It was quite impossible to persuade the dog to return to the ship, so it was left behind when the barque sailed. The dog is regularly fed by the locals near the cemetery, and his vigil is much admired. [Translated from the Swedish newspaper *Tidning för Wenersborgs Stad och Län*, October 13, 1893][12]

A DOG FALLS EIGHTY FEET
BIG NEWFOUNDLAND PRECIPITATED FROM A PASSAIC RIVER BRIDGE AND LIVES – Newark, May 27. James Coley of West Arlington started to walk across the Midland Railroad Bridge over the Passaic River yesterday afternoon. His big Newfoundland dog Rex persisted in following him. There is no foot path on the bridge, and the only means of crossing is by walking on the ties which are about two feet apart. Mr. Coley tried to prevent the animal following, but did not succeed. He did not dare to make him turn around after he was once upon the ties. The dog followed his master in safety until in the middle of the bridge, where the bridge is eighty feet above the water. Then the dog lost his footing and fell into the water. Mr. Coley expected the brute would be killed, but he came to the surface, and swam ashore on the Arlington side. He did not seem discomfited by his dive, and after

The Newfoundland dog presented to the Prince of Wales

A detective saved by a Newfoundland dog: 'Blackbeard' comes bursting into the room to save Inspector Druscovich. From the *Illustrated Police News*, May 8 1897

shaking the water from his fur ran home. [*New York Times*, May 28, 1897]

The celebrated Newfoundland dog, Sultan, which, for his acts of devotion to man and for his courage, was, on the 9th of May, 1894, solemnly rewarded by the Society for the Protection of Animals with a collar of honour, has just fallen a victim to his fidelity to his master. Among the feats performed by Sultan are the arrest of a robber, the capture of a murderer, the saving of a child thirteen years old who was drowning in the Marne, and the saving of a man who had thrown himself into the seine from the Pont Neuf. He first belonged to the publisher, M. Didier, who, however, gave him to Madame Foucher de Careil. She kept him at her residence near Corbeil, where Sultan was the terror of tramps and malefactors, one of whom, it is probable, killed him, for he was yesterday found lying dead by a hedge, poisoned by a piece of meat. [*Standard*, August 7, 1897][13]

A Victorian scrap of a rescue scene.

CHAPTER 15.
NEWFOUNDLAND DOG MEMORABILIA
BY DI SELLERS

> Of more than gentlest manners, unprovok'd;
> If rous'd, of strong resentments well restrain'd;
> For active service, and for truth renown'd;
> For fondest, purest, and most firm regard,
> Thro' all the changes of a lengthen'd life:
> Worthy, most worthy of that famous breed,
> That in Newfoundland's climate first was rear'd:
> Poor Dash farewell! – thy merit's deep impress'd,
> In the retaining tablet of my heart;
> Thy better great grac'd a master's side, -
> And if the presage of my heart be true,
> And mourning of thy loss, and to thy worth
> All graceful and alive, I fear it is,
> 'I shall not look upon thy like again.'
>
> Elegy on a Newfoundland dog,
> from G.H. Harley, *Poems* (London 1796).

Because of the popularity of the Newfoundland dog in the 1800s, there is a wide variety of memorabilia and collectables of these dogs to be found, from very expensive to moderately priced items. As we have seen earlier in this book, there are paintings of Newfoundlands dating back at least to the mid-1700s, although it was not until the 1790s that artists like George Morland produced a large number of Newfoundland dog paintings. These were mainly beach scenes. George Stubbs painted the breed more than once. His most famous portrait of a Newfoundland, painted in 1802, is 'A Newfoundland Dog, property of the Duke of York'. It is thought that the same dog is included in the 1807 painting of the Duchess of York, by Peter Edward Stroehling. Among other well-known painters of Newfoundland dogs were Philip Reinagle, Ben Marshall and Sir Abraham Cooper.

Sir Edwin Landseer painted a number of Newfoundlands, most of which were white and black, or in some instances white and brown. There has been speculation that he painted a few portraits of solid black dogs as well, one entitled 'Friends' or 'Hours of Innocence' and the other 'Head of Caesar' But as we have seen earlier in this book, Caesar may well have been a black and white dog with a black face-mask, and the dog in 'Hours of Innocence' does not look particularly Newfoundland-like. The debate is likely to continue about this particular question. Other paintings of Newfoundland dogs from Landseer's prolific output include 'Neptune,' 'My Dog,' 'Saved,' 'Off to the Rescue,' Lion,' 'Princess

George Earl's painting of Cato, from a private collection in the United States, reproduced by permission

Mary and a favourite Newfoundland dog' and 'A Distinguish Member of the Humane Society'. The latter must be the most famous of all Newfoundland dog paintings in the world. It is through the enthusiasm and dedication of the late Ron Pemberton in the USA that this painting has been restored and will now be enjoyed for decades to come. Ron bred Newfoundlands and was also a well known international dog judge. He came over to England on a number of occasions and on two different visits he tried to see the painting that was in store at the Tate Gallery after flood damage in the late 1920s. He did not manage to see it either time.

In 1996, Ron Pemberton came up with the idea of trying to get the 'Distinguished Member' restored. A committee was formed and so began the process of raising funds by contacting Newfoundland Clubs around the world, and through auctions and donations, $18,000 was raised for the restoration of the painting and a new frame. An agreement was made with the Tate that once the work was completed, the painting would go to America for three years. The transportation across the Atlantic was paid for by the Newfoundland Club of America. Finally, on April 17 2002, the painting arrived at the Philadelphia Museum of Art and was hung within a few days. For the first time in many decades it was on public display. That year the Newfoundland Club of America held its National Specialty (23-27th April 2002) in Carlisle, Pa. and a number of Newfoundland dog people went to see it whilst at the show. Funds also had to be raised for the transportation of the painting back to the Tate. Once again it went back into storage until the Tate agreed to loan the painting to the Kennel Club. It was the major artwork in the Kennel Club Art Gallery 'Pets & Prizewinners' Exhibition (6th July 2009-29th January 2010). It is now on a three-year extended loan to the Kennel Club for Newfoundland dog lovers to see, and you should make haste to see it if you have not already done so.

* * *

Up to the early 1800s most of the Newfoundland dogs in art were either white with black markings or white with brown markings. In 1829, John Fernley Sr. painted 'Mr Pare's Coachman and a black Newfoundland' (Leicester City Art Gallery): a solid black dog with white on his chest. Thomas Woodward painted at least one black Newfoundland dog, as did Thomas Musgrave Joy. In 1851, George Horlor painted 'Portraits of Favourites' which included a black Newfoundland with white on his chest (Cheltenham Art Gallery and Museum). In the 1860s Richard Ansdell painted at least two pictures which included black Newfoundlands, his most famous being 'On Guard'. This painting has been reproduced many times. Also in the 1860s George Earl painted the head of a black Newfoundland, entitled 'Cato'. Sometimes artists painted more than one copy of their paintings, and this seems to be the case as there is one 'Cato' in The Dog Museum, St. Louis, Mo. and a larger one in a private collection in the USA. One very nice 1866 painting by Edmund Swift, 'Best of Friends' illustrates a boy in Highland dress asleep on a black Newfoundland. John Emms (1843-1912) painted a Landseer with a small terrier type dog on a beach, 'Dogs Watching Bathers' (Southampton City Art Gallery). Auguste Renoir (1841-1919) painted 'Madame Charpentier and her children' in 1876, with a Landseer Newfoundland.

Joseph Henry Sharp (1859-1934) was born in Ohio. He travelled to Europe before he became famous for his American Indian works. At least three of his paintings included a Landseer Newfoundland dog. Set in the same garden scene, including a kennel and a little girl with a drum. In the first one, painted on board, the dog lying in the kennel with the girl sitting with her back to the garden wall, her arms straight up in the air, holding a drumstick in one hand and the drum on the ground. The other drumstick is in the dog's mouth. The second one, painted on canvas and entitled 'Disturbed but not Perturbed,' is slightly different. The girl is much closer to the kennel that the dog is lying in, and there is a chain hanging from its neck. The girl is holding a drumstick but her arms are differently positioned; the drum is on the ground and the other drumstick is in the dog's mouth. The third one is entitled 'Full House'. This one shows both the girl and dog inside the kennel but no drum or drumsticks.

George Earl's daughter Maud (1864-1943) painted at least two Newfoundlands, one black (head and shoulders) and the other white and black. A Landseer lying on a quayside with a small white terrier dog between its front paws entitled 'A Grand Spirit'. Prints of it were used as an advert for James Buchanan's Scotch Whisky and appeared in 'The Illustrated London News'. Some of the coloured prints were framed and the name James Buchanan & Co. Ltd. embossed into the frame. F.T. Daws painted a number of Newfoundland dogs; one was a side view of a Landseer head ('Ch. Prince of Norfolk'). In 1905 he painted a full face head study of 'Ch Shelton Viking' who was the sire of 'Ch Gipsy Duke', who he also painted. 'Ch Gipsy Duke' is his most famous Newfoundland painting and has been reproduced many times over the years either the full painting or just as a head study. 'Ch.

Gipsy Duke' held the Newfoundland Club breed record for 70 years with his 22 CC wins.

Over the years, some of these important paintings of Newfoundland dogs have been lost, but most of them are now in art galleries, museums, stately homes, the Queen's collection, or those of other Royal families. Only a few are in private collections, and fewer still are owned by Newfoundland dog enthusiasts.

* * *

Many etchings, engravings and prints of Newfoundland dogs have been issued over the years. These can be 'official' or 'unofficial' with slight changes, or even reversed to get round the copyright of the original painting. Most of Landseer's paintings can be found either as engravings or prints, and these are of course much more readily available to the private collector. In the 1990s, these could be had for £50 or even less, but today they are worth a fair amount more than that. Engravings of Newfoundland dogs can also be found in many magazines from the early 1800s. 'The Illustrated London News', 'Vanity Fair', 'Animal World', 'Harpers Weekly', 'American Tract Society', 'Boys & Girl's Weekly', 'The Penny Magazine', to mention but a few. The diligent searcher of eBay and other online marketplaces may find a single page, a number of pages or the full magazine, sometimes for a paltry sum. The January 11 1831 issue of 'The Penny Magazine', has an engraving entitled 'Newfoundland Dog', illustrating a dog with a sailor lying on a beach, in the background are rocks and a ship sinking in the rough seas. The 'Book of Beasts' published before 1876 shows virtually the same engraving in the 'Dogs' chapter. A starfish has been moved and the rocks are slightly different, as well as the dog's tail. An engraving of Landseer's 'Carlo' takes up the whole of the front page of the New York 'The Illustrated Christian Weekly' for November 16 1872. The August 28, 1886 issue of the 'National Police Gazette' has an engraving of a lady on a 'raft' being pulled through the water by two Newfoundlands. And the caption underneath states 'She drives in double harness - a unique and novel turn–out - a southern belle glides through the surf, off Watch Hill, Westerly, Rhode Island.'

There are many beautiful lithograph prints of Newfoundland dogs to be found. One entitled 'Nellie's Guardian' is just slightly different from a design on a Victorian chocolate box lid, painted by Richard Cadbury. Both show a white and brown dog standing alongside a pram with a child in it. The difference between them is the clothes the child is wearing. Another entitled 'The Garden Tea Party', shows the head and shoulders of a Landseer with one paw on the table, two cats sitting on the table as well as plates of food with a girl pouring milk from a jug into a tea cup.

Many prints involving Newfoundland dogs are rescue scenes, often entitled 'Saved' or 'Rescued'. A very nice print is of a white and black dog lying on a rock, and a mother with a child in her arms in the sea, just below the dog. A very similar scene is depicted on a Carte de Visite (CDV) card entitled 'A Friend in Danger'. There are two prints that have the same background, with the same little girl and her toys, but the dogs are totally different. The first is entitled 'Asleep and Awake' shows a white and black dog. The dog's front paws are over an upturned toy. The girl is lying asleep against the dog holding a doll. This print is rarer than the second one entitled 'Companions', with a much heavier built dog facing the opposite way. The girl is lying asleep and wearing the same dress but this one is trimmed with pink not blue, her shoes are pink not black and she is holding a different doll. Many different prints and cards have been produced from this print. Another nice print shows a standing Landseer with a little girl in a pink and white dress, one arm around the dog the other holding part of her dress. Many of Currier & Ives lithographs have been produced from paintings, and not only issued as prints, but used as illustrations in books.

Maud Earl's 'A Grand Spirit', here used by James Buchanan & Co. Ltd to advertise their Scotch whisky

THOSE AMAZING NEWFOUNDLAND DOGS

Illustrated dog books from the 1860s often had engravings. 'Birdie & her Dog' and 'Our Dumb Companions' both had engravings of Newfoundlands by Harrison Weir. Many old dog books included a chapter or pieces about Newfoundlands: 'Dogs and their Doings,' 'Brave Bobby', 'Dog Life', 'Dog Stories & Dog Lore' all included engravings of Newfoundlands. The oldest storybook involving a Newfoundland is the 'Dog Crusoe' by R.M. Ballantyne, first published in 1860, and since then many different editions have been published. The colour of the dog varies in the pictures with each edition; sometimes he is white and black, white and brown or nearly all brown. Another very rare storybook is the 1890 'Captain' by Mme P. de Nanteuil, and translated by Laura Ensor, with 76 very fine illustrations, most of which include 'Captain' the black Newfoundland. The beginning of the story is set around the waters of Newfoundland and St. Pierre. Not only is 'Captain' involved with rescues from the sea, but he saves a baby from a cabin fire as well.

* * *

Following on from paintings, came the start of photographs. In the late 1830s Daguerreotype, in the 1850s Ambrotype, followed by images on tin. You can find the occasional one which includes a Newfoundland in the image. These were followed by CDV: a small thin paper photograph mounted on either thicker paper or cardboard. They started as visiting cards; some illustrated dogs on their own, with people and some were of paintings, often those of Sir Edwin Landseer. There is also one of Ulysses S. Grant with his son's Newfoundland dog 'Faithful'. By the early 1880s the larger Cabinet cards had superseded the CDV's and there must be hundreds of these showing both blacks and Landseers, some on their own, others with children or with family groups. Stereo view cards came out in the 1880s until the late 1930s. Some of these were of scenes from the Klondyke gold rush, showing teams of dogs, Romey the hero dog of the May 31, 1889 Johnstown Flood, Newfoundlands with a child or children, and one even shows the 1872 Parian ware figurine by D. C. French of 'Retribution'.

Hundreds of postcards depicting Newfoundland dogs have been published since the late 1800s. The early ones mainly featured Landseers as they showed clearer details than solid black dog. The dogs were often shown in sentimental poses with children, adults, small dogs or even cats. Often these cards were produced in sets of six different poses but the same dog and background. A lot of artists' paintings appeared on postcards. Many of Sir Edwin Landseer's paintings were illustrated, but his painting of 'A Distinguished Member' must have been issued by more publishers than any other card. Real photographic cards show illustrations of people's pet Newfoundlands, as well as winning show dogs. ('Wolf of Badenoch', 'Merry Boy', 'Landseer Don', 'Waterbaby'), regimental mascots, charity collecting dogs, and harnessed dog teams. Even the writing on the back of some of these cards sometimes makes very interesting reading.

From the 1890s onwards, there have been many sets of cigarette and trade cards featuring Newfoundland dogs, more often solid blacks than Landseers. In 1890, the American company H. Ellis & Co. issued a set, 'Breeds of Dogs', with a black dog, swimming among water lilies, with a cane in its mouth. Also in 1890, Goodwin & Co. (USA) issued an un-numbered 50-card set named 'Dogs of the World,' including a standing solid black Newfoundland dog. In 1891, Wm. S. Kimball & Co. (USA) issued an un-numbered set of 25 cards, 'Household Pets', one of them showing a lady and a Landseer.

It was not until 1898 that a set of cigarette cards was issued in the U.K. that included a Newfoundland, when T.P. & R. Goodbody issued 'Dogs,' an un-numbered set of 67 cards. Depicting a standing, solid black dog, this is a very rare card and extremely hard to find. In 1900, Taddy & Co. issued another 'Dogs,' a set of 50 cards that illustrated the heads of different breeds, of which No. 2 shows the head of a Landseer. Between 1900 and 1902 Ogdens Ltd. issued a number of sets that include a Newfoundland.

THOSE AMAZING NEWFOUNDLAND DOGS

These were included in their all photographic sets of 'General Interest'. Some of the cards illustrated named Newfoundlands.

The first non cigarette card set to include a Newfoundland was issued in 1902 by Church & Dwight (Baking soda) USA. No 4 in their 30 card set 'Ch Dogs', produced in two sizes, shows a lovely black Newfoundland lying on a stone bridge, very similar to Thomas Fall's photo of 'Wolf of Badenoch'. The artist for the set was Gustav Muss-Arnolt, (1858-1927). The next trade card set was issued in 1910 by Spratts Patent Ltd. (Pet food), a set of 12 'Prize Dog's cards, in which No. 5 shows a Landseer head. In 1926, they issued a set of 36 'Champion Dogs' cards. The illustrations for this set were from paintings of champion dogs by F.T.Daws. The Newfoundland dog card included in the set was 'Ch. Gipsy Duke'. The same champion dog illustrations were used for a set of postcards also issued by Spratts Patent Ltd. Since then over 30 different companies have issued sets that included a Newfoundland dog card. Some of the illustrations in the sets have also appeared on postcards. Sometimes different companies issued the same sets.

From the 1850s onwards, many colourful embossed single sheet greetings cards and cut-outs were imported. They became popular as decorative additions for Christmas, New Year and Valentine cards and also to illustrate historical events. They were often used to decorate the folding screens for draughty rooms. These were followed by Victorian scraps (cut outs) which also depict more Landseers than black dogs. Those that are head studies vary in size from very large to very small. There is a wide variety of different 'subjects', standing dogs, rescue scenes or dogs with children. The scraps were often put into albums and now sold as either the full album or singe pages. One rare beautiful large scrap show a Landseer with a child riding on its back and a small pug following behind.

* * *

Other paper items featuring Newfoundland dogs include cigar bands, tobacco duty labels, blotters, chocolate boxes, matchbox labels, fruit labels, beer labels, theatrical playbills, sheet music, Reward of Merit cards, advertising cards (Continental and American), calendar cards and advertising calendars. One 1901 calendar advertising Oliver Oliver & Co., Tea, Coffee & Cocoa Merchants, 231, Southgate Rd., London has a large sepia illustration of a boy in a sailor suit standing alongside a large white and black Newfoundland dog. He is holding the dog's collar, and it is entitled 'Comrades'. There are also prints with the same illustration.

Many American and Canadian banks issued cheques, promise to pay notes, paying-in slips etc with illustrations of Newfoundland dogs in the design. The breed has been featured on postage stamps since 1887, when Newfoundland issued a ½ cent stamp. It is believed that this was the first time any breed of dog appeared on a stamp. It was rose/red coloured and showed a Landseer head. It was designed by J.S. Rolph of Toronto. The stamp was re-issued a number of times in different colours, black (1894), orange/red (1896) and (1898). Since then, over 50 different countries have issued stamps, mini sheets, and first day covers/cachets that included a Newfoundland dog in their design. Mostly they show black dogs, but a few show Landseers, and even fewer are browns. A stamp was issued in 1888 for Adams Express which operated a parcel delivery service in Kristiania, Norway. It was issued in two different values, the 10 öre is pale rose and black and the 20 öre is pale green and black. The design is the same on both stamps, a dog holding a parcel in its mouth. This was the company trade mark.

In 1913 the Berlin Zoo issued a publicity label, (known as a Cinderella item) that illustrated Sir Edwin Landseer's 'A Distinguished Member'. Not only were Landseer's paintings illustrated on many paper items such as old share certificates; cheques, pay-in slips, promise to pay notes, continental advertising

A trade card depicting a Newfoundland dog, issued in 1910 by Spratts Patent Ltd

cards, Victorian scraps, but on furniture (chairs with tiles inserted in the back showing the dog) grandfather clocks, coal buckets, papier mache items, (fold down tables, plates, trays, fire-screens), chocolate boxes, children's building blocks, jewellery, as well as ceramic items, plates, mugs etc.

John Derbyshire (1840-1900) of Manchester produced pressed glass models on a ribbed plinth (1873-1877) (jelly moulds) in pairs, modelled on 'A Distinguished Member' in various colours, clear, two shades of green, a white opaque and a blue opaque, two shades of blue, amber and a very dark purple which is nearly black. These models have their head turned the same as the painting but there is a rarer model in clear glass that looks straight ahead over its front paws. In the early 1900s Crown Devon (Fieldings) produced a limited edition of a glazed uncoloured version of the dog on a base which looks like a quayside. Some models have the same uncoloured base and others have a black coloured base.

One pair of ceramic dogs, also modelled on the image of the 'Distinguished Member' is glazed and colourful; one is white with a black head the other is white with a brown head, facing each other and both lying on a base representing a quayside. Many ceramic items have been manufactured in great variety, punch bowls, chargers, plates, mugs, jugs, vases; tobacco jars, pot lids, tiles, dishes, lustre ware items and crested miniatures.

Models were made by various potteries. A number of bisque models were produced, some of them Continental. Sometimes the same dog was used with various children, either sanding alongside or sitting on the dog's back. Other bisque models show a lady sitting side-saddle on a 'running' white and black dog; another version of this has a jockey sitting on the dog. One bisque model is of a dog lying down with a child lying asleep on it and there is a Staffordshire model the same but just slightly larger in size.

There are different models from unknown potteries, one that I think must be from the Continent, possibly made in France, is free standing and decorated with small flowers with a blue 'collar' around its neck. Another model is a seated dog with a basket and is very pale blue in colour with some black on it. A very nice green and white statue is of a little girl sitting on a bench with a Landseer sitting beside her and the girl has her hand in the dog's mouth. One very unusual and fine detailed model is made of slag glass, pink in colour, and is of a lady with a dog sitting beside her. In one hand she is holding the dog's chain linked lead and her other hand is resting on the dog's head.

Various Parian ware models have been produce. An early pair of Minton figures on bases show children sitting side-saddle on standing dogs, representing 'War and Peace'. D.C. French's pair (1872) 'Imposing on Good Nature' and 'Retribution' are a very fine detailed pair. Others are of 'rescue scenes', dogs with children on their backs or of standing dogs with one or the other of Queen Victoria's children in Highland dress.

The same figurines were produced by the Staffordshire potteries along with a number of other different models that have the Royal children standing alongside, sitting on the dog's back or lying across their backs. There are two sizes of free standing models without children, they too come in pairs. There are spill vases to be found and these normally were produced as single items. There are at least two different spill vases that included a white and black Newfoundland. One is a 'rescue scene' of the dog holding up a child by its dress and the other, a seated dog is watching over a sleeping child. Newfoundland Staffordshire dogs were painted white with black or brown markings but never solid colours. Very early models were made with a plain white flat back.

A rare pair of Staffordshire models (c1851) illustrates the 'Dog and Snake' story, with one showing the standing dog, crushing a snake beneath its paw with a young child alongside and the other of the

A trade card depicting a Newfoundland dog, issued in 1910 by Spratts Patent Ltd.

snake with its head off and the child with its arms around the seated dog's neck. The story is that an Indian prince's son was saved from a snake by a Newfoundland dog. There are many other items on the same theme. Two Staffordshire plates were produced entitled 'The Deliverer' both illustrating a slightly different scene. There is at least one pair of opaque glass pictures that illustrates the same scene. Ausguste Lechesne was the artist for the stone statues on the top of the gate posts at Harlaxton Manor in Lincolnshire; also he exhibited a plaster cast, (No. 573) in the Great Exhibition in 1851. There is also at least one pair of very nice 18" bronzes that was cast after this but the artist is not identified for these. A pair was auctioned a few years ago at Skinners Auction Rooms in Boston, USA.

Wedgwood produced a series of plates with dogs heads on, one of these showed a full faced Newfoundland and the same design was used on a tile and some of these were made into tea pot stands. Many different types of plates have been produced including ribbon plates, pierced plates, even alphabet and baby's plates. Richard Ansdell's painting 'On Guard' was painted by James Rouse onto a pierced plate. An alphabet plate entitled 'The Guardian' has the same design that is on a 1860/70 longcase clock by Alfred Smith. It shows a Newfoundland standing over a child. According to the text about the clock there is a snake's head under the dog's paw. A sale price is quoted at over £3000 (2012).

A great number of mugs have been produced by various well known potteries as well as unknown ones. Paragon Fine Bone China (British Breed Dogs) shows a black standing Newfoundland along with two other breeds around the side, another from E.M. & Co. (Field Sports) shows a solid colour dog with a pheasant in its mouth with two greyhounds or whippets on the other side. One from the Goss factory shows a similar dog to 'A Distinguished Member' but with hair standing up on its head. In one Goss reference book it is referred to as a Lion. A larger Sunderland lustre mug show a child on the dog's back holding a flag and another child standing alongside holding the dog's lead.

Royal Dux produced at least three different Newfoundland dog models. The first one has the dog pulling a cart, in a sand and green colour, the second one has a standing dog with a child being held on its back by a figure standing alongside the dog. This model was produced in colour, and also in a white with gilt version. The third model is of a plain white standing dog on a base representing rocks, the dog is very similar to the one pulling the cart but this one has its head turned.

There are glass items of Newfoundland dog memorabilia to be found. Three of the rarer items are a clear glass dog pulling a cart that is a toothpick holder, this was patented by Jonathan Haley in October 1890. In 1881, Gillender & Sons factory in Philadelphia produced a number of various sizes of glass comport dishes, with two different patterns around the rim of the dishes, one know as the 'Deer and Dog', the other 'Dog and Hunter'. Both designs have a frosted dog finial on the top of the lid. The third is a covered butter dish; on the lid is a recumbent Newfoundland dog.

Many items of Newfoundland dog memorabilia have been produced in various metals: not only free standing models, but ink wells, nodding dogs, bookends, and a variety of different chocolate moulds, (large, medium and small, standing and seated). Various cast iron items include door stops and money boxes in the shape of dogs. Mainly, these consist of a standing dog (two different sizes) some stood on all four paws, others have one front leg raised, and some have packs on their backs. One rarer type that only comes in the larger size has 'I hear a call' on the straps of the pack on the dog's back. A different type is in the shape of a model bank building. The dog is on a turntable, with a tray in its mouth. A coin is put on the tray, a handle turned and the dog enters the bank, deposits the coin and returns with the tray empty. Mechanical money-boxes include 'Speaking Dog,' with a seated dog and a girl, and 'Trick Dog,' with a standing clown with a hoop. When the catch is released the dog tips up and the dog and coin goes trough the hoop to deposit the coin. Cast iron nutcrackers featuring Newfoundland dogs were produce in two sizes, some free standing and others on bases with dishes to catch the nuts in. There are many forms of them, with different tails, some more rare ones include a squirrel or tobacco cutters in their design.

Another Victorian scrap with a boy and two Newfoundland dogs

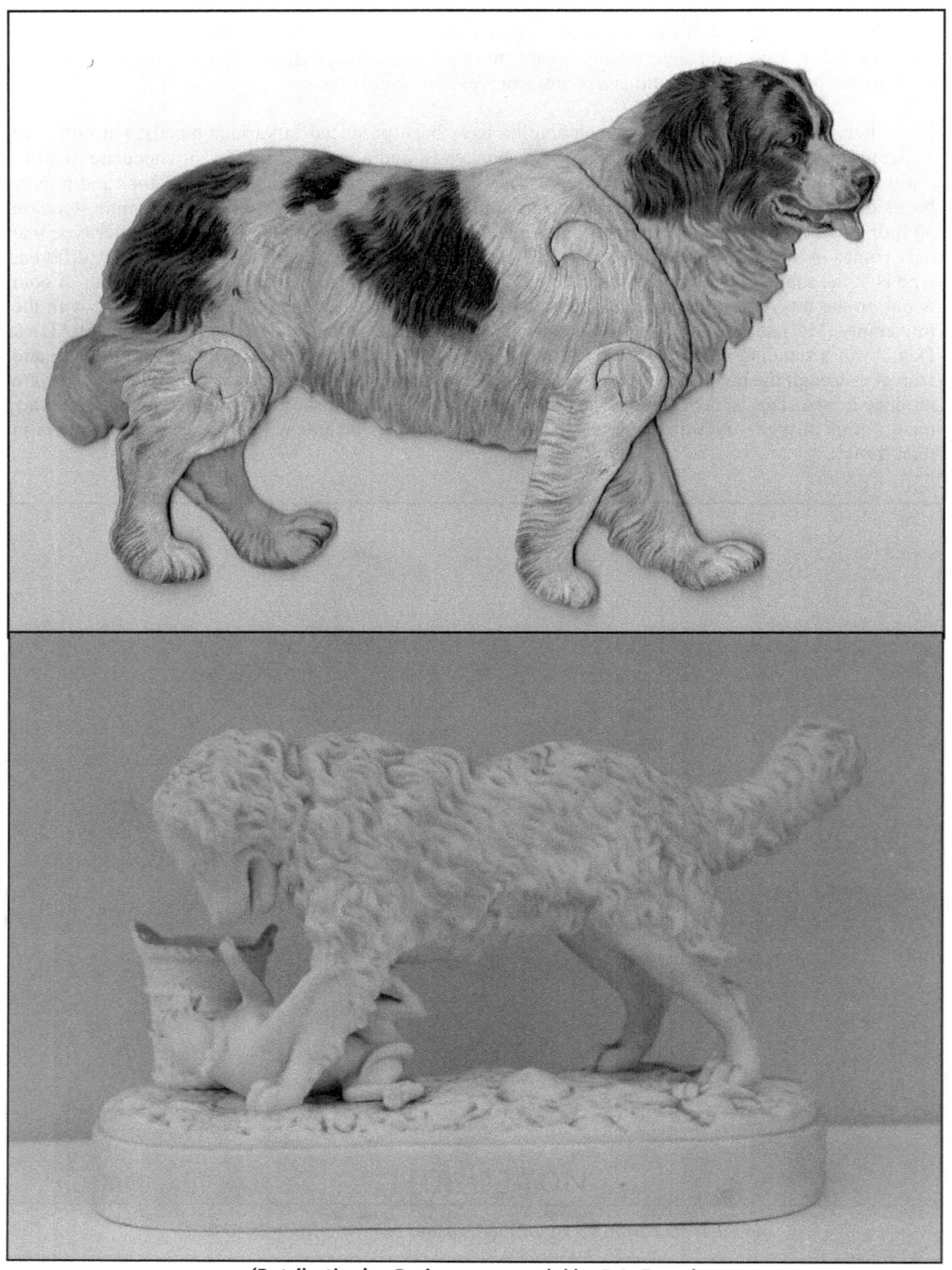

An articulated white and black Newfoundland dog, from a series of different breeds of dogs published by Raphael Tuck & Sons Ltd

'Retribution', a Parian ware model by D.L. French

THOSE AMAZING NEWFOUNDLAND DOGS

From the 1850s onwards, life-size cast iron and cast zinc models of Newfoundlands were produced in America. There were a number of different models and sizes of the dogs, some standing, some lying down, some have different shaped heads, and different tail settings, and some have wavy coats whereas others have smooth coats. Haward, Bartlett & Co. were the main foundry for producing the models and then in 1863 J.W. Fisk started a foundry that produce both cast iron and zinc items including dogs. These life-size dogs must have been produced in large numbers at the time but over the years some of them have been melted down. They have stood on either side of the main doors of buildings, in museums, cemeteries or even on hotel lawns. They do come up for auction from time to time either in pairs or singular. When cast these dogs sold for around $100 each, but now when they come up at auction, they can go for more than $10,000 for a single dog.

An attractive statue of a girl and a Newfoundland dog sitting together on a bench, from an unknown pottery

Spelter models give much finer details than other metal models. These could be free standing or on a base. Sometimes the same model of the Newfoundland dog was used, with a child added either standing alongside or sitting on its back, and some dogs carry baskets in their mouths. A different freestanding model has a hole in its back for putting items in, like toothpicks, pens or matches. It also has a hook under its jaw, perhaps intended to hold a pocket watch. Mantel clocks can be found with a gilded figure of a Newfoundland standing on the top of the clock. Others clocks come in the form of freestanding dogs with a clock face fitted into the dog's side or back. Some have a figure sitting on the back of the dog, carrying a flag with a company advertisement on. A rare silver model is of a Newfoundland pulling a sleigh, being 'driven' by a man and the clock is on the back of the sleigh.

A few bronzes featuring Newfoundland dogs can be found, but these are rare. There are cold-painted Austrian bronzes, free standing models, some of these have nodding heads and a few of the dogs carry a cane in the mouth. A number of silver plated inkwells can be found, one is a Newfoundland lying down with a child pulling itself up with the dog's fur. The dog's head lifts up to reveal the ink pot. An illustration in 'Dog Stories and Dog Lore' by Thomas W. Knox, entitled 'The Baby's Playmate' shows a very similar scene. Children's items featuring Newfoundlands include building bricks, wooden money boxes, jigsaw puzzles, school exercise books, rubber squeaky toys in the shape of a dog, celluloid figures, various tea sets, baby plates, and pull along toys as well as push along toys.

There are many samplers, tapestries, rugs, cross stitch and silk embroidery pictures to be found, many featuring the 'Distinguished Member'. Rarer items include tin plate toys, candle snuffers, pipes and cheroot holders, napkin rings, tape-measures, sovereign cases, silver baby's rattles in the shape of a

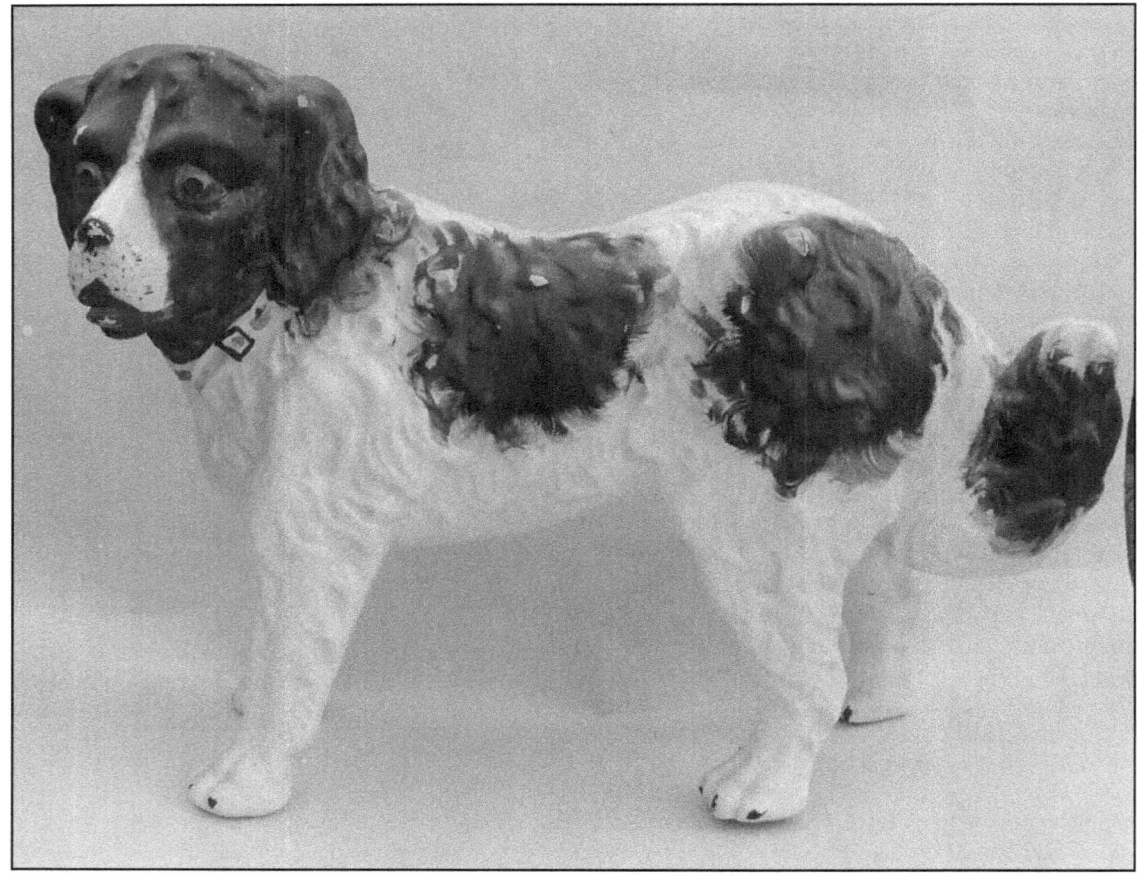

A large free standing statue of a Newfoundland dog

seated dog, small solid silver standing models, (the same model can be found made of lead), silver pin cushions in the shape of a standing dog, buttons, including cape fastening buttons and different items of jewellery including stick pins.

The Kennel Club was founded on the 4th April, 1873 and records have been kept from then on. The Newfoundland Club was founded in 1886 and registered with the Kennel Club in 1891. It is one of the oldest breed clubs in the world. Highly sought after are the silver medallions from the late 1800s to the early 1900s that were given to the winners at some shows, particularly those that have the name of the winner and the show at which it was originally presented.

Undiscovered items of Newfoundland dog memorabilia are being found all the time, be it a few pages from a magazine that includes an engraving, a print, a children's book, a piece of jewellery or a major painting. Long may items continue to be discovered.

A Newfoundland keeping watch over a sleeping child.

THOSE AMAZING NEWFOUNDLAND DOGS

ABOVE: The alphabet plate 'The Guardian' by Elsmore & Foster
BELOW: A metal free standing clock featuring a Newfoundland dog, with a company advertisement on the flag

CHAPTER 16.
SOME SPECTRAL NEWFOUNDLAND DOGS

I'll not believe it, Carlo, I
Will fetch you with me when I die,
And standing up at Peter's wicket,
Will urge sound reasons for your ticket;
I'll show him your life saving label,
And tell him all about the cable,
The storm along the shore, the wreck,
The ninety souls upon the deck.

From the poem 'Carlo' by E.J. Pratt.

There is a widespread folklore concerning the ghosts of dogs. In his *Animal Ghosts*, the ghost-hunter Elliott O'Donnell collected many examples of spectral canines.[1] One of his stories concerned a lady named Miss Lefanu, who was followed by a strange Newfoundland dog when she walked in a country lane. She called to the dog, but it stayed at a respectful distance. Suddenly, two murderous-looking tramps jumped out from a hedge, ready to strike at her with their bludgeons. The Newfoundland uttered a low, ominous growl and flew at them. The terrified tramps fled yelling, like if the salvation of their souls depended on it. After the dog had followed Miss Lefanu home, she decoyed it into her back yard, which was surrounded by a high wall, and shut it up in there. She ordered her cook to prepare a hearty meal for the heroic dog, but when it was to be delivered, the dog was nowhere to be seen. Clearly, it must have been a ghost! Miss Lefanu later heard that on the very spot where the tramps had been lurking, a pedlar and his Newfoundland dog had been found murdered many years before. A sceptic would of course instead suspect that it had been a *real* Newfoundland dog, which had made use of its superior intellect to effect its escape from the rear yard, losing out on its free meal as a result.

The statue of Captain John McNeill Boyd in St Patrick's Anglican Cathedral is a well-known Dublin monument. The heroic Captain Boyd was lost at sea while attempting to rescue the crew of another stricken ship in the Irish Sea during the terrific gales of February 1861. According to tradition, his Newfoundland dog was the sole survivor, and this dog walked alongside his coffin to the Glasnevin cemetery. Here, the faithful Newfoundland refused to leave the grave and died of hunger. Rationalists have doubted this story, objecting that to commit suicide would have been a strange thing to do for a dog that had recently narrowly escaped death at sea, and also expressing doubts whether Captain Boyd was really buried in this particular cemetery. Afictionados of Irish ghosts have retorted that a spectral Newfoundland dog has often been seen in the cemetery, or even sitting at the base of Captain Boyd's statue in the cathedral. Yet the truth about this spectral Dublin 'Greyfriars Bobby'

THOSE AMAZING NEWFOUNDLAND DOGS

'The Con-Foundland dog', a cartoon from Punch alluding to some Anglo-French quarrel over Newfoundland. John Bull has plans to whip the French lobster, but the Con-Foundland dog impedes him.

remains obscure.

In an old Devon legend, written down by a certain Mrs Hewitt in 1900, a man crossing Roborough Down, Dartmoor, on a cold and moonlit December night, could hear the footfall of a dog. When he stopped to listen, the dog stopped also. Suddenly there appeared close to his right side an enormous Newfoundland dog. Since he was fond of dogs, he spoke to it and lifted his hand to stroke it. But his hand passed straight through the body of the spectral canine. When the dog yawned, a stream of sulphurous breath issued from its throat. Terrified, the man ran away, pursued by the dog, until they reached a crossroads. There was a huge crash and flash of lightning, which knocked the man to the ground. The next morning, he was found senseless in a ditch.[3]

This story clearly concerns the Black Dog. These large, black, shaggy dog ghosts haunt certain roads or bridges; others appear in churchyards to frighten grave-robbers with their large glowing eyes and vaporous breath, or haunt certain families to whom they have taken a dislike. Most of them are silent, although some can growl, bark or even scream. Some of them are headless, others make up for this deficiency by having several heads. Some Black Dogs are helpful ghosts, warning people from unseen dangers; others have been definitely harmful. The Black Dogge of Newgate was supposed to have been the ghost of a prisoner murdered for cannibalistic purposes, haunting this ancient prison in the guise of a large black dog walking on its rear legs. The Black Dog of Bungay, Suffolk, appeared in St Mary's Priory Church in August 1577; it ran down the nave, wrung the necks of two people, and disappeared. Within minutes, the spectral dog also appeared in the Holy Trinity Church in Blythburgh, seven miles from Bungay. Again, it ran down the nave, killed two men and a boy and burnt the hand of another, before again abruptly disappearing; the church door still exhibits the claw marks of this demonic dog.[4]

A colleague of mine once had a spooky canine ghost story to tell. He lived in Richmond just outside London, with his wife and their three Newfoundland dogs. One of these dogs was not less than thirteen years old. She had problems with arthritis and seemed frustrated by not being able to play and run with her two younger friends. One day, the old dog was discovered to have died in her sleep, and she was buried in the large garden. The other two dogs did not do a 'Greyfriars Bobby' on their grandmother's grave, but instead were unseemingly hilarious, insisting on being let out at all hours, to romp in the garden barking vigorously, and even leap a fence and dig a large hole in a neighbour's flower-beds. When the old lady neighbour came to call, my friends believed she was about to complain about the barking dogs and the vandalized garden, but instead she turned out to be a great canophile. She had been admiring these *three* magnificent Newfoundland dogs playing in the garden, the old dog with the grey nose leading the way and playing pranks on the other two. The old lady saw the ghost dog once more, just as dusk; when she opened an upstairs window, it looked up at her, before slowly moving away. For several days, the other two dogs vainly searched for it.

* * *

A most extraordinary story about the adventures of a Newfoundland dog goes as follows [with spelling and grammar as per the original]:

> "Boatswain was brought to England as a young puppy by a captain of the royal navy in 1801 and presented to the prince regent at the age of two. In a letter from this period he is described as the most beautiful dog of his breed. His coat was spotted steel grey and brown, he had a 'majestic head', eyes full of fire and yet gentleness, and his beautifully shaped broad tail was in permanent motion. Boatswain began his part in history on one evening in 1804. At the time he was the prince's bodyguard in Carlton-House in London. This night there was a reception for diplomats accredited to the court of St. James, and there were whispered rumours stating that England was on the bridge of breaking alliance with France. Nevertheless, the French envoy and the ambassador who had left Paris specially for this occasion, were chatting away quite harmlessly. They assured the neutrality and goodwill of the Prussian envoy, and Prussia was the final block in the alliance Pitts was striving for. While the Prince tried in vain to convince the Prussian diplomat of the advantages of a connection with England against France, Boatswain entered the prince's room, happily wagging his tail. He was carrying something in his mouth, and the prince called him to his side. Boatswain handed him a letter that without doubt had been dropped on the floor of the nearby salon. The door to the adjacent salon was ajar, and while the prince, deep in though, handed over the letter to the Prussian delegate, he saw the French envoy searching his pockets next door. The letter was addressed to him".
>
> > 'Monsieur, I am writing to my envoy at the same time, the matter is of utmost importance. Any rapprochement between the Court of St. James and the Prussian envoy must - at all costs - be prevented. The latter is a man of a silly and complacent nature. You will have no difficulty in dealing with him. Bonaparte, first Consul.'"

THOSE AMAZING NEWFOUNDLAND DOGS

Six weeks later the first coalition against the military tyranny of France has been signed and sealed. The prince some time later gave the Newfoundland dog to his friend Brummel, the world known dandy, who sold him to the Duke of Richmond for 7500 franc. After the peace of Amiens Boatswain, who because of his outstanding character was a dog in great demand, came to live with Lord Ross, a famous scholar. Lord Ross was granted permission to visit France and brought the dog with him. During an audience with the Emperor at St Cloud the dog made his way to Lord Ross and was very much petted by Napoleon. In 1814, as the Emperor was a prisoner on Elba, planning to escape to France, Boatswain through a legacy came into the possession of a captain of the royal navy. He commanded a ship anchored outside Elba, and was very surprised as he, while walking on the island, encountered the emperor, and the Newfoundland dog ran after Napoleon and greeted him with great joy. Napoleon petted him, since he remembered the dog and even knew his name still. During the following night, in the tumult of a thunderstorm, Napoleon carried out an attack for the escape to France. As the emperor boarded the ship, an Englishman was brought on board by some officers, who had protected him from the soldiers with great difficulty.

As the emperor stepped on deck, he slipped and fell into the deep water right

A life-saving corps station in New York, complete with a Newfoundland dog. From *Harper's Weekly*, April 1879

> beside the ship. In the darkness, the excitement and the confusion of the moment, his disappearance went unnoticed, and Napoleon could not swim. A dark form dived after him, and after diving under twice he rescued the helpless emperor, by holding him above the water while swimming. It was Boatswain, the English prisoner was the captain, his master, who had been arrested as a spy as he wanted to return from a visit ashore. As proof of his gratitude the emperor made the captain and Boatswain part of his entourage until they reached Paris, from which they were escorted to Boulogne. There they were safely brought on board an English frigate. The Newfoundland returned to his former home with the prince regent in Windsor Castle, and the heir to the throne was a few months later present at the funeral of his old friend as well as at the erection of a marble memorial in Windsor Castle."[5]

The immediate reaction to this farrago of nonsense is that the story is too good to be true. It seems like if some half-educated foreigner with an indifferent grasp of history has made up a fantasy, using some of the most famous historical personages of the time as actors, with the Newfoundland dog taking centre stage. George Prince of Wales did keep dogs, but there is nothing to suggest that he ever had a Newfoundland. Beau Brummell [so spelt] was not interested in dogs, and although he was a friend of the Prince at the time, it was not customary for the royal family to give away valuable favourite dogs. The price for the dog appears quite exorbitant, since 7500 francs would have bought you a nice town house.[6] The Peace of Amiens took place in 1802, indicating that the heroic Boatswain would have added time-travelling to his other accomplishments. There is not, and never has been, any monument to a dog named Boatswain at Windsor Castle, and the academic biographers of George IV, Beau Brummell and Napoleon I do not refer to the 'Boatswain' incidents.

* * *

One of the best-known stories of Newfoundland dog sagacity and heroism is that of 'Hero', the Newfoundland saving 92 people at the wreck of the S/S Ethie in 1919. The Ethie was a 400-ton coal steamer, used to carry passengers and goods between various Newfoundland fishing communities, An old ship, constructed in 1901 with a single boiler and a small propeller, she was due to be replaced with a more modern vessel. On December 10 1919, the Ethie hit a fearsome hurricane off Bonne Bay. Buffeted by the waves and covered with ice, the vessel was in serious danger of sinking. Captain Edward English decided to beach the Ethie in a sandy cove behind Martin's Point. Thanks to a combination of luck, courage and good seamanship, this manoeuvre was performed according to plan; a rope was floated to the beach using a buoy, where it was made fast by local resident Reuben Decker and some other mariners. Through this route, all 92 passengers were successfully evacuated from the ship. An 18-month-old child was transported to shore in a mailbag.

The earliest accounts of the wreck of the Ethie and the rescue of the passengers mention nothing about any dog taking part. But a few days later, the *Western Star* alleged that one of the people at Martin's Point had sent out a very sagacious dog to bring one of the ropes from the Ethie ashore. 'Newfoundland Dog Rescues Crew!' exclaimed the *Evening Advocate*: one of these extraordinary dogs had been on board the Ethie, and it had swum ashore with a rope. The *New York Times* regurgitated this variant of the story, under the headline 'Dog lands Lifeline, Saves 92 on Wreck!'[7] The *Western Star* stuck to its own version, however, adding that the sagacious Newfoundland dog was owned by none less than Reuben Decker, the Martin's Point man who had first become aware of the stricken Ethie.

In early 1920, down in mainland America, the *Philadelphia Ledger* had a scarcity of good news stories. The journalist Fullerton L. Waldo thought the Ethie story might become capital stuff, if it was 'spiced up' a little further. This meant that the sagacious Newfoundland dog 'Hero', property of Reuben Decker of Martin's

Point, made his bow (wow) to the newspaper readers for the first time. This sagacious animal was solely responsible for the rescue of the passengers and crew of the Ethie, since he had swum out to the ship, seized a rope, and brought it ashore!

The story of Hero was syndicated in quite a few American newspapers, and even made it into the *Daily Mirror*, under the heading 'Dog Saves Ninety-two Lives!'[8] In Philadelphia, a humanitarian organization called the Starry Cross wanted to present Hero with a special collar trimmed with silver. A *Ledger* journalist was of course present when the collar was unveiled. It was enormously big, made from a 28-inch piece of leather, and had a silver medallion with the inscription 'The Starry Cross, a symbol of universal mercy, presented to 'Hero' by the Starry Cross of Philadelphia, PA. In token of appreciation for his rescue of 92 souls from the Ethie on December 10, 1919.'

A poet named E.J. Pratt wrote a long and heartfelt poem about the Hero Dog of the Ethie, giving the lifesaving dog the name Carlo, and containing the lines:

> But from the way you held the cable
> Within those gleaming jaws of sable,
> Leapt from the taffrail of the wreck
> With ninety souls upon its deck,
> And with your cunning dog-stroke tore
> Your path unerring to the shore ...

In the unintentionally funny ending of the poem, used as an epigraph to this chapter, Pratt personally undertook to facilitate the heroic dog's entrance into a Better World.[9]

From Philadelphia, Hero's collar was duly transported to Newfoundland, where it was handed over to the astounded Reuben Decker. He had never owned a Newfoundland dog in his life, and his only dog at the time of the shipwreck had been a small collie cross names Wisher. Being frightened of storms and high waves, this animal had done nothing worthwhile during the rescue of the survivors from the Ethie. Still, Decker collected the handsome collar; after all, it might come in handy one day.

A showman named William Orum, who had read about Hero, made a cunning plan to exploit the heroic canine. What if he bought the dog and took it on tour to various country fairs? He travelled to Martin's Point and tracked down Reuben Decker. His jaw probably hit the floor when he saw the rather mangy-looking little collie cross, and the enormous collar. Still, he made a bid of $30 for them, but Reuben Decker drove a hard bargain, and he only got the dog for that sum. Three months later, Orum returned with another $30, and left with the collar.

The little dog Wisher soon became surplus to requirements for Orum, since people did not take him seriously as 'Hero', and since he could not wear the collar. He was replaced with a sturdy black Newfoundland, who wore the collar like a champion. Acting the part of Hero to perfection, this dog became quite popular for a while. In late 1922, people had started to get fed up with Orum and Hero, however, and the showman decided to sell the dog and the collar. He had the good fortune to meet a proper 'mug' to sell the animal to: the millman Dennis 'Dinty' Kane.

Dinty had served as an army soldier in 1918 and 1919, before returning to his old job in Chipman, New Brunswick. He was far from a clever man, and could easily be persuaded into buying Hero and the collar. Dinty set out exhibiting the dog, telling the story of the wreck of the Ethie and the hero dog with great pathos. He was fond of doing a 'pub crawl' around town, telling the story of this extraordinary dog to every

An engraving by an unknown artist of a sailor lying on a beach with a Landseer Newfoundland standing over him. (The Penny Magazine of January 11, 1834)

person who bought him a whisky. Dinty's wife, a fierce and angry woman who disapproved of him adding a large, expensive dog to the already impoverished household, which contained a crippled son, sometimes refused to let her husband into the house when he returned from these drinking binges. Dinty had to sit shivering in a tent in the back yard, clutching a bottle of whisky, with the hero dog as his only source of warmth.

In 1923, Dinty travelled to Camp Hill Hospital in Halifax, for treatment of some nondescript malady. This was a military hospital, free of charge for veterans, and Dinty soon perked up once he was supplied with a warm room, nourishing food, and non-alcoholic beverages. He had brought Hero with him, and the dog became a great favourite among the other patients. Dinty made sure that they knew all about the heroism of his large, furry companion. In May 1923, a second medal was added to Hero's collar, with the inscription 'Presented to 'HERO' by the sick soldiers at Camp Hill Hospital Halifax, NS May 7 1923'. Not long after, Dinty left the hospital and returned to Chipman, but the lure of the bottle became too much for him on the way home, and he once more ended up sharing the tent in the back yard with his large, furry canine companion.

Fed up by his wife's mean-spirited attitude, Dinty went to Alaska, leaving his house, wife and two sons behind. He settled down in a town named Wrangell, where he lived in a shed and cooked his food over an open fire. Not much money was to be gained from exhibiting the hero dog in this dismal outback, so Dinty had to work as a farm hand, sharing a mud hut with the dog. In 1931, when Hero had been dead

A rare 1904 black and white postcard entitled "Saved" showing a very nice looking Landseer dog with a child lying across its paws.

for some years, his luckless master died from alcohol poisoning, although some suspected that Dinty had been poisoned for agreeing to witness against the owner of a local still for moonshine whisky.[10]

For several decades after Dinty's demise, garbled variations of the 'Hero' yarn were published in various newspapers and magazines. One of them introduced the heroic Newfoundland dog 'Tang', the ship's dog of the *Ethie*, who had been sent overboard to retrieve the tangled rope after one sailor had perished in the attempt. Tang was given 'a Meritorious Service medal from Lloyds of London' and he wore it on his collar until his death in St John's, at an advanced age. When the local journalist Cassie Brown wanted to write up the story in 1964, she was puzzled by the contrasting accounts of Hero and Tang. She interviewed the surviving crew members of the Ethie, who assured her the ship had not carried any dog, and that the story of the heroic canine had just been newspaper hokum. Reuben Decker, who was still alive, told her about the clever deal he had made back in 1920, selling the little dog and the enormous collar for a very good price.

When local historian Bruce Ricketts investigated the story of S/S *Ethie* and the Hero Dog some thirty years later, he unravelled the full story of the substitution of dogs, and the sad fate of the pathetic 'Dinty' Kane. He managed to find several eyewitnesses who had seen Hero: a large, black, benevolent-looking Newfoundland dog, wearing his fine silver collar. Ricketts also tracked down the collar itself, with both medals intact, to Dottie Olson, a hotel owner in Wrangell, who had been given it as a present by a neighbour who found it while clearing out an attic. He made sure it was exhibited at the Newfoundland Museum in 2001. An old lady named Hilda Menchions was present at the ceremony when the collar was formally received by the museum; 82 years earlier, she had been the little baby taken to shore from the *Ethie* inside a mailbag.

Ricketts later published a full account of the 'Hero' hoax and the odyssey of the dog's collar.[11] But his book has not prevented the story from living on; on a number of Internet pages, the Hero Dog of the Ethie is still swimming through the heavy waves, his powerful jaws grasping the rope,[12]

Another oft-repeated yarn of Newfoundland dog heroism is that of 'Rigel, Hero Dog of the *Titanic*'. This sagacious dog belonged to William Murdoch, the First Officer of the *Titanic*, and after the ship had sunk, Rigel swam in the freezing water for three full hours, searching for his master. It had been Rigel's barks that attracted the *Carpathia's* notice to a boatload of *Titanic* survivors. Far from tired after his three-hour swim, the heroic dog swam ahead of the lifeboat, making himself known to the rescuers with his booming bark.

The earliest version of the Rigel story was published in the *New York Herald* in April 1912:

> **"Survivor's Cries Weak, Dog's Bark Causes Rescue of Boatload.**
>
> **Rigel, whose master sank with the *Titanic*, Guides the *Carpathia*'s Captain to Suffering Passengers Hidden Under Rescue Ship's Bow.**
>
> Not the least among the heroes of the *Titanic* was Rigel, a big black Newfoundland dog, belonging to the first officer, who went down with his ship. But for Rigel, the fourth boat picked up might have been run down by the *Carpathia*. For three hours he swam in the water where the Titanic went down,

A Victorian scrap of a white and black Newfoundland with a small boy sat on its back, another child holding him on and two other children around the dog

THOSE AMAZING NEWFOUNDLAND DOGS

A drawing by Gray-Parker picturing two children going for a sleigh ride accompanied by the Newfoundland dogs Castor and Pollux. Around the main illustration are smaller images of the two Newfoundlands chasing and catching a hare. It is entitled *Leaving Home* and was illustrated in the February 2, 1886 issue of *Harpers Young People*.

evidently looking for his master, and was instrumental in guiding the boatload of survivors to the gangway of the *Carpathia*.

Jonas Briggs, a seaman aboard the *Carpathia*, now has Rigel and told the story of the dog's heroism. The *Carpathia* was moving slowing about, looking for boats, rafts or anything which might be afloat. Exhausted with their efforts, weak from lack of food and exposure to the cutting wind, and terror stricken, the men and woman in the fourth boat drifted under the *Carpathia's* starboard bow. They were dangerously close to the steamship, too weak to shout a warning loud enough to reach the bridge.

The boat might not have been seen were it not for the sharp barking of Rigel, who was swimming ahead of the craft and valiantly announcing his position. The barks attracted the attention of Captain Rostron and he went to the starboard end of the bridge to see where they came from and saw the boat. He immediately ordered the engines stopped and the boat came alongside the starboard gangway.

THOSE AMAZING NEWFOUNDLAND DOGS

> Care was taken to take Rigel aboard, but he appeared little affected by his long trip through the ice cold water. He stood by the rail and barked until Captain Rostron called Briggs and had him take the dog below."[13]

The *New York Herald* story of Rigel was syndicated in some other American papers, but just like the Titanic itself, the tale of the hero dog failed to cross the Atlantic. Still, Rigel's heroism has been described in more than one book about Newfoundland dogs. The Hero Dog of the *Titanic* has also been able to sink his fangs into Internet popular culture, with a vengeance: his story is retold on pages about dogs, accounts of notable shipwrecks, and educational stories for schoolchildren.[14] At least one novel have been based on his antics.[15] But the only true part of Rigel's story is that the *Titanic* went down, and that there were dogs on board. Twelve dogs were paying passengers, and there may well have been some others hitching a free ride across the Atlantic. Three of these dogs survived, a Pekingese named 'Sun Yat Sen' and two Pomeranians; all these animals were tucked away into the clothing of their masters and mistresses, who were among the passengers evacuated from the *Titanic* at an early stage, in lifeboats not filled to capacity. No person on board the *Titanic* had encountered a Newfoundland, and there is nothing to suggest that the first officer, William Murdoch, had a dog on board.

The likely origin of the 'Rigel' hoax is that stories about the *Titanic* were hot news in 1912. If there were no truthful ones, then the unscrupulous American journalists used their imaginations. Or perhaps the person 'Jonas Briggs' who verified the story, was a hoaxer who wanted to collect some money from the *New York Herald* for a spicy *Titanic* story. There is no listing of a Jonas Briggs as a crew member of the *Carpathia*.

The time has come to leave fictions like 'Boatswain', 'Hero' and 'Rigel' behind: the stories are blatantly untrue, and give as little credit to the knaves who invented them as to the fools who are repeating them. Whereas the ghostly Newfoundland dogs described in the first part of this chapter are timid, retiring spectres, and not harmful ghosts, the formidable trio of Boatswain, Hero and Rigel have become malevolent Internet poltergeists. They ought to be thoroughly exorcized before they cause any further mischief. There are better *true* stories about Newfoundland dog heroism out there, and it detracts from the breed's long and illustrious history that such ludicrous falsehoods are regurgitated.

The Newfoundland dog Diane rescues a man from the Seine, from the *Supplément Illustré* of *Le Petit Journal*, June 22 1902

CHAPTER 17.
THE LIFESAVING NEWFOUNDLAND DOGS OF PARIS

> Life saver! Wave stemmer!
> Deep diver! away!
> Night's shadows are closing
> The portals of day;
> On the breast of the billow
> We hear his low wail,
> We have put up the rudder,
> And furl'd up the sail.
>
> From Henry Russell's song
> 'The Newfoundland dog'

In 1900, the Paris police prefect Louis Lépine founded the *Brigade Fluviale*, a police squad that would devote itself entirely to policing the Seine. M. Lépine was a far-sighted police official, who had been greeted with a mixture of admiration and hilarity when he had initiated the cycling police a few years earlier. The *Brigade Fluviale* would consist of forty constables, under the command of Inspector Guillemin. Their duties were to save drowning peoples, rescue suicides leaping into the river, and pursue thieves who took refuge in the water.

Later the same year, it was decided to finally act upon an idea that had been twice discussed in the previous century, and to provide the *Brigade Fluviale* with some life-saving dogs. Two purebred adult Landseer Newfoundland males were purchased, for £20 each. They were named 'Turc' and 'César'. In addition, a police constable named Dubois was recruited to the force, since he had an old Newfoundland dog named 'Sultan' that already possessed some degree of prowess in water rescue. In addition, one of his neighbours gave Constable Dubois another Landseer Newfoundland named 'Félix', because she could no longer cope with the boisterous young dog. Another of the canine lifesavers, a black Newfoundland named 'Paris', was retrieved from the dog pound, where he had been imprisoned for savaging another dog.[1]

The dogs were housed in a comfortable kennel adjoining the police station at the *Quai de la Tournelle*. They underwent an ambitious training programme, using a large floating dummy, and a series of commands aiming to make the *chiens plongeurs* leap into the Seine and grasp the dummy. The old dog Sultan was by far the most successful of them, but both Turc and César were showing promise. The black dog Paris took to the water only when he wanted to, but his fierce and angry temperament

Constable Dubois and his dog 'Sultan'

convinced the constables that he would become a useful asset to their unit; few thieves and burglars would be able to resist such a formidable animal, when he was set on them.

Since M. Lépine was keen to observe the progress of his four-footed recruits, the dogs were ordered to give him a demonstration in late 1901. All the dogs were reasonably competent at executing a number of commands, including 'Au pied!', 'A terre!', Va chercher!' and 'Apporte!'; since they were quite excited and barked in their stentorous voices, the command 'Silence!' did not have the desired effect. The dog Sultan competently retrieved the dummy when it was thrown into the river, and was applauded by M. Lépine.

But the police prefect also wanted to see the two younger dogs, on the purchase of which so much money had been spent, show off their skills. Accordingly, 'M. Mannequin', as the dummy was called, was again thrown into the river, and César brought it to shore. But the dog Turc very much resented being left out. He ran up to the dummy, and started tearing at M. Mannequin with his powerful jaws. César joined in the fun, until M. Mannequin was well-nigh unrecognizable. A journalist wrote that this extraordinary display must have convinced the onlookers that death by drowning would be preferable to being dismembered by the so-called 'lifesaving dogs'.

But in spite of this mishap, M. Lépine kept faith in his four-legged lifesavers. At another review of their accomplishments, the old dog Sultan again rescued the replacement 'M. Mannequin', this time aided only by signs. The expansive police prefect envisioned a force of twenty constables, each of whom would have a Newfoundland dog. But Inspector Guillemin did not find it advisable to make a wholesale purchase of fifteen more expensive Newfoundlands. First, a large kennel needed to be built, with housing for all these dogs, each in its own apartment. A special dog-kitchen should also be constructed, with a huge copper for the cooking of their food. The Inspector also urged that the usefulness of the dogs, in practical situations, needed to be established before more animals were recruited.

* * *

In early 1902, a force of eight Newfoundlands were inhabiting the kennel at *Quai de la Tournelle*: the five original dogs, two Newfoundland crosses donated by members of the public, and a handsome young Landseer Newfoundland bitch named 'Diane', purchased for another £20. Unlike the other dogs, she received water rescue training from an early age, and soon became very proficient. M. Lépine was much impressed with the team of dogs. He ordered that although their main purpose would be to save drowning people, or would-be suicides jumping into the river, they should also be used to catch thieves who tried to evade the police through swimming the Seine, or taking refuge on a barge. A 1902 illustration shows Diane, the youngest of the dogs, leaping into the Seine from the embankment. Approvingly, the March 15 issue of the *Annuaire des Commissaires de Police* wrote that these robust Newfoundland dogs would become valuable assets to the *Brigade Fluviale*, since they were well suited to save drowning people, and to pursue dangerous vagabonds taking refuge near the Seine or its tributaries. But not long after, the old dog Sultan died, and the dogs Turc and César were sold, because these boisterous animals were up to all kinds of mischief.

The remaining five *chiens plongeurs* were also given some basic police dog training, in order to be useful also on dry land. This part of their education was tested later in 1902, when a thief came rushing out of a shop right in front of some of the river constables. The constables immediately gave chase, releasing Diane and her fellow Landseer Félix when the miscreant refused to stop. The great dogs were slow starters, but they gradually caught up with the exhausted thief. He suddenly veered into an alley, with the dogs in hot pursuit. The constables had high hopes of a vital success for their team, but all they found inside the alleyway were the two police dogs, who were greedily eating some bread and sausages strewn on the ground. The constables were nonplussed, but a waiter from a restaurant nearby explained that the clever thief had grabbed a large plate of bread and sausages from a table, and emptied it in front of the pursuing dogs, before running off unharmed.

A few months later, there was further farce when the black Newfoundland Paris, the most fierce of the river police dogs, was sent to sniff out a dangerous criminal, who was believed to be hiding on board a barge. Just seconds after the great dog had boarded the barge, a yell of pain was heard, and a man came lurching out on deck, clutching his buttocks. The river constables took him into custody, but he turned out to be the owner of the barge, who had been sleeping on board; the criminal had once more escaped.

Later in 1902, when the *chiens plongeurs* were formally tested in front of the *commissaire*, they gave a dismal account of themselves. Only Diane could be coaxed to leap into the Seine, whereas the other four dogs obstinately refused to take to the water. One of the Newfoundland crosses was sacked for being entirely uneducable, but the other four dogs were grudgingly given another chance, since M. Lépine remained a strong supporter of the river police dogs. And the police prefect's confidence in his canine life-savers seemed to have been vindicated when, on June 5, the dog Diane plunged into the river without any word of command, and seized a man who had just thrown himself into the water. She held him by his coat until the constables arrived to pull the would-be suicide up onto the embankment. Several witnesses to this extraordinary rescue stood to attention and applauded Diane, and an old lady came up to embrace the soaking wet dog. The journalists, who had previously been quite unimpressed with the *chiens plongeurs*, now applauded Diane's heroism, which was not less astonishing, they wrote, since the dog was just twenty months old. Even the faraway *Illustrated Buffalo Express* briefly noticed this incident: "Seeing a man jump into the Seine, one of the life-saving dogs kept by the Parisian police jumped in after him, and, seizing the would-be suicide by his clothes, brought him safely ashore. Some of the spectators of the incident were so affected by the dog's bravery that they wanted to embrace it." The only dissenter was the would-be suicide, not because the histrionic Frenchman had really intended to destroy himself, but since he had been badly bruised by the dog's powerful jaws when hauled to safety.

* * *

The four remaining river police dogs remained active throughout 1903 and 1904. In 1905, a photograph in the *Quiver* magazine shows them all alive and well.[2] But their performance still left much to be desired; they jumped into the river only when they wanted to, and could be very obstinate. During another review of their willingness to take to the water, the constables were asked to detail the rescues made in the last twelve months. The only success had been scored by the black Newfoundland Paris, who had once attempted to retrieve a corpse from the Seine. He had only 'rescued' the coat and hat, however, since the body sunk. More than once, the unpredictable dogs had jumped into the Seine on their own accord, to retrieve hats and sticks that mischievous individuals had thrown into the water to tempt them. On other occasions, they could not be persuaded to take to the water at all, lying down on the Seine embankment to watch a corpse float by, or a thief swim away. Diane had not performed any further rescues, but she had once retrieved valuable evidence, the constables claimed, namely a large ham stolen from a grocer. This was hardly an exacting task for a highly trained police dog, however, particularly when it turned out that she had been discovered while in the process of eating it. By this time, the river police and their unpredictable dogs had become figures of fun. On a cartoon illustrating a popular song, a red-nosed police constable and a jolly-looking Newfoundland dog stand on the Seine embankment, watching two corpses float by. There were many newspaper jokes about the bumbling police dogs, of which the following is a fair example:

THOSE AMAZING NEWFOUNDLAND DOGS

The mess-room of the river police

> A Newfoundland dog on the probationary staff of M. Lépine one day distinguished himself by rescuing a child from drowning. The grateful father presented the canine life-saver with a large, juicy beefsteak. Two days later, another child was saved by the dog in a similar manner, and then yet another one. The dog was again praised and rewarded, and the sentimentalists wanted to give it a medal. The police were busy chasing the maniac who was throwing children into the Seine. They soon found the culprit: for the sake of the beefsteaks, the Newfoundland dog had been pushing children into the river and then rescuing them! M. Lépine made sure it was dismissed in disgrace from his force of canine lifesavers.[3]

In September 1905, when the river police dogs were briefly featured in the *Daily Mirror*, there are only two animals in the photograph, probably the Landseers Diane and Félix, indicating that the police were scaling down its force of canine life-savers.[4] There are much fewer mentions of the life-saving dogs in 1906 and 1907.[5] It turns out, however, that least one of the *chiens plongeurs* became an ordinary police dog, patrolling the streets instead of the river embankments. In late 1909, a thief took refuge in a large indoor food market, pursued by a police constable and his large Newfoundland dog Diane. When the dog

Sultan and the dummy used for training the dogs

was released, she bounded after the fugitive with alacrity, and tackled him into a fishmonger's stall But again there were no thanks to the gallant former *chien plongeur*: far from praising the canine thief-taker, various people pushed over by the dog demanded compensation, and the fishmonger vociferously lamented his broken stall. Similarly, a painting exhibited at the 1910 *Salon* shows two sturdy river policemen travelling on the Seine in a dinghy, with their black Newfoundland dog Paris, obviously yet another survivor from the original squad of *chiens plongeurs*.

Why were the life-saving dogs of Paris such a failure? After all, one rescue and one corpse nearly retrieved in more than five years of active service were not particularly favourable statistics for the dogs and their handlers. Firstly, it was unwise to leave their training to ordinary police constables, who possessed neither experience with dogs, nor any particular water rescue skills. Secondly, the river police were very much mistaken when they paid such exorbitant prices to purchase adult dogs, who were not amenable to be taught new tricks. For a Newfoundland dog to become fully competent in water rescue, the animal has to be actively taught since quite a young age. Thus it is no coincidence that Diane, the youngest of the dogs, ended up becoming the most competent of the canine life-savers. Furthermore, it was probably not a good strategy to try to make the dogs into jacks-of-all-trades; it would seriously tax their intellects to determine whether a person swimming in the Seine was an absconding thief, or a drowning person calling for assistance. The disbanding of the river police dog force seems to have been a result of the adverse newspaper publicity, and the gradual realization that the animals were not up to the task. Mischievous people throwing coats, hats or sticks into the river to distract and tempt the unpredictable dogs cannot have done them any favour either.

Vindicating the opinion of M. Lépine back in 1901, many Newfoundlands have since been successfully trained as professional life-saving dogs. Both in France and in Italy, Newfoundland dogs have patrolled

The original force of canine life-savers, with the constable to the left holding Turc and César, and Constable Dubois holding Sultan and Félix. The black Newfoundland Paris is lying to the right. Like the previous three, it is from a feature in *The Windsor Magazine*, 1902.

The *chiens plongeurs* practicing their skills, an engraving from the *Petit Parisien* (No. 678, 1902)

the beaches at least since the 1960s. The Italian school for lifesaving dogs has a formidable force of Labradors and Newfoundlands, some of them trained to jump out from a helicopter to save swimmers in difficulties.[6] The United States has several Newfoundland dogs trained for water rescue. In an amazing story from 1995, vouched for by *National Geographic* magazine, a 10-month old Newfoundland named Boo was taken out for a stroll by his master, along the Yuba River in Northern California. When Boo, who entirely lacked water rescue training, saw a man desperately trying to stay afloat in the swollen current, he leapt into the water and pulled him safely to shore. The man turned out to be a deaf-mute who had fallen into the water while gold-dredging. The Newfoundland Club of America awarded Boo a medal for his heroism in 1996.[7]

The scientific study of Newfoundland dog water rescue is a neglected area. In two articles published in 1991, M. J.-M. Durand, president of the Fédération Nationale des Maitres Chiens Sauveteurs Nautiques, pointed out that the Newfoundland was the superior breed of dog for water work.[8] Its strength, endurance, calmness, tenacity and resistance to cold combined to make it the ideal water dog. These useful animals were equally adept in the open sea as in lakes and rivers, and could also prove valuable in flooding incidents. The Newfoundland puppy should be exposed to water from an early stage, and taken out in a boat to see the adult dogs perform.

In another article, a team of Polish scientists aimed to investigate the behaviour of water working dogs in a simulated rescue incident.[9] They recruited two Newfoundlands, three German Shepherds and a Labrador retriever, which all had around five months of basic water rescue training, and a variable amount of experience. An unknown person pretended to be drowning, and the dog's handler ordered it into action. One of the Newfoundlands was the only dog to immediately leap into the water after receiving the command, whereas the other dogs needed to be encouraged by their handlers. The other Newfoundland, and one of the German Shepherds, once refused to take to the water altogether, nor were the other dogs particularly reliable performers. They sometimes returned to land before reaching the drowning person, and one of the German Shepherds once climbed onto him to play. Although the German Shepherds were quick short distance swimmers, the Newfoundlands were superior in towing the person to be rescued. Unfortunately, the low number of dogs in this study renders it practically worthless. To properly compare the Newfoundlands and the other rescue dogs, at least ten animals would have been needed in each group.

In Britain, the Swansea division of the Royal Navy reservists has a team of life-saving dogs, trained by Mr David Pugh, who has also set up the charitable organization Newfound Friends to promote Newfoundland dog water training. Its leading light has been the 13-stone white and black Newfoundland dog Whizz, who has been trained to leap into the chilly waters of the Bristol Channel, together with his two-legged sidekick, schoolgirl Ellie Bedford. The remarkably intelligent Whizz is likely to be Britain's finest professional water rescue dog. Once, when going for a walk near Clevedon, Whizz darted off into the bushes, to save an Irish setter named Topper, who had fallen into a disused water tank. Just like he had been taught, Whizz plunged into the tank, resolutely grabbed Topper by the scruff of his neck, and pulled him to safety. A dog saving the life of another is always news, at least in Britain, and Whizz was featured in the evening newspapers; in one of the photographs, a rather apprehensive-looking Topper was depicted seated next to the hulking Newfoundland. Mr Pugh and his team of dogs regularly perform at various events, being one of the headliners of the Bristol and Cardiff Harbour Festivals, to very considerable acclaim.[10]

Whizz is still alive and well, having survived a near-fatal bout of leptospirosis. He lives with his younger friend Ted, another massive white and black Newfoundland male, who is making good progress as a water rescue dog himself.

RÉPERTOIRE FÉLIX MAYOL
à Maurice RHÉYAL

Les Chiens Sauveteurs

Paroles de
PAUL MARINIER

Musique de
EUGÈNE PONCIN

Deux p'tits a_mou_reux, un ma_

_tin, Qu'avaient le cœur très cha_grin Et l'âm' tout a fait en pei_ne. Comm' des gens

qu'ont d'mauvais des_seins Sui_vaient d'un pas in_cer_tain Les bords malsains de la

Sei_ne. Le public prompt à s'a_mas_ser Se di_sait 'Sa_cré_dié! Qu'est-c'qui va bien s'pas_

_ser? 'Ils ont tout deux mi_ne ha_gard; Bah! s'ils veul'nt se pé_rir, a_près tout ça les

r'garde.' Et les chiens sauv'teurs, m'direz-vous, oui da, Qu'est-c'qu'ils fichaient donc pendant tout c'temps

_là? Tranquill'ment as_sis sur leurs gros der_rières Ils s'disaient entre eux: 'V'la un' sal' af_

_faire! Tout ça, c'est cer_tain, n'finira pas bien Que c'est bêt' l'amour, sacré nom d'un chien!"

Paris, HACHETTE & Cie Editeurs, 79, Bd St Germain.

Tous droits d'exécution publique, de reproduction, de traduction et d'arrangements réservés pour tous pays, y compris la Suède, la Norvège le Danemark. H.12

The funny song ridiculing the life-saving dogs of Paris, who are said to be sitting on their large behinds to watch the corpses of two suicidal young lovers float by. The punch-line is that for any suicidal person to qualify for being rescued by the dogs, destroy themselves

II

Soudain l'amoureux fait un bond,
Une cascade, un plongeon
Disant: "Qui m'aime me suive!"
Et l'amoureuse, pour plonger,
De son pied le plus léger,
Comme lui quitte la rive.
Dans le public on crie: Au s'cours!
Ah! mon Dieu! quel malheur! Ils attent'nt à leurs jours!"
Chacun en grands mots se dépens',
Pourtant, pour les r'pécher, personne ne s'élance.
Et les chiens sauv'teurs, m'direz-vous, oui da,
Qu'est-c'qu'ils fichaient donc pendant tout c'temps là?
Tranquill'ment assis sur leurs gros derrières
Ils r'gardaient couler l'eau dans la rivière
Et pensaient entre eux: "Faut il êtr' nigaud,
Par un temps pareil, pour se fiche à l'eau!

III

Dans le public ce n'fut qu'un cri
Puis, soudain'ment, on apprit
(Ô décevante ironie!)
Que les cabots qui v'naient d'manger
Ne pouvaient s'mettre à nager
Sans risquer un' gastralgie.
Ah! sacredié, disaient les gens
"Vraiment c'est enrageant! Nous donnons nos argents
"Pour entret'nir des sinécur's
"Faut aller réclamer jusqu'à la Préfecture!"
Et les fonctionnair's, m'direz-vous, oui da,
Qu'ont ils répondu à tout c'potin là?
Tranquill'ment assis sur leurs gros derrières
Ils dir'nt "Nous faisons une circulaire;
"Ceux qui s'suicid'ront d'vront, dorénavant
"Nous prév'nir au moins vingt quatr' heur's avant!"

Three funny postcards showing a river police constable sitting just by the quayside, with his Newfoundland dog. He is busy reading *Le Figaro* and does not see that a little girl falls into the Seine, but the dog is the hero of the day

3. — Le bébé allait se noyer.

5. — Dans l'eau se jeta courageusement.

Bilbo, another lifesaving Newfoundland dog, patrolling the beach at Sennen Cove in Cornwall, has been no stranger to controversy. After stopping a foreign woman from entering the surf on a windy day, through simply blocking her way, Bilbo was widely featured in the newspapers. And the benign-looking 14-stone brown Newfoundland did not look back. Already a local hero, he made celebrity appearances, and visited schools to help teach beach safety. He beat 70 human contestants in a mile-long open water swimming race from Newlyn to Penzance. Sponsorship from a dog food company kept his food-bowl well filled, and he was invited to Crufts as a guest of honour. A film of Bilbo leaping from a raft towed by a water scooter, to save a person waving for help, became a Youtube favourite. Bilbo soon had a web site, and his own fan club; he made regular TV appearances, and his biography was published in 2008.[11]

It would appear as if some of the lifeguard bosses did not like all this publicity for a mere dog, or appreciate the newspaper hints that Bilbo was a fully trained lifeguard capable of doing the job of his two-legged colleagues. Ignoring Bilbo's good work to promote beach safety education, they decided to ban Bilbo from the Sennen Cove beach, allegedly because dogs were not allowed, and because there were health and safety concerns about the 14-stone dog riding on the back of a quad bike. Newspapers all over the country scented a good story. In tabloid press parlance, the lifeguard bosses had to be *barking* to *hound* Bilbo out of his job, and demand that this *four-legged Hasselhoff* would *bow-wow* out of *Baywoof*. All the odium in the newspapers, and thousands of people petitioning the Queen and the Prime Minister to reinstate Bilbo, finally had the desired effect: in March 2009, he was allowed to return to duty at the Sennen Cove beach.[12] According to a recent newspaper article, he is still alive and well, and made an appearance in a Cornish school in February 2012 to help teach the children about water safety.[13]

A curious old French postcard, depicting the life-saving dog Paris hitching a ride with two river constables. Another scarce postcard, using a rather murky photograph of the dog Diane and another Newfoundland, is in a private collection in Paris, valued at a very high amount by its owner

CHAPTER 18.
NEWFOUNDLAND DOG WATER RESCUE
BY MR DAVID PUGH OF NEWFOUND FRIENDS

>Ho! Carlo! Newfoundland!
>Go follow his cry,
>As it gaspingly answers
>The sea moaners sigh;
>
>The boat shall be lower'd,
>The men shall belay,
>Life saver! Wave stemmer!
>Deep diver, away!
>
>From Henry Russell's song 'The
>Newfoundland dog',
>in his *Musical Bouquet*.

The Newfoundland is renowned for its reputation as a swimming dog. Much is said about its webbed feet and its double coat, but my observations over the years lead me to believe that the immensely strong Newfoundland dog's unique swimming action is not equaled by any other breed. Unlike lesser breeds of water dogs, the Newfoundland swims with all four legs, a canine four wheel drive if you like. They may not be the fastest of swimming dogs, since after all there is an awful lot of dog that has to travel through the water, coupled with a very shaggy coat that makes for a much less streamlined animal than some other aquatic counterparts. The Newfoundland's strength in the water is unequaled among the canine tribe. These dogs can, with ease, tow ten or more people to safety, something no human can achieve. Most lifeguards will tell you that it is a real struggle to pull two people at a time.

The Newfoundland dog's double coat acts like a wetsuit enabling it to withstand colder temperatures than most other dogs can tolerate, or humans for that matter. The outer coat has an oily base, aiding water resistance. The double thickness of the coat traps a layer of air that gives buoyancy in a similar manner to a human's wetsuit. The tail of the Newfoundland dog is much the same as a boat's rudder and acts as its steering mechanism to guide it through the water.

I have now given an understanding of the attributes the Newfoundland has that makes it the swimming champion of the canine world. Then how does the beginner dog develop into a life-saving water rescue dog? Well, I have often been asked this question, and the answer always remains the same. We

THOSE AMAZING NEWFOUNDLAND DOGS

Whizz jumps from a rubber dinghy

encourage the new dog to swim, and provide its owner with tuition how to treat their beloved friend. Let me explain. Each and every dog is an individual in its own right and just like its human counterpart we have to learn about their temperament, physical ability and their willingness to learn. On the whole, the dogs are not the overall problem. They usually possess the ability to learn very quickly and very often pick up all the information they need to progress by just watching the more experienced dogs at work. The Newfoundland dog is the original Stonewall Jackson and if it does not want to do something, then it is just not going to do it willingly. There's no way you are ever going to produce a water rescue dog with a heavy-handed approach. Encouragement, reward and the chance for the dog to fulfil its true love of the water is the only way forward.

A puppy can start to swim as soon as it has had all the initial injections, at a time when the water temperature is warm enough not to cause a problem to a young dog. Some Newfoundland puppies will just take to the water of their own accord, and with others, we just support their body weight, with one person either side of them, to give them confidence. After a short time most will take to swimming naturally. There may be a little splashing stroke until they gain more and more confidence and we always encourage the owner to be part of their dog's first swimming lesson by being in the water to give their puppy that little extra encouragement. Now we have a dog that swims and later I will explain how we gradually advance the exercises and equip the Newfoundland to its full potential as a water rescue dog

So how does the inexperienced owner learn about water rescue dogs? It's not as if you can go to night school, or take up a degree course and there are no books on the subject. The only way to learn is to find experienced people that you know swim with their Newfoundlands. This has to be researched and

THOSE AMAZING NEWFOUNDLAND DOGS

the Internet is a good place to start. The chances are that this will mean some sort of self-assessment on how far you want to travel, and the amount of time you can commit to the cause. Newfound Friends always welcome people and their dogs to our lake, to evaluate the level of commitment and understanding that it takes to produce a water rescue dog. This allows their dog to work with very experienced handlers who can assess the ability of their dog, and allows us to evaluate the dog's owner and their willingness to listen and learn. Working with the dogs is a huge commitment in time, and a large expenditure in personal equipment, like wetsuits and rescue aids. A wet dog does not travel well in the back of a car, so more often than not a change of car to an estate or van is required. This is in no way a cheap pastime, but the chance to swim and spend time with a happy dog makes all the sacrifices worthwhile.

* * *

So how and why did I start to swim with Newfoundlands? Back in 1987, my first Newfie was a solid black boy named Thomas. After we had owned German Shepherds for what seemed like a lifetime, a change of breed came about. With no real intention to swim with the new arrival, and with the thought that a Newfoundland was no more than a 'pipe and slippers dog', swimming never crossed my mind, although I was well aware of the Newfoundland's reputation as a water dog..

Not long after the new canine recruit became a member of the family it soon became apparent that this was a totally different type of dog. A short stay in a rented cottage in a remote part of Scotland, brought about Thomas' own intentions to become a swimming dog. On arrival at the cottage after a lengthy trip

Whizz and Ellie in action

Whizz sitting on the beach, looking very handsome and dignified

from the south of England, Thomas was out of the car, across two fields and into the river Tweed. Now how he knew there was a river and where it was I just don't have a clue. It was just Thomas telling me that above all else he wanted to be a water rescue dog just like his forefathers.

With the knowledge that I was the proud owner of a dog that just loved to swim how was I going to get the best out of him, and more importantly I was keen to find out the safest and most productive way that I could learn about water rescue work. I approached the Newfoundland breed club for information, and if there was anybody locally that I might be able to approach to teach me and Thomas the art of water rescue. The reply was that there was no one local to my home, so I had a choice of either Southampton or Plymouth. As Southampton was slightly less distance to travel, I made contact with the group at that location, only to be told that they thought I lived too far away, that they had a waiting list of people, and that they did not think I would be suitable anyway.

Their loss was Plymouth's gain. The people in Plymouth were like a breath of fresh air, very welcoming and informative. Although this was a greater distance to travel (240 mile round trip), I found that the experience and information I gained far out weighed the fact that I had to travel all that way. Tony Mayor and Tom Rudd, the founders of Plymouth Sporting Newfoundlands, were miles ahead of any other people in the U.K with regard to water rescue work. They had better equipment, much more knowledge, and two of the best Newfoundlands I had ever seen working at the time.

The French group T.N.S (Terra Nova Sportive) was popularly regarded as the best in the world at this time working with Newfoundlands in the sea, often travelled to Plymouth to exchange ideas and information about the dogs and the way to obtain the best out of them in the water. Although they could not bring their own dogs with them at the time, T.N.S were more than willing to travel to England, to work with our dogs, exchange views and opinions with us, and train us humans the safe and responsible way and respect of the open water.[1]

Plymouth Sporting Newfoundlands encouraged all its members to join the Royal Life Saving Society and take their life saving qualifications, and to obtain Royal Yachting Association boat and skipper certifications. After all, the water can be a dangerous place, and no one can have enough skills to work in this environment. Most of the swimming with the dogs took place in the sea off the coast of Plymouth, and longer trips could involve a fifty mile boat ride off the sunny shores of Cornwall. Exercises with the dogs would take place along the way. Often, one of the boats would travel ahead of the rest, to set up an incident that the lifeguard and dog would have to evaluate and react to. There is no doubt that a Newfoundland dog's real home is the sea: they just love this experience, and the salty water gives them extra buoyancy.

Each year, there is the Newfoundland International event on the Continent, held in either Italy, Germany, Switzerland or France, where the countries come together to exchange views and opinions and demonstrate the skills of their beloved Newfoundlands. If you ever have the opportunity to attend this event, then don't miss out, since you will be made most welcome

* * *

After three years learning and working with the Newfoundland dogs at Plymouth it became clear that these dogs are indeed very special and that they have a mindset of their own. It takes time and a huge amount of commitment to gain a true understanding how to get the best from the dogs. Each and every Newfoundland dog is an individual in its own right, just like us humans, and has to be treated accordingly: whilst most of the basic exercises suit all the dogs, the mindset of each dog has to be

THOSE AMAZING NEWFOUNDLAND DOGS

The Newfoundland dog Ty

considered. There is no doubt that any person working with these dogs in the water has to be a proficient swimmer, able to keep up with the dog, and confident in the water. Especially with a young dog, this inspires confidence in the animal, and builds up the handlers' understanding of what they are asking of the Newfoundland. Open water can be a very dangerous place and conditions can change very quickly. There are currents, tide movements and weather conditions that might catch the most proficient person out, and the basic rule is that "if you're not prepared to enter the water yourself then don't expect your Newfoundland to." If you cannot respond to a situation yourself, then do not swim your dog, since a dog can get into difficulties as well as humans.

I can remember, twenty years ago, that when a young man was swimming with his Newfoundland dog, he got caught up in weeds at an inland lake in the south of England and drowned. I can recall also an incident when two Newfoundlands went over board from a vessel in the English Channel and were lost. Once when I was swimming with the dogs off a beach in Devon, with my friends from Plymouth, a family with their two Newfoundlands came along to see what we were doing. They engaged in conversation with us and told us how well their dogs worked in the water. The family moved along the beach to swim their dogs and after a short amount of time came running back towards us. Their dogs certainly could swim, it was just that they would not come back to shore! Looking to the horizon, we only just made out the shape of two objects in the water, rapidly disappearing from view. It was fortunate that we had two inflatable boats with us, which we made use of to pursue the disappearing dogs. The two Newfoundland dogs were reunited with their owners, and all ended well, but if there had

Whizz shakes himself

THOSE AMAZING NEWFOUNDLAND DOGS

been no boats to hand, those dogs would have been lost. There is a thought in my mind that they had been caught in an ebbing tide, and were on their way to France, not that they would ever have made those distant shores. Please, if you intend to swim your dog, make sure that you can understand the conditions, and that you are able to respond to any situation that may arise.

Never swim with your dog by yourself. It is almost impossible to get a 13-stone Newfoundland back into a boat without the help of others, and when the dog is wet it is at least a stone heavier. To enable a safe entry into the boat, our dogs have special harnesses made from pigskin leather, with stainless steel fittings. The handles on the top of the harness enable us to lift the dog safely into the boat. The harnesses also have a secondary use: a casualty can hold on to them, and be pulled to safety. The equipment we use is proven and used by most continental training groups. It also should be made very clear that you should never tie anything on to the harness or the body of the dog, since the Newfoundland should always be able to swim free from any encumbrance. Sometimes it may appear to the untrained eye that the dog swims a longer distance than you might think is necessary, but don't be fooled: the Newfoundland has a canny knack of understanding the tidal movements and wind direction, and the dog knows the best way to use the conditions to its advantage.

There is a growing trend that people make water dogs of all kinds using life jackets. It is becoming a fashion

Whizz flying.

THOSE AMAZING NEWFOUNDLAND DOGS

Whizz showing off his skills.

accessory that people use when their dogs are in and around the water. Well that is all well and good for lesser breeds of dogs, but not one I would recommend for a Newfoundland. Firstly, the jackets are not strong enough for a dog of such size, since the weight of a wet Newfoundland will break the fixing straps. Secondly a floatation aid for a dog that has a coat much better than any life jacket is an encumbrance to the dog, since the compression of a tight fitting jacket stops the layers of the dog's coat from being effective. With a trained eye, you can tell when a Newfoundland is beginning to struggle in the water, since the back end of the dog starts to disappear under the water. An artificial flotation aid will hide these telltale signs and disguise the fact the dog is starting to tire. Above all else, we are writing about the canine swimming champion. Like a fully trained lifeguard, the Newfoundland dog does not need a life jacket unless they have a medical condition that makes it necessary.

* * *

When we are confident that the dog is swimming properly, and that it is comfortable in the water, then the time has come to start teaching the dog and handler the basics of water rescue. Firstly we ask the handler to swim a little way out, say about five meters, and then ask their dog to swim to them. As the dog approaches, the handler taps the water to attract the dog's attention, and then gradually turns in a semi circular movement, tapping the water along the way. The dog should follow the body movement of the person and end up facing the shore. Then the handler can hold onto the dog and be towed back to dry land, lying flat on his or her back. There is no point in a water rescue dog taking a casualty further away from safety, so the object of this exercise is to control the dog in the water. We practice this

Whizz pulls the dinghy with the greatest ease.

exercise until it is clear that the Newfoundland is comfortable with the word 'Shore' that is the only word we use to explain were we want the dog to travel to. As with all the exercises, it is very important that only one person instructs the dog, and the less commands the better. If two or three people call to the dog, the sagacious Newfoundland merely gets confused and ends up wondering just what those silly humans are trying to do.

We then move on to holding exercises. Most Newfoundlands have a natural ability to retrieve, and make a habit of holding things in their mouth already at the puppy stage. Training the dog fetching and retrieving toys can start at an early age. Large plastic bottles can also be used, since the noise these containers make when held in the puppy's mouth gives added interest to the young dog. Just make sure you throw the bottle tops out of harms way. Throw a float with a rope attached to it a little way out into the water, and ask the dog to fetch: make this into a game, and before very long it will become great fun. After each and every successful exercise, praise the dog and show you are proud of its achievements. Every one likes to be told they have done well and that most definitely goes for Newfoundlands, because if they don't enjoy what they are being taught, they will not be obedient.

Once the Newfoundland dog gets used to holding objects in their mouths, there are a number of holding exercises they can perform. One is tow a boat, holding a rope that is held by someone in the boat. We never attach the rope to the dog or the boat, for safety reasons, so that the rope can be released at any time ether by the dog or the person. Then there is holding a life ring, with a rope around the ring which the dog can hold onto, and then take to the casualty in the water. When the person puts an arm through the inner part of the ring, the dog tows him and the ring to safety. A very similar exercise you can do with a lifeguard's torpedo, just like in the Baywatch TV show. In this exercise the lifeguard swims with the dog to the casualty, then gives the attached rope of the torpedo to the dog to pull the casualty to safety. A more difficult holding exercise, which goes against the Newfoundland's natural instincts to retrieve, is for the dog to swim out to some person, holding a life saving aid or rope in its mouth. This takes a little more practice, and not all dogs are comfortable with this exercise.

From an early age, the Newfoundland puppy should be taken out in the boat. This will give it the chance to understand the movement and sensation of traveling across the water with the wind in its coat. Since most dogs really enjoy this experience, it soon becomes hard to keep them out of the inflatable boat. When the dog has shown that it has confidence of all the basic exercises that it has been taught at the waterfront, the time has come to see what it can achieve from the boat. We use an inflatable boat, since it is more stable in the water. The tubes are rounded so there are no sharp edges, and they tend to sit lower in the water, making it much easier to help the dog back into the boat. Because the Newfoundland is by now used to swimming with its handler, we ask the handler to dive out of the boat with the dog. We can usually tell by the dog's reactions whether it is willing to follow, or better still jump with, the handler. Some dogs will do it, others will not; it's just a matter of building confidence with the dog. As I have said before, a Newfoundland has a mind of its own. The training is all about encouraging the dog and building its confidence, and remembering that the dog will only do what it feels comfortable with. Over-eager owners can at this stage very easily ruin their dogs. I have experienced people being so impatient that they physically throw the dog out of a boat and that, I'm sad to say, is the ruination of the Newfoundland and that dog may never go near a boat again.

Once we have the satisfaction that the dog is comfortable coming in and out of the boat, most of the exercises are as before. We can build up the speed of the boat gradually and there are few more amazing things to experience than a dog of this size jumping at speed from a moving boat. This is not for every Newfoundland dog, only the really accomplished and confident ones. We always train the handler to work with the dogs and in a real-life situation you would never ever send a dog alone to

A close-up of 'Bear', *Daily Mail* **Dog of the Year for 2004**

THOSE AMAZING NEWFOUNDLAND DOGS

rescue a drowning person. A person in distress and in danger of his life has the strength of ten people, and in a panic would almost certainly pull the dog under. The lifeguard works as a team with the dog, and is there to do the only job the Newfoundland cannot do, namely to reassure and comfort the casualty; the dog does the rest and takes the person to safety.

The rewards of a fully qualified Newfoundland dog doing the job it always was intended for are unequaled. It takes time and a deal of patience, and the dog will only work if it is comfortable in its environment. In my experience it's 60 % teaching the handler and 40% the dog. Most people expect their dogs to be water rescue trained in weeks. I'm afraid that is not the way it works, and if you are impatient and cannot devote the time to your dog, then it is never going to happen.

* * *

After serving my apprenticeship with my good friends from Plymouth and T.N.S (Paris), and traveling for five years to the south coast, it was time to start somewhere nearer home. The South West of England is a popular tourist destination and most of the recreational open water venues are fully exploited. I live only ten minutes from the Bristol Channel, but with the second highest rise and fall of all tidal waters in the world, the Channel is impossible to use for training dogs. A friend suggested that I try the Cotswold Water Park, the largest in the UK. Arranging a meeting with the Warden, he did not appear all that keen, but suggested that we could try a one off charity day. With nothing else on offer, we took up the idea, and went about arranging a Newfoundland rescue day for the Clic (Sargent)

The dog 'Boswell' shows what he is capable of.

charity, which look after children suffering from leukemia and other cancers. With help of close friends, business connections, and the boys from Plymouth the day turned out very well. This went on to become an annual event held each year at the same venue, but since it was a public lake, it was not suitable for routinely working the dogs. However, the Cotswold Water Park were able to point us in the right direction, namely to the owners of the other lakes that encompass the park. Most of the lakes in the area were formed by the flooding of areas dug out for the extraction of gravel; they are privately owned by aggregate companies. These lakes are excellent because the gravel filtrates the water, providing good clean quality conditions. A number of letters were sent to the various quarry owners and thankfully we had a positive response from A.R.C., since taken over by the multi national group Hanson's. Their estates manager thought that there was a lake we could use, and after a visit and agreeing terms we had at long last our very own lake for training.

Now when we had a private lake to use to train the new owners and their Newfoundland dogs, Newfound Friends was born. Mark and Sue Pawson joined the new team at the lake at Lechlade, and I am glad to say that they are still with us to this day. Mark and Sue's attitude has been first class from day one, quite simply they just love the dogs, not just their own but all Newfoundlands and if every owner followed their example, life would be much easier.

Over the past twenty years, Newfound Friends have produced a number of excellent working dogs, Don't just take my word for that statement: they have achieved a number of national awards. These have all been judged by independent people outside of the breed, with no favours to ask for their adjudication. The Animal Health Trust and Pet Plan acknowledged the work of Newfound Friends by awarding three of our dogs with their Talent award. The host of other awards our dogs have attained over the years which can be found on newfoundfriends.co.uk.

The Newfoundlands Barny, Bruce, Tess , Boswell and Whizz have all been outstanding working dogs. Barny was the first to obtain the highest level at the breed club's water tests. Barny's owner entered his dog into the tests from his own choice. Set tests for Newfoundlands had previously been tried on the continent, but were quickly abandoned as not to be the way forward to advance the best relations between dog and owner. The breed clubs in the UK have continued with these tests, and in my opinion, they have not moved forward since Barny was involved twenty years earlier. These tests are all about people and very little about the skill of the dogs. If you look at the number of judges, it far exceeds the number of dogs that enter the trials. Nor do those judges always have the qualifications to make judgments on these magnificent animals. Let's put it this way: if you take a driving test or want to learn to drive, you have to have a person that is qualified beside you. If you test a Newfoundland, anybody will do, something that ridicules the whole reason to test in the first place.

So what makes a good working Newfoundland? Most of the best dogs have a little edge to them, full of themselves and no shrinking violets. These spirited dogs probably do not have the type of temperament for someone's first Newfoundland. Tess and Whizz had both been in other homes for the first year of their lives, and came to us at a year old, It was noticeable that once given the attention, home life and love that these dogs crave, they were able to give all they had. Because they had experienced the other side of life, they become 'cling ons' and wanted to please their owners as much as they could. I got Whizz in 2005, when he was one year old, since his previous owner found him quite a handful. Whizz has without question been a fantastic dog and the awards and media attention he has attained have been unequalled. The Dogs Trust acknowledged Whizz for his outstanding bravery and intelligence when he saved the dog Topper from drowning. Topper, an elderly Irish Setter, had gone missing and fallen into a disused ground level water tank. On a cold and rapidly darkening January evening, Whizz's rescue training came to the fore. Sensing where Topper was, and the danger he was in, Whizz set off to save

THOSE AMAZING NEWFOUNDLAND DOGS

his canine friend. Following Whizz, and wondering what had attracted his attention, I found him pulling Topper to the side of the tank. The steep sides of the tank were an obstacle for both dogs, but luckily I was at hand to pull both of them out. There is no doubt that due to the failing light, and the cold temperature of the water, Topper's fate would have been sealed but for Whizz's instinctive reactions. Whizz was awarded the very first Dogs Trust Honor's medal, given to him at a prestigious ceremony at London's Guildhall.[2] Whizz has appeared in every major national newspaper in the UK. Martin Ellard's amazing pictures of this huge dog flying through the air from a speeding lifeboat caught every picture editor's attention. This media interaction brought about an appearance on the BBC programme *The One Show*. Whizz was also asked to appear live on the programme and to this day is one of only a handful of dogs to attend the live show.

What makes Whizz the most outstanding of water rescue dogs is that his confidence in his own ability enables him to work with a number of handlers. Most trained dogs only work with one person, either their owner or handler; that includes police dogs, drug detection dogs, and even obedience trained dogs. But we teamed Whizz up with eleven-year-old Ellie Bedford. While Ellie was keen to learn about the dogs, she was not so confident in the water. Teaming the two together proved to be inspirational. Whizz took with ease to his young companion and Ellie gained huge belief in herself working with an exceptional Newfoundland. Ellie has now gone on to be one of the Royal Life Saving Society's top lifeguards, winning a host of medals along the way. Newfound Friends are very proud of Ellie and have high hopes for another rookie lifeguard, Chloe.

The Newfoundland dogs of Newfound Friends have been honoured by the Royal Life Saving Society, for their life saving skills and promotion of water safety; they are the only dogs to attain such awards and commendations from the Society. The BBC news featured the dogs and the work they undertake to promote water safety with the Rookie Life Guard scheme in a feature that went worldwide promoting water safety for children. The dogs are great 'ice breakers' and a dog that swims and knows what it is about when it comes to water safety can impress children far more than words of advice from adults - who always get it wrong in the minds of children anyway. Olympic Gold medalist Sharron Davies was so impressed with the dogs and what they do to promote safety in and around the water, that she has become a patron of Newfound Friends.

A pivotal point in the history of Newfound Friends came when the *Daily Telegraph* published a feature about the organization by Celia Haddon, coupled with some outstanding action pictures of the dogs at work.[3] The response from this article was amazing and gave Newfound Friends a huge boost. Twelve television production companies were soon in touch, and we received over seven hundred letters, some even from prisoners, proving that some inmates in jail read good quality papers! The feature in the *Telegraph* was only sixteen years ago, and how times have changed: we hardly ever receive a letter these days, since nowadays it's all emails!

The *Telegraph* feature also brought about an invitation from St.John Hartnell OBE, the man behind the 500th anniversary of the founding of the 'New Found Lands' by John Cabot, an Italian who had set sail from Bristol in a ship named the *Matthew*. Costing well over two million pounds, a replica of this ship was built in Bristol to replicate the epic journey. St.John asked the dogs of Newfound Friends to be part of these historic celebrations and the dogs to be the official mascots of the *Matthew*. The Newfoundlands played their full part in the anniversary, from the launch of the *Matthew* in Bristol to its arrival at Bonavista, Newfoundland. I was invited to the *Matthew's* arrival at Bonavista, which was attended by H.R.M. the Queen and a host of dignitaries. Canadian and American owners of Newfoundlands attended in large numbers, some traveling the full width of the vast continent of America in their camper vans with their dogs, an expedition they aptly called the Great Newfoundland

Dog Trek. The Queen, a well know dog person herself, was greatly intrigued with the Newfoundland dogs and the distance their owners had crossed to be part of this historic reenactment. St.John Hartnell OBE, patron of Newfound Friends, thank you.

The Newett family from Oxfordshire, renowned for their generosity approached us after a TV programme that featured the work of Newfound Friends with children. Each year the Newett family raises funds for special good causes. They asked if we would like to have a dog purchased especially for us to train to work with children. The dog was to be owned by us, and trained to become the first dog to work with terminally ill children. This had to be a very special dog indeed, and as it turned out he was a tremendous ambassador for the Newfoundland breed. Bear was a Landseer Newfoundland, and I often likened him to Cary Grant: tall (36 inches to the shoulder), handsome and a true gentleman. Bear's work as a companion to terminally ill children at the Children's Hospice South West was rewarding, in the way that he tended to bring people together, out of their own environment.

Extract from the *Western Daily Press* –"The friendly way in which Bear greeted a family and their daughter Courtney, whose heroic fight to survive an illness that will not take her beyond childhood, is an example of his loving disposition . As he held out a large paw the little girl instinctively stroked the big bundle of fur in front of her. It was a magical moment for everyone as the pain and heartache of an incurable condition faded from their minds. The often forgotten siblings of terminally ill children can also benefit from the dogs and Courtney's brother and sister were all at the meeting to have fun with

The Newfoundland puppy 'Ted', eight weeks old. Ted is now a strapping Newfoundland male, and shows promise at water rescue

Bear as well. Adam aged ten, struggled to keep pace with Bear as he lolloped along, his floppy ears pinned back by the wind. Bear weighs thirteen stone but moves like a Greyhound with his long legs. Adam, who found it hard to understand the enormity of his sister's condition, could hardly contain his delight as he raced with the huge dog. Later Hayley also joined in the fun and although she and Bear were as tall as each other, he did not intimidate the seven year old in any way. The whole meeting was a perfect example of the very special affinity between Newfoundland dogs and children."[4]

Jill Farwell and Jo Hern were two inspirational women that set about raising the funds to provide a Children's Hospice in the South West of England. Each of the ladies had terminally ill children of their own, and the long trip to Oxfordshire to get support from a Hospice there proved to be taxing. With the use of a kitchen table that acted as an office, and with houses to run and terminally ill children to look after, they set about raising literally millions of pounds to establish a hospice closer to home. A children's hospice offers very sick children suffering from conditions which mean they will die in childhood and their families, providing respite and relaxation, friendship and a sense of community, sharing in the 24-hour care of the very sick child, expert palliative and terminal care, and support for the whole family into bereavement. Impressed with the dedication of these wonderful ladies, Newfound Friends has supported their valiant efforts unstintingly over the years. Jill Farwell MBE stressed the value of dogs like Bear in disarming tension, worry and fear in children faced with incurable illness. She said "you can see in their faces, they can hardly contain their excitement, I think Newfoundlands have a sixth sense." Bear described as "a spectacular dog" was awarded the *Daily Mail* 'Dog of The Year' award for 2004, and received a gold medal for his work as a companion dog to terminally ill children.[5]

Newfound Friends has over the years supported a host of children's charities, and always welcome children to be part of our organization. We have hosted children from Belarus affected by the nuclear disaster at near by Chernobyl, children that still are and have been in the foster care of our members and many disadvantaged and disabled young people. The Newfound Friends attend all the major festivals such as The International Festival of the Sea in Dartmouth and the Bristol and Cardiff harbour festivals, to give displays of the life saving skills of their highly trained dogs. To date well over £750,000 has been raised for various good causes and this year it has been back to the beginning! Our youngest member, six-year-old Tol, has leukemia. This very brave little boy, who is in the care of Newfound Friends, has two more years of treatment ahead of him to fight off this very serious illness. We intend to support Tol as much as we can and show our support that we are with him in every way. Tol asks that we raise funds for other children fighting against cancer, which we will try our best to achieve, but this appeal is in no way all about money: it is showing our support for our youngest member. The first fundraising day we held was for the Clic (Sargent) charity, and it now appears we have turned full circle with Tol's Appeal.

NEWFOUND FRIENDS
by Ellesha Bedford

I have been working with Newfoundland dogs for five years now and I believe they have changed my life. My name is Ellesha Bedford, a lot of people call me Ellie, and I am 16 years of age. My first encounter with a Newfoundland was when my parents decided to get one, at this point I had no idea what they were capable of. This was our first Newfoundland, Amy. After a couple of weeks we were told about their love of water so decided to join the Newfound Friends water rescue club, and to be honest I am glad we did. Every Sunday we train with the Newfoundland dogs and each week I learn more and more about what they can do. Since joining Newfound Friends we have gained two new additions to our family, Ozzie and Frankie.

After about two months of coming down to the lake, Dave, the founder of Newfound Friends, decided to pair me up with Whizz, a very experienced dog when it came to water rescue. My first thoughts where, "great, I can learn from a pro" but then Dave explained what I had to do. To be honest, I probably should have told you before that I was not the most confident in water, but I trusted Dave and knew he would not just throw me in at the deep end! So from then on, each week Dave would have me swimming alongside Whizz, and slowly we built a connection, Whizz was giving me the confidence I needed. Not long after this me and Whizz where diving off the boat into all sorts of water and I found myself no longer scared of the deep waters as long as Whizz was there. During the time I spent working with Whizz, Newfound Friends made newspaper headlines and many TV appearances, including The One Show which was a great experience for me, one of which I will never forget. Newfound Friends itself is made up of many people each with their own number of dogs, each working together to make a day run smoothly or a display look good.

Each year the club partake in various displays and sponsored rescues, including; Mumbles, Bristol Harbour festival, Isle of Wight, Dartmouth, Portishead, each are amazing events and are only a few that Newfound Friends participate in. At Bristol people are crowding the walls, and there are crowds of people to see in each direction, edging closer to see the Newfoundlands perform. Portishead is where most of the sponsored rescues take place and there is always a mass turn out of family and friends, ready to support their loved ones as they jump into the cold waters. Portishead was also the first event I was involved in when I joined Newfound Friends and I remember it well. I had to run down the pontoon, Whizz close behind, dive off the end and rescue the person in the water. While working with Whizz I found a love, not only in working with the dogs but jumping in to save someone, so I decided to take up Lifesaving, which would also give me some qualifications for doing such work, and make it safer for the people around me and myself. So I joined Wantage Lifesavers, and to date, I have participated in all kinds of lifesaving competitions, doing well in a lot and frequently being placed. Furthermore I have achieved numerous qualifications, of which there are; lifesaving 1, 2 and 3, life support 1 and life support 3, Bronze medallion and more recently, Bronze and Silver cross and my Award of Merit. I continually train twice a week and without the Newfoundland dogs, without Newfound Friends, I would not have found this love for lifesaving, which I can put to practice each time we train at charity events and at sponsored rescues.

Personally, over the next few years, while continually raising money for charities, I want to make people aware of the dangers of water and I believe the dogs will be a great help in this. So many young people are unaware of the dangers of open water or do not know what to do if there friends get in to trouble in the water. I want to change that, and help prevent these accidents from happening. In 2011, Newfound Friends held a lifesavers day at the lake we train in, the young lifesavers loved watching the dogs do their work. Doing rescues they often re-enact in a pool, simply one of the Newfoundlands pulling ten people in to safety, any lifesaver knows how hard that is! With the help of the dogs we were able to show the lifesavers the dangers of the cold water whilst giving them an experience they would not forget. To date I continue working with Newfoundlands each week, and would not wish to be doing anything different. I love participating in the charity events and sponsored rescues; I enjoy raising money and seeing the excitement on people's faces when a massive dog jumps towards them. I am determined to continue working with Newfoundland dogs throughout my life, during which I am sure I will learn so much more about these amazing animals.

MY LIFE WITH NEWFOUND FRIENDS,
by Victoria Welsh

My first experience of Newfoundland dogs was at the Annual Bristol Regatta in Bristol Docks. There was a display of the dogs rescuing people from the water. I was immediately taken in by the power and size of these beautiful dogs, so much so that I went along to the tent where they were operating from, to see the dogs close up and find out more about them. It was there I met my good friend David Pugh, founder of Newfound Friends.

Since David could see that I was quite impressed and enthusiastic about the dogs and the work that they do, and asked a lot of questions, he asked me if I would like to be 'rescued' by one of the dogs. With no doubt in my mind I said yes. David told me that the Newfoundland dog team went to various venues around the country, to raise money for various charities like children's hospices, Guide Dogs for the Blind, and Hearing Dogs for the Deaf. He invited me to come along to the Portishead Marina to participate in a charity event they were going to do.

The day had come and on my arrival I was given a wetsuit to wear during the event. I cannot describe the feeling I had when I was 'rescued' by David's dog Whizz. Before I knew it I was in the water with David by my side, telling me what I had to do when Whizz reached me. Then I saw Whizz jump from the boat and come swimming towards me. I held on to his harness like I had been told and he towed me back to the boat, and safety. It was a fantastic feeling, and it was then that I understood how powerful the dogs are.

Realizing that I was now in love with the dogs and the wonderful charity work they do, I eagerly accepted when David asked me if I would like to become a member of the team. I did all my training with David's dog Whizz, and we now have a bond together, built up over a period of time. During that time I got to know Whizz and his way of working so that I was learning from him too. The training is all about hard work and dedication, in all winds and weathers, along with a lot of patience.

Also, I had to be prepared to give up my time every weekend throughout the season, something that I did very willingly. During my period of training and watching the other members of the team with their dogs, I became more and more aware of the needs of the dogs, like their diet, grooming and healthcare. Even after two and a half years working with the Newfoundland dogs, I am still learning.

Fourteen months ago, I was asked whether I would like to have a dog of my own. Without hesitation, I said yes, knowing about the dogs and what I was going to take on. Along came my dog Indy, a five-month-old Landseer Newfoundland. He is now nineteen months old and still a puppy really, but you would not think it to look at him. Indy has now been in training with David and me for the past twelve months. Indy and I have built up a tremendous trust between us. Together with the other team members, we go to various venues to talk about our work with the dogs, and raise awareness of the charities we support.

Indy and I have featured in the TV documentary 'Extraordinary Dogs' and another called 'You and Your Dogs'. Indy has also taken part in a photo shoot for a fundraising event that we very much enjoyed doing. Having Indy has changed my life in so many ways, and for the better. The things we do together and the places where we go. He is my companion, my shadow, my new life, he makes me happy and he is always there for me like I am for him. My lookout on life has changed since I got my Indy, and I now have a meaning in life, doing the things I love the most, and being a team member in Newfound Friends and helping as many charities as we can. I bless the day I saw the dog display by Newfound Friends at the Bristol Regatta. None of this would have been possible if I had not met David Pugh and his dog Whizz, a truly remarkable man and a wonderful dog.

Whizz looks rather quizzically at the madcap former 'Baywatch' actor David Hasselhoff, at a recent newspaper photo shoot.

CHAPTER 19.
THE CHANGING NEWFOUNDLAND DOG

> I am the noble Newfoundland,
> My voice is loud and deep;
> I keep a watch all through the night
> While other people sleep.
>
> Another children's rhyme, about a
> watchful Newfoundland dog.

It is today generally accepted that animals, dogs not excluded, also have a history, although this (cultural) history is largely a product of their interactions with human beings.[1] Some of the most distinctive breeds of dog, like the Newfoundland, the St Bernard dog and the Irish Wolfhound, have histories of their own.[2] Even the lowly Turnspit dog, a today extinct breed that ran inside a dog-wheel to propel kitchen machinery, has left behind enough lore for its history to have been recently compiled.[3] The problem is that the human fascination with dogs has corrupted canine history through centuries of distortion, sentimentality, and deliberate falsification. A prime example is the legend of Greyfriars Bobby, the little Edinburgh terrier supposed to have kept vigil on his master's grave for fourteen years. Although the cult of this saintly dog is still promoted by the Edinburgh tourist office, it has been demonstrated that Bobby was an unconscious impostor, taking advantage of the sentimental Victorian notions of how a dog ought to behave, to make a comfortable life for himself in the cemetery. So many people came to see this supposedly faithful dog that the verger and a local restaurateur made good money from exploiting Bobby; when the original canine paragon died of old age, these two got hold of a second Bobby to continue their profitable scheme.[4] Nor has the history of the St Bernard dog been free from distortion. Two veritable cornerstones in the annals of these dogs, namely the keg of brandy they carried attached to their collars, and the famous dog Barry rescuing a child by having it ride on his back, are both sentimental falsifications.[5]

As we have seen, the history of Newfoundland dog has not been free of various undesirable additions, like the yarns about that spectral trio, Boatswain, Hero and Rigel. Much more seriously, the falsifications introduced into Newfoundland dog history by Dr William Gordon Stables and two other Victorian dog fanciers have never been rebutted. As demonstrated in this book, the solid black Newfoundland is not the original breed, and there were white and black (or white and brown) spotted Newfoundlands in Britain for a century before the first solid black dogs with a similar phenotype were introduced. Being dominant over 'spotted', the 'Solid' gene soon made an impact on the Newfoundland dog phenotype, particularly since the solid black dogs became highly fashionable in late Victorian times, with selective breeding playing a part. The term 'Landseer Newfoundland' is a misnomer, since the white and black dogs can be proven to have occurred in Britain many years before Landseer's time.

THOSE AMAZING NEWFOUNDLAND DOGS

A postcard posted from Bonn in 1910. The text on the back explains that it was fashionable among the Bonn students to walk their large dogs in the boulevards. If one dog barked at another, as this Landseer Newfoundland seems on the verge of doing, the students had to fight a duel with swords, to obtain one of those scars in the face that were considered desirable among the Teutonic youngsters in those days.

In this book, the 'Newfoundland Dogs in the News' chapters have introduced some extraordinary true stories about sagacious and brave Newfoundlands in history. Not only could these amazing dogs catch crayfish, or fish for salmon, but they were able to victoriously fight a seal, or a shark, in the open sea. The Newfoundland dog's use of water shows many instances of problem solving and creative action. A Newfoundland dog pursued after biting a child took refuge in the water, relying on its superior swimming ability. A Newfoundland annoyed by a smaller dog might drop it into the water; in a fight with another large dog, it might pull its antagonist into the water and deliberately drown it. The Newfoundland's strong instinct to retrieve objects from the water, or to save a drowning dog or human, has been very much in evidence. It has been clearly demonstrated that there is a multitude of true accounts of Newfoundlands being ordered into the water by their masters to save a drowning person, or spontaneously plunging into the water to go to the rescue. There are also many true accounts of Newfoundlands either swimming to shore from a ship, carrying a rope, or taking a rope from the shore to a stricken vessel. The sheer power of these dogs in the water is something to be marvelled at, like the dog swimming fifteen miles against a very strong wind, for eighteen hours, or the extraordinary story of the Newfoundland dog surviving a shipwreck by standing on some wreckage.

This postcard was posted on Dec. 24th 1904, and printed in Prussia. Most likely, it is from a series of Christmas cards showing similar Landseers with children.

Already the dog author Rawdon Lee found it peculiar that so many early Victorian authors extolled the superior intellect of the Newfoundland dog; in his opinion, they were much like other dogs. He has had support from Professor Stanley Coren's influential *The Intelligence of Dogs*, which ranks the Newfoundland as number 34 out of 78 breeds, with regard to obedience and working intelligence. Dr Stables and his fellow Victorian dog fanciers would have considered this an insult to their sagacious breed. Nor have some of the present-day Newfoundland dog enthusiasts appreciated Professor Coren's ranking of their breed, objecting that intelligence does not equal obedience. They have pointed out that although the Newfoundland is hampered by its independent nature and short attention span, the dogs (Landseers more so that solid-coloured dogs, some say) are definitely more clever than most large breeds, particularly with regard to problem solving. An anecdote in Professor Coren's book would support their case: a tired Newfoundland bitch was annoyed by a yapping little Maltese terrier wanting to play. In the end, the great black dog seized the little terrier by the scruff of the neck and walked out to the bathroom. Here she deposited it into a large, empty bathtub, where it was securely confined, before contentedly returning and settling down to sleep.[6] This not only shows a very good example of creative action in dogs, but also that the old stories of sagacious Newfoundlands ducking annoying little dogs in ponds or ditches are likely to be true.

Professor Coren also has a very low opinion of the Newfoundland as a watchdog. In my opinion, this is true for most bitches, and also many male dogs, due to their placid and friendly nature, and lack of suspicion towards strangers. Any burglar who takes on a large and alert Newfoundland male used to guard his territory, and being protective of the other members of the household, may well be mistaken to rely too much on the Professor's advice, however. It is curious to note that many of the early Newfoundland dogs in Britain, Lord Byron's Boatswain prominent among them, were known for their pugnacious nature. According to many sources, they were also excellent watchdogs: vigilant and wary of strangers. In 'Newfoundland Dogs in the News', we have encountered many accounts of these dogs protecting their masters against robbers, or fighting off burglars. The *Times* newspaper provides many examples of burglars emerging second best from encounters with fierce Newfoundlands, and even reports of smugglers and thieves themselves keeping Newfoundlands to set on the police and customs officers.[7]

To analyze the problem of the changing Newfoundland, it is it important to take into account the work of Professor Jasper Rine and coworkers, with regard to canine genetics.[8] A Border Collie is a very intelligent dog, concentrated and intense; it has a strong herding instinct: crouching and 'giving eye' when it sees some recalcitrant sheep, or sometimes even a human being it considers to require some herding. The present-day Newfoundland is friendly and easygoing, has webbed feet and loves water, and holds its tail high. Rine and his colleagues cross-bred a male Border Collie with a Newfoundland bitch; the union of this mis-matched couple produced seven healthy puppies, which were in turn bred with each other, resulting in a third generation of 23 'grandchildren'. These dogs exhibited a seemingly quite random combination of 'Border Collie' and 'Newfoundland' traits: for example, one of the dogs might be very intelligent but also friendly and easygoing, holding its tail high but hating water, and possessing the herding instinct to 'give eye'. It is important that the typical traits of these dogs appear to be inherited separately.

With these arguments in mind, let us return to the early Newfoundland dogs. These dogs were selectively bred to have webbed feet and a talent for water work, but also to be intelligent and altruistic, with a strong instinct to rescue some person falling into the water. The dogs should also be watchful and wary of strangers, not fearful to 'have a scrap', and ready to defend their masters. Unlike the sheepdogs, mainly trained to follow the signals of their masters, the working Newfoundlands were bred to take initiatives of their own; it would not do if the ship's dog stood waiting for orders when a net full

This a single thin cardboard sheet, New Year card with a verse, and a very nice illustration showing a large mainly black Newfoundland with a small child.

of fish was lost, or a sailor drowned. Understandably, these remarkable dogs were widely admired in Georgian and Victorian Britain. The stories of Newfoundland sagacity recounted in this book are only the tip of the iceberg; there is no wonder these amazing dogs were so widely featured in magazines, children's books and books of anecdotes on natural history. We will never know what genetic event triggered the development of these remarkably intelligent early Newfoundland dogs.

A recent study aimed to determine whether dogs would seek help from a bystander if their owner feigned a heart attack, or pretended to be trapped underneath a falling bookcase; they did not.[9] There is a marked contrast between these very Ordinary Dogs standing by uselessly when their owner was in trouble, and the heroics of the Newfoundlands described earlier in this chapter; for example, the extraordinary 'Princess May' not just sensing danger to the child on the tram line, but taking appropriate action with commendable alacrity. There was clearly something special about the Newfoundland dogs in those days, something that set them apart from other breeds of dog.

With time, the Newfoundland dog fanciers valued different qualities in their dogs, and adapted their breeding accordingly. For example, since they were not used as watchdogs, there was no need for them to be watchful and wary of strangers; in recent times, the dogs have become increasingly placid and friendly, not just to their owners, but to everyone else. A calm and stolid temperament, great size and

A postcard of a winning Landseer Newfoundland dog, named Landseer Don. This rare card was most likely published by the dog's owner, since not only does it have some of the dog's show wins from 1904/5 printed on the front, but also hand-written entries on the back about its wins at Yeovil and Crystal Palace dog shows.

solid black fur were considered as valuable characteristics, whereas the spirit and watchfulness formerly exhibited by the dogs was no longer appreciated. The dog Boo who rescued the drowning American gold-dredger, and the remarkably intelligent Whizz, seem to be throwbacks to the earlier type. It is interesting that in his chapter, David Pugh describes Whizz as a 'special' dog, more spirited and edgy than most Newfoundlands. It would appear as if selective breeding in the last 150 years has led to the Newfoundland dogs losing a good deal of their pugnacity and guarding instinct along the way – and also some of the intelligence for which these amazing dogs were once rightly admired.

NOTES

CHAPTER 1.
INTRODUCTION
1. There is a profusion of Newfoundland dog breed monographs, of variable quality. Among the more cerebral of them is M. Booth Chern, *The Complete Newfoundland* (Richmond, Va 1955), revised and considerably improved as *The New Complete Newfoundland* (Howell Book House 1975). C. Cooper, *The Newfoundland* (Pontypool 1975) and K. Maynard Drury, *This is the Newfoundland* (Neptune City NJ 1978) are also valuable sources. There are also many foreign-language breed monographs, notably A. Heim, *Das Neufundländerhund* (Mannheim 1934), K. Brönnecke, *Das Neufundländer Buch* (Osnabrück 1994), R. Gravero, *Le Terre-Neuve* (Paris 1998) and B. Gothen Christensen, *Newfoundlandshunden* (Västerås 1981). There are fewer books dealing with the history of Newfoundland dogs. F. Pratt & C. Cooper, *A Friend in Deed* (Penryn 2002) is a useful contribution. B. Hynes, *The Noble Newfoundland Dog* (Halifax, NS 2005) is an interesting jumble of true and false stories. N. Waters, *The Newfoundland in Heritage and Art*, (the Hague 2006) is a very valuable book, profusely illustrated and with a long bibliography of relevant works. The Deutscher Landseer Club has produced three valuable monographs, or rather *Zuchtbücher*, of which the second *Zuchtbuch* has particular merit.
2. Mrs Di Sellers and Mr David Pugh have provided a chapter each for this book, about areas where they have special expertise. Another chapter has been adapted from Edward Jesse's old dog book *Anecdotes of Dogs*. All illustrations in this book are from the private collections of Jan Bondeson and Di Sellers, unless otherwise stated. All images in Chapter 18, and also the fourth image in Chapter 13, are photographs by Martin Ellard or David Pugh, copyright Newfound Friends. The second, third, fourth and sixth images in Chapter 4 are copyright Nottingham Museums and Galleries, Newstead Abbey.

CHAPTER 2.
THE ORIGINS AND EARLY HISTORY OF THE NEWFOUNDLAND DOG
1. For reviews of Newfoundland dog history, see E.C. Ash, *Dogs, their History and Development* (London 1927), Vol. 2, 565-87; M. Booth Chern, *The Complete Newfoundland* (Richmond, Va 1955), 15-42; C. Cooper, *The Newfoundland* (Pontypool 1975), 1-17; K. Maynard Drury, *This is the Newfoundland* (Neptune City NJ 1978), 22-43.
2. B. Hynes, *The Noble Newfoundland Dog* (Halifax, NS 2005), 8-19
3. H.G. Parker *et al.* (*Science* 304 [2004], 1160-4).
4. Y. Li *et al.* (*Animal* 5 [2011], 1868-73)
5. E.C. Ash, *Dogs, Their History and Development* (London 1927), Vol. 2, 566.
6. Anon., *The Gentleman Farrier* (London 1732).
7. National Archives ADM 106/905/197.
8. C. Matenaar in the *Zuchtbuch Nr. 2* of the Deutscher Landseer Club (Pfungstadt 1989), 98-100. The alleged 17th century portraits of Newfoundland dogs in this valuable article do not depict Newfoundlands, however. The dog in the 1625 portrait of Sir Humphrey Styles is a Great Rough water dog, the one with the young Sir Henry Sidney is a setter, and the animals in various early German paintings are hunting dogs.

The dog 'Luttine' in Jean-Baptiste Oudry's 'Misse et Luttine' is likely to be a *Gredine*, a spaniel-like French breed fashionable at the time.
9. *Times* Feb 29 2008.

CHAPTER 3.
SOME EARLY NEWFOUNDLAND DOGS IN BRITAIN
1. *London Chronicle* Oct 8 1789.
2. *Bath Chronicle* Oct 15 1789.
3. *Felix Farley's Bristol Journal* Oct 10 1789.
4. Sir W. Gilbey, & E.B. Cuming, *George Morland, His Life and Works* (London 1907); C. Matenaar in the *Zuchtbuch Nr. 2* of the Deutscher Landseer Club (Pfungstadt 1989), 104-5.
5. *Leeds Mercury* Feb 22 1894
6. *Pall Mall Gazette* June 14 1879
7. http://www.greatbradley.suffolk.gov.uk/familyhistory/wilder/wilderhistory.htm
8. *Animal World NS 3 [1908], 87.*
9. F. Pratt & C. Cooper, *A Friend in Deed* (Penryn 2002), 48.
10. E. Jesse, *Anecdotes of Dogs* (London 1873), 154-6.
11. www.southbucks.gov.uk/includes/.../t/taplow_list_descriptions.pdf
12. *Times* April 8 1803 3a; April 28 1803 2d. Admiral Macnamara's obituary is in the *Age* Jan 29 1826.
13. H. Belsey (*Burlington Magazine* 129 [1987], 735-6); J. Egerton, *George Stubbs, Painter* (New Haven 2007), 92-4, 616-7.
14. *Morning Post* June 30 1832.
15. F.L. Carter (*Connoisseur* 77 [1927], 215-21).
16. J. North, *The Chronicles of Oatlands* (Oatlands 1875), 64-6; J.W. Lindus Forge, *The Dog's Cemetery, Oatlands* (Walton and Weybridge Local History Society Monograph No. 18, 1974); M. Symes (*Garden History* 9 [1981], 136-56); H. Belsey (*Burlington Magazine* 129 [1987], 735-6);

CHAPTER 4.
NEW LIGHT ON LORD BYRON AND 'BOATSWAIN'
1. *Daily Mirror* Nov 14 1903, 5.
2. T. Moore, *Letters and Journals of Lord Byron* (London 1901), 38, 44, 80.
3. C. Smith (*Kennel Gazette* 113(8) [1991], 48-9); C. Kenyon-Jones (*Byron Journal* 28 [2000], 85-8).
4. *Sunday Times* June 22 2008.
5. R. Lloyd-Jones (*Byron Journal* 26 [1998], 91-7) and A.M. Stauffer (*Byron Journal* 26 [1998], 82-90).
6. *Chambers's Journal* May 3 1884; B.R McElderry Jr (*Modern Language Notes* 58 [1943], 553-4); see also N.B. Penny (*Connoisseur* 192 [1976], 298-303), C. Kenyon-Jones, *Kindred Brutes* (Aldershot 2001), 23-50, K. Guthke (*Zeitschrift für Volkskunde* 99 [2003], 1-28) and I.H. Tague (*Eighteenth-Century Studies* 41 [2008], 289-306).
7. W. Parry, *The Last Days of Lord Byron* (London 1825), 75.
8. British Library Add Mss 56549.
9. British Library Add Mss 56549, 131.
10. N. Waters, *The Newfoundland in Heritage and Art*, (the Hague 2006), 205-9; R. Preece & J. Clewlow (*Veterinary History* 15 [2009], 10-15).
11. *Bury & Norwich Post* Oct 12 1825.

CHAPTER 5.
NEWFOUNDLAND DOGS IN THE NEWS 1750-1800
1. This advertisement for what must have been a fairly odd-looking animal is the earliest mention of a Newfoundland dog in any British newspaper.
2. This brief advertisement, which is unlikely to have the desired result due to the absence of a description of the dog, is the earliest recorded newspaper use of the term 'Newfoundland dog'.
3. A most remarkable story, which has the semblance of truth; how could an 18th-century journalist invent

4. This is the earliest example of life-saving Newfoundland dogs in any UK newspaper.
5. This 'bull-dog' is very likely to have been an Old English Bulldog, a breed today extinct; they were larger and more formidable that the present-day bulldogs.
6. A satirical account of 'John James Rousseau', a philosopher not held in high esteem in Britain in 1796.

CHAPTER 6.
EDWARD JESSE'S ANECDOTES ON NEWFOUNDLAND DOGS
1. Edward Jesse is in the Oxford DNB. His obituary was in *Times* March 31 1868 and *Gentleman's Magazine* 4s. 5 [1868], 682.
2. This dog really existed, see *Chatterbox* May 26 1879.
3. This yarn, emanating from the hometown of Greyfriars Bobby, is quite hard to take seriously. Like most of his contemporary accumulators of anecdotes on animals, Edward Jesse was quite a credulous man.

CHAPTER 7.
CARLO THE ACTING NEWFOUNDLAND DOG
1. J. Boaden, *The Life of Mrs Jordan* (London 1831), vol 2, 149-51; D. Donald, *Picturing Animals in Britain* (New Haven and London 2007), 136; also the useful homepage www.dogdrama.com. Onstage canines and their significance is discussed by M. Dobson (*Performance Research* 5(2) [2000], 116-24), M. Peterson (*The Drama Review* 51(1) [2007], 33-48), and T. Grant in B. Boehrer (Ed.), *A Cultural History of Animals* 3 [2007], 95-117. Other articles of relevance to onstage animals are those by S Duffy (*British Art Journal* 3 (3) [2002], 25-35), J. Stokes (*NTQ* 20 [2004], 138-54) and M. Pomerance in B.K. Grant (Ed.), *The Schirmer Encyclopedia of Film* (New York 2007), vol. 1, 79-84.
2. *Derby Mercury* Dec 15 1803; *Hampshire Telegraph* Jan 16 1804; Morning Chronicle Feb 13 1804; *Spirit of the Public Journals* for 1804, 42-3.
3. *Morning Chronicle* Dec 15 1803.
4. *Hampshire Telegraph* Feb 29 1804.
5. *Morning Post* Dec 9 1803.
6. *Morning Post* Dec 8 1803.
7. *Times* Nov 5 1804 2f.
8. E. Fenwick, *The Life of the Famous Dog Carlo* (London 1809); *Sporting Magazine* for 1804; see also *Dublin University Magazine* 58 [1861], 224-5 where Carlo is described as "a splendid specimen of the Newfoundland breed."
9. *Morning Chronicle* Oct 12 1805; *New York Times* Dec 11 1898.
10. M.D. George, *Catalogue of Political and Personal Satires* (London 1978), vol. 8, 232-3, 251-2, 270, 379. 573, 702-3, 881.
11. *Bentley's Miscellany* 13 [1843], 372.
12. *Times* May 31 1811 3b.

CHAPTER 8.
SOME OTHER ACTING NEWFOUNDLAND DOGS
1. *Weekly Entertainer* 59 [1819], 415-8. There are short accounts of Victorian dog drama in H. Chance Newton, *Crime and the Drama* (London 1927), 84-6, and M.R. Booth, *English Melodrama* (London 1965), 86-7.
2. *Times* April 11 1820 2c and March 26 1821 3b.
3. A.H. Saxon, *Enter Foot and Horse* (New Haven 1968); M. Kwint (*Past & Present* 174 [2002], 72-115.
4. P. Fitzgerald, *The World behind the Scenes* (London 1881), 80-2.
5. *Age* Oct 8 1826, 591.
6. *Times* March 18 1828 3c; *Era* March 18 1828.
7. *Harlequin* June 13 1829, 13; *Times* Jan 19 1829 4a, Nov 3 1830 6c, Dec 6 1830 5c, Dec 17 1830 2e and Oct 26 1831 2b.

8. On Cony and Blanchard, see M. Morley, *The Old Marylebone Theatre* (London 1960), 3-17; M.H. Winter, *Theatre of Marvels* (London 1964), 175-89; G. Odell, *Annals of the New York Stage*, various entries in volumes 5-9; G. Morice (*Notes and Queries* 188 [1945], 250-2); *Caledonian Mercury* June 13 1842; *Times* July 8 1846 4a; *Theatrical Journal* 3 [1842], 204, 4 [1843], 268 and 7 [1846], 401. Also various texts at www.circushistory.org.
9. *Era* Oct 18 1840, 5.
10. *Blackburn Standard* June 13 1849.
11. *Era* Oct 12 1856 and Aug 22 1858.
12. *Era* Nov 11 1860.
13. R. Lee, *Not so Dumb* (New York 1970), D. Rothel, *Great Show Business Animals* (San Diego 1980), 66-183, A. Lloyd, *Hollywood Dogs* (London 2004) and P. Haining, *Lassie* (London 2006).

CHAPTER 9.
NEWFOUNDLAND DOGS IN THE NEWS 1800-1850
1. An extract from a long account of the tremendous gales at Lowestoft.
2. The end of a long pursuit of a thief.
3. From an account of some poachers on trial at the Aylesbury assizes.
4. Reprinted from the *Lincoln Gazette*.
5. From an account of the rescue of the *Chance* of Speydrove, in a hurricane off the bay at St Margaret's Hope, South Ronaldshay.
6. From an account of the rescue of the crew of the *Mary*, of St John's, N.B., off Whiting Bay, near Youghal.

CHAPTER 10.
THE CULT OF THE NEWFOUNDLAND DOG
1. E. Jesse, *Anecdotes of Dogs* (London 1873), 133-84; W.H.G. Kingston, *Stories of Animal Sagacity* (London 1874); Rev. C. Williams, *Dogs and their Ways* (London 1893), 154-72.
2. L. Johannesson in H. Brander Jonsson et al. (Eds.), *Historiens Vingslag* (Stockholm 1987), 232-60.
3. *Times* Nov 5 1812 4a.
4. 4. *Morning Post* March 11 1834.
5. *Times* Sept 14 1839.
6. *Times* Oct 9 1839.
7. *Liverpool Mercury* June 19 1829.
8. E.C. Ash, *Dogs, Their History and Development* (London 1927), vol. 2, 571-3.
9. *Illustrated Police News* July 4 1868.
10. *Manchester Times* March 16 1872; *Cheshire Observer* March 16 1872; *Illustrated Police News* March 30 1872.
11. *Star* June 17 1875.
12. *Western Mail* Aug 8 1892.
13. *The Age* Nov 15 2011; www.nma.gov.au/collections.
14. *Daily Mirror* Feb 12 1914; *Northern Advocate* June 16 1914.
15. See footnotes 4, 7.8, 8, 8.1 and 8.2 above, and chapter 8 footnote 10; also 'Newfoundland dogs in the News' Oct 28 1793, May 7 1801, Aug 20 1825, Nov 7 1829, Aug 24 1832, Aug 20 1836 and Aug 20 1882.
16. See Footnotes 3 and 7 above; also 'Newfoundland dog in the News' Aug 19 1782, Sept 15 1787, Aug 4 1796, Dec 31 1803, June 9 1804, Aug 6 1806, July 9 1808, Sept 30 1808, Dec 20 1809, May 15 1815, Dec 23 1819, Sept 14 1821, Jan 13 1850, April 1 1860, July 14 1868.
17. 'Newfoundland Dogs in the News' May 25 1821, June 9 1829, Dec 4 1837 and Dec 7 1838.
18. Anon. (*Notes and Queries* 4s. 11 [1873], 10-1).
19. *Freeman's Journal* Nov 10 1896; *Lloyd's Weekly Newspaper* Nov 15 1896; *Daily News* Dec 16 1896.
20. For more information about collecting dogs, see J. Bondeson, *Amazing Dogs* (Stroud 2011), 104-18.
21. *Times* Aug 27 1912 4e; *Daily Mirror* March 23 1912, 10 and April 22 1913, 3.
22. *Animal World* 31 [1900], 40-1. A Dachshund named Fritz would hardly have been made welcome at one of these conventions for patriotic collecting dogs.
23. On the Victorian dog-stealing racket, see P. Howell, Flush and the Banditti, in C. Philo & C. Wilbert (Eds),

Animal Spaces, Beastly Places (London 2000), 35-55.
24. *Daily News* March 19 1858.
25. *Daily News* June 2 1856.
26. *Era* November 20 1842. On the impostor Naundorff's eventful career, see J. Bondeson, *The Great Pretenders* (New York 2004), 13-71.
27. *Morning Post* December 15 1842 and January 17 1843
28. The standard biography of Henry Russell is A. Lamb, *Life on the Ocean Wave* (Croydon 2007).
29. *Bristol Mercury* Oct 28 1895.
30. *Era* March 31 1850.
31. *New York Times* Dec 7 1900.
32. J.A. Rupert-Jones (*Notes & Queries* 158 [1930], 6-7)
33. N. Waters, *The Newfoundland in Heritage and Art*, (the Hague 2006), 44-6, 50-1.
34. N. Waters, *The Newfoundland in Heritage and Art*, (the Hague 2006), 47, 51.
35. N. Waters, *The Newfoundland in Heritage and Art*, (the Hague 2006), 47, 51.
36. A. Heim, *Der Neufundländerhund* (Mannheim 1934), 10.
37. B. Gothen Christensen, *Newfoundlandshunden* (Västerås 1981), 131.

CHAPTER 11.
SIR EDWIN LANDSEER AND THE NEWFOUNDLAND DOG
1. F.G. Stephens, Sir Edwin Landseer, RA (London 1880); R. Ormond, Sir Edwin Landseer (London 1981); D. Conlon in the *Zuchtbuch Nr. 2* of the Deutscher Landseer Club (Pfungstadt 1989), 14-55.
2. D. Conlon in the *Zuchtbuch Nr. 2* of the Deutscher Landseer Club (Pfungstadt 1989), 14-55.
3. On Wyatt and Bashaw, see *Lloyd's Weekly Newspaper* Jan 19 1862 and *Era* Jan 19 1862. Also J. Harris, *Country Life* 122 [1957], 1085 and J. Bryant, *Bashaw by Matthew Cotes Wyatt* (London 1983).
4. *Morning Chronicle* Feb 28 1834; *Morning Post* Feb 18 1834.
5. *Morning Post* July 8 1834.
6. J. Bryant, *Bashaw by Matthew Cotes Wyatt* (London 1983).
7. *Pall Mall Gazette* March 5 1870.
8. *Times* Sept 20 1882 4e.
9. *Morning Post* April 18 1887.
10. *Illustrated London News* June 18 1960, 1054.
11. *Morning Post* Sept 24 1866.
12. D. Donald, *Picturing Animals in Britain* (New Haven and London 2007), 127-58.

CHAPTER 12.
WILLIAM GORDON STABLES AND SOME OTHER VICTORIAN NEWFOUNDLAND DOG FANCIERS
1. William Gordon Stables is in the Oxford DNB; see also S. Graham, *An Introduction to William Gordon Stables 1837-1910*, Twyford and Ruscombe Local History Society 2006.
2. W.G. Stables, *Aileen Aroon* (London 1884) details all his adventures with Theodore Nero.
3. For evidence, see Chapter 10, note 5 and 'Newfoundland dogs in the News', Nov 17 1791, July 15 1848 and April 30 1889.
4. *Bradford Observer* Aug 25 1873.
5. W.G. Stables in *Boy's Own Paper* May 1 1880.
6. *Manchester Times* Dec 11 1875.
7. W.G. Stables in *Fancier's Gazette* March 25 1875.
8. E.C. Ash, *Dogs, Their History and Development* (London 1927), vol. 2, 582-3.
9. W.G. Stables in *Fancier's Gazette* March 25 1875 and *Boy's Own Paper* May 1 1880.
10. R. Guttridge, *The Evening Echo Book of Heritage in Dorset and the New Forest* (Southampton 1991), 32-3.
11. H. Ritvo (*Victorian Studies* 29 [1986], 227-253) and *The Animal Estate* (Cambridge, Ma 1987), 82-121.
12. There was one less of them in 1791, deliberately drowned in the Thames by a Newfoundland dog, after a dog fight staged by two 'gentlemen'.

13. Quite wrongly so, since the bulldog is at the very bottom of the canine pecking order with regard to its intellect; see S. Coren, *The Intelligence of Dogs* (London 2006), 193.
14. W.G. Stables, *Our Friend the Dog* (London 1884), 164-74.

CHAPTER 13.
HISTORICAL ANALYSIS OF NEWFOUNDLAND DOG FUR COLOUR GENETICS

1. M. Booth Chern, *The New Complete Newfoundland* (Howell Book House 1975), 38; K. Maynard Drury, *This is the Newfoundland* (Neptune City NJ 1978), 45-58.
2. A, Barlowe, *Newfoundland* (Dorking 2001), 2-9, and J. Kosloff, *Newfoundlands* (New York 2006), 5-11.
3. A. Heim, *Das Neufundländerhund* (Mannheim 1934), 7-11.
4. J. Bondeson, *Amazing Dogs* (Stroud 2011), 196.
5. M. Booth Chern, *The New Complete Newfoundland* (Howell Book House 1975), 38-42, 109.
6. R.D. Lee, *A History and Description of the Modern Dogs of Great Britain* and Ireland (London 1894), Chapter III.
7. A. Heim, *Das Neufundländerhund* (Mannheim 1934), 10. 41.
8. E.C. Ash, *Dogs, Their History and Development* (London 1927), Vol. 2, 565-87.
9. E.H. Mellencamp (*Newf Tides* 7(4) 1976).
10. E.H. Mellencamp (*Newf Tides* 9(1) 1978). Both Dr Mellencamp's articles are reproduced on the homepage of the Newfoundland Club of America.
11. D. Conlon and C. Matenaar in the *Zuchtbuch Nr. 2* of the Deutscher Landseer Club (Pfungstadt 1989), 14-55 and 57-200 respectively.
12. N. Waters, *The Newfoundland in Heritage and Art*, (the Hague 2006)
13. C.C. Little, *The Inheritance of Coat Colour in Dogs* (New York 1957).
14. O. Winge, *Inheritance in Dogs with Special Reference to the Hunting Breeds* (Ithaca, NY 1950).
15. H. Pape (*Genetica* 80 [1990], 115-28).
16. E.K. Karlsson *et al.* (*Nature Genetics* 39 [2007]. 1321-6).
17. S.M. Schmutz *et al.* (*Journal of Heredity* 100 [2009], S66-S74)
18. *Times* May 21 1785 4b.
19. W.G. Stables, *Our Friend the Dog* (London 1884), 164-74.

CHAPTER 14.
NEWFOUNDLAND DOGS IN THE NEWS 1850-1900

1. From a French newspaper.
2. From the *Glasgow Examiner*.
3. From the *New York Daily News*.
4. The Prince's Newfoundland dog was brought back to England, and won the first prize at the Agricultural Hall dog show in 1864.
5. An account of the collapse of the skating arena in Regent's Park, where many people lost their lives.
6. From an article entitled 'Will the ice bear?'
7. From an account of the floods in South of France.
8. From a lecture by Charles Bradlaugh MP.
9. From an article about Newfoundland.
10. Proof that the dog-thieves were still active.
11. From an article about the old actor Edmund Kean playing Richard III.
12. The story of this Newfoundland dog doing a 'Greyfriars Bobby' must be suspected to be a newspaper canard. Would the captain really have left a valuable dog behind in such a manner?
13. The dog Sultan really existed, see M. Booth Chern, *The New Complete Newfoundland* (Howell Book House 1975), 188.

CHAPTER 16.
SOME SPECTRAL NEWFOUNDLAND DOGS

1. E. O'Donnell, *Animal Ghosts* (London 1913).
2. C.F. Lowth on www.mariner.ie.
3. J. Westwood & J. Simpson, *The Lore of the Land* (London 2005), 199.
4. P. Dale-Green, *Dog* (London 1966), 47-53; J. & C. Bord, *Alien Animals* (London 1980), 77-111; C. Stubbs (*Fortean Times* 195 [2005], 30-5); D. Waldron & C Reeve, *Shock! The Black Dog of Bungay* (Bungay 2010).
5. This version of the 'Boatswain' yarn is from the CKA Canadian Forums homepage, translated from K. Brönneke, *Das Neufundländer Buch* (Osnabrück 1994), 48-9. This account in turn gives the source as 'Die Hundevelt' of 1941; were the Nazis up to their old tricks again, spreading desinformation about canine history? Alternative versions of the story are in B. Hynes, *The Noble Newfoundland Dog* (Halifax, NS 2005), 39-42; F. Pratt & C. Cooper, *A Friend in Deed* (Penryn 2002), 21-2; and P. Pickett, *Heroic Companion* (Grand Falls-Windsor 2001); A. Barlowe, *Newfoundland* (Dorking 2001), 10-11 and J. Kosloff, *Newfoundlands* (New York 2006), 6-7.
6. And the sum of £7500, indicated by Hynes, *Noble Newfoundland Dog*, 40, would have secured you a nice country estate.
7. *New York Times* Dec 17 1919.
8. *Daily Mirror* Jan 3 1920, 2.
9. It was published in the *Canadian Forum* for November 1920, 55.
10. M. Bridson (*Newfoundland Quarterly* 96(2) [2003], 56-9); B. Ricketts, *The SS Ethie and the Hero Dog* (Quebec 2005).
11. B. Ricketts, *The SS Ethie and the Hero Dog* (Quebec 2005).
12. See also B. Hynes, *The Noble Newfoundland Dog* (Halifax NS 2005), 48-53 and P. Pickett, *Heroic Companion* (Grand Falls-Windsor 2001), 28-9.
13. *New York Herald* April 21 1912.
14. B. Hynes, *The Noble Newfoundland Dog* (Halifax NS 2005), 108-110; A. Barlowe, *Newfoundland* (Dorking 2001), 10-11. The 'Hero' and 'Rigel' yarns are also retold, albeit under the subtitle 'Legend or Fact' on the homepages of the Newfoundland Club of America.
15. C. Jamesson, *The Legend of Rigel, Hero Dog of the Titanic* (Bloomington, Ind. 2006).

CHAPTER 17.
THE LIFESAVING NEWFOUNDLAND DOGS OF PARIS

1. *Petit Parisien* No. 678, 1902; a valuable article from *The Windsor Magazine* of 1902 is reproduced by N. Waters, *The Newfoundland in Heritage and Art*, (the Hague 2006), 229-33.
2. H.B. Philpott (*Quiver* 137 [1905], 573-8).
3. Repeated in the *Colonist* May 18 1908.
4. *Daily Mirror* Sept 7 1905, 8.
5. A later article about the Paris police (*Almanach Pratique du 'Petit Parisien'* 1911, 17-25) has a section about police dogs, but does not mention any *chiens plongeurs*.
6. *Daily Mirror* July 22 1975, 16; *EasyJet Magazine* 84 (December 2008), 47-51.
7. M. Mott in *National Geographic News* Feb 7 2003.
8. J.-M. Durand (*Receuil de Médecine Vétérinaire* 167 [1991], 619-22, 719-22)
9. T. Orlowski et al. (*Animal Science Papers and Reports* 19 [2001]. 157-66)
10. *Sun* Feb 2 and Aug 8 2007; *Daily Mail* Aug 8 2007; *South Wales Echo* Aug 29 2009.
11. S. Jamieson & J. Hevizi, *The True Story of Bilbo* (Penwyn 2008).
12. *Daily Express* July 22 2006, 3; *Daily Mirror* Feb 28 2008, 55 and May 19 2008, 29; *Independent* March 28 2009.
13. *Cornish Guardian* Feb 15 2012.

CHAPTER 18.
NEWFOUNDLAND DOG WATER RESCUE BY MR DAVID PUGH OF NEWFOUND FRIENDS

1. The French group still exists but is no longer as active as it once was, and Tom Rudd also still takes an interest in Newfoundland dogs.
2. Whizz is still alive and well, and his younger successor Ted is making good progress as a water rescue dog.
3. *Daily Telegraph* June 3 1995.
4. *Western Daily Press* May 17 2003.
5. Bear sadly passed away two years ago.

CHAPTER 19.
THE CHANGING NEWFOUNDLAND DOG

1. R. Delort, *Les Animaux ont une Histoire* (Paris 1984); M.E. Thurston, *The Lost History of the Canine Race* (Kansas City 1996); see also the six-volume series *The Cultural History of Animals*.
2. R. & R. Beaver, *All about the St Bernard* (London 1988); M. Nussbaumer, *Barry* (Berne 2000); J. Bondeson, *Amazing Dogs* (Stroud 2011), 189-205.
3. J. Bondeson, *Amazing Dogs* (Stroud 2011), 149-161.
4. J. Bondeson, *Greyfriars Bobby* (Stroud 2011).
5. M. Nussbaumer, *Barry* (Berne 2000); J. Bondeson, *Amazing Dogs* (Stroud 2011), 189-205.
6. S. Coren, *The Intelligence of Dogs* (London 2006), 65-6.
7. *Times* Jan 7 1805 4a, June 9 1806 3a, Sept 27 1824 3e.
8. R. Mestel (*Discover* Jan 10 1994); D. McCraig (*Smithsonian* 27(8) [1996], 126-35); M.W. Neff *et al.* (*Genetics* 151 [1999], 803-20); E.A. Ostrander *et al.* (*Trends in Genetics* 16 [2000], 117-24).
9. K. Macpherson & W.A. Roberts (*Journal of Comparative Psychology* 120 [2006], 113-9).

HOW TO START A PUBLISHING EMPIRE

Unlike most mainstream publishers, we have a non-commercial remit, and our mission statement claims that "we publish books because they deserve to be published, not because we think that we can make money out of them". Our motto is the Latin Tag *Pro bona causa facimus* (we do it for good reason), a slogan taken from a children's book *The Case of the Silver Egg* by the late Desmond Skirrow.

WIKIPEDIA: "The first book published was in 1988. *Take this Brother may it Serve you Well* was a guide to *Beatles* bootlegs by Jonathan Downes. It sold quite well, but was hampered by very poor production values, being photocopied, and held together by a plastic clip binder. In 1988 A5 clip binders were hard to get hold of, so the publishers took A4 binders and cut them in half with a hacksaw. It now reaches surprisingly high prices second hand.

The production quality improved slightly over the years, and after 1999 all the books produced were ringbound with laminated colour covers. In 2004, however, they signed an agreement with Lightning Source, and all books are now produced perfect bound, with full colour covers."

Until 2010 all our books, the majority of which are/were on the subject of mystery animals and allied disciplines, were published by `CFZ Press`, the publishing arm of the Centre for Fortean Zoology (CFZ), and we urged our readers and followers to draw a discreet veil over the books that we published that were completely off topic to the CFZ.

However, in 2010 we decided that enough was enough and launched a second imprint, `Fortean Words` which aims to cover a wide range of non animal-related esoteric subjects. Other imprints will be launched as and when we feel like it, however the basic ethos of the company remains the same: Our job is to publish books and magazines that we feel are worth publishing, whether or not they are going to sell. Money is, after all - as my dear old Mama once told me - a rather vulgar subject, and she would be rolling in her grave if she thought that her eldest son was somehow in `trade`.

Luckily, so far our tastes have turned out not to be that rarified after all, and we have sold far more books than anyone ever thought that we would, so there is a moral in there somewhere…

Jon Downes,
Woolsery, North Devon
July 2010

Other Books in Print

CFZ Yearbook 2012 edited by Jon and Corinna Downes
ORANG PENDEK: Sumatra's Forgotten Ape by Richard Freeman
THE MYSTERY ANIMALS OF THE BRITISH ISLES: London by Neil Arnold
CFZ EXPEDITION REPORT: India 2010 by Richard Freeman *et al*
The Cryptid Creatures of Florida by Scott Marlow
Dead of Night by Lee Walker
The Mystery Animals of the British Isles: The Northern Isles by Glen Vaudrey
THE MYSTERY ANIMALS OF THE BRTISH ISLES: Gloucestershire and Worcestershire by Paul Williams
When Bigfoot Attacks by Michael Newton
Weird Waters – The Mystery Animals of Scandinavia: Lake and Sea Monsters by Lars Thomas
The Inhumanoids by Barton Nunnelly
Monstrum! A Wizard's Tale by Tony "Doc" Shiels
CFZ Yearbook 2011 edited by Jonathan Downes
Karl Shuker's Alien Zoo by Shuker, Dr Karl P.N
Tetrapod Zoology Book One by Naish, Dr Darren
The Mystery Animals of Ireland by Gary Cunningham and Ronan Coghlan
Monsters of Texas by Gerhard, Ken
The Great Yokai Encyclopaedia by Freeman, Richard
NEW HORIZONS: Animals & Men *issues 16-20 Collected Editions Vol. 4* by Downes, Jonathan
A Daintree Diary -
Tales from Travels to the Daintree Rainforest in tropical north Queensland, Australia by Portman, Carl
Strangely Strange but Oddly Normal by Roberts, Andy
Centre for Fortean Zoology Yearbook 2010 by Downes, Jonathan
Predator Deathmatch by Molloy, Nick
Star Steeds and other Dreams by Shuker, Karl
CHINA: A Yellow Peril? by Muirhead, Richard
Mystery Animals of the British Isles: The Western Isles by Vaudrey, Glen
Giant Snakes - Unravelling the coils of mystery by Newton, Michael
Mystery Animals of the British Isles: Kent by Arnold, Neil
Centre for Fortean Zoology Yearbook 2009 by Downes, Jonathan
CFZ EXPEDITION REPORT: Russia 2008 by Richard Freeman *et al*, Shuker, Karl (fwd)

Dinosaurs and other Prehistoric Animals on Stamps - A Worldwide catalogue by Shuker, Karl P. N
Dr Shuker's Casebook by Shuker, Karl P.N
*The Island of Paradise - chupacabra UFO crash retrievals,
and accelerated evolution on the island of Puerto Rico* by Downes, Jonathan
The Mystery Animals of the British Isles: Northumberland and Tyneside by Hallowell, Michael J
Centre for Fortean Zoology Yearbook 1997 by Downes, Jonathan (Ed)
Centre for Fortean Zoology Yearbook 2002 by Downes, Jonathan (Ed)
Centre for Fortean Zoology Yearbook 2000/1 by Downes, Jonathan (Ed)
Centre for Fortean Zoology Yearbook 1998 by Downes, Jonathan (Ed)
Centre for Fortean Zoology Yearbook 2003 by Downes, Jonathan (Ed)
In the wake of Bernard Heuvelmans by Woodley, Michael A
CFZ EXPEDITION REPORT: Guyana 2007 by Richard Freeman *et al*, Shuker, Karl (fwd)
Centre for Fortean Zoology Yearbook 1999 by Downes, Jonathan (Ed)
Big Cats in Britain Yearbook 2008 by Fraser, Mark (Ed)
Centre for Fortean Zoology Yearbook 1996 by Downes, Jonathan (Ed)
THE CALL OF THE WILD - Animals & Men issues 11-15
Collected Editions Vol. 3 by Downes, Jonathan (ed)
Ethna's Journal by Downes, C N
Centre for Fortean Zoology Yearbook 2008 by Downes, J (Ed)
DARK DORSET -Calendar Custome by Newland, Robert J
Extraordinary Animals Revisited by Shuker, Karl
MAN-MONKEY - In Search of the British Bigfoot by Redfern, Nick
Dark Dorset Tales of Mystery, Wonder and Terror by Newland, Robert J and Mark North
Big Cats Loose in Britain by Matthews, Marcus
MONSTER! - The A-Z of Zooform Phenomena by Arnold, Neil
The Centre for Fortean Zoology 2004 Yearbook by Downes, Jonathan (Ed)
The Centre for Fortean Zoology 2007 Yearbook by Downes, Jonathan (Ed)
CAT FLAPS! Northern Mystery Cats by Roberts, Andy
Big Cats in Britain Yearbook 2007 by Fraser, Mark (Ed)
BIG BIRD! - Modern sightings of Flying Monsters by Gerhard, Ken
THE NUMBER OF THE BEAST - Animals & Men issues 6-10
Collected Editions Vol. 1 by Downes, Jonathan (Ed)
IN THE BEGINNING - Animals & Men issues 1-5 Collected Editions Vol. 1 by Downes, Jonathan
STRENGTH THROUGH KOI - They saved Hitler's Koi and other stories by Downes, Jonathan
The Smaller Mystery Carnivores of the Westcountry by Downes, Jonathan
CFZ EXPEDITION REPORT: Gambia 2006 by Richard Freeman *et al*, Shuker, Karl (fwd)
The Owlman and Others by Jonathan Downes
The Blackdown Mystery by Downes, Jonathan
Big Cats in Britain Yearbook 2006 by Fraser, Mark (Ed)
Fragrant Harbours - Distant Rivers by Downes, John T
Only Fools and Goatsuckers by Downes, Jonathan
Monster of the Mere by Jonathan Downes
Dragons:More than a Myth by Freeman, Richard Alan
Granfer's Bible Stories by Downes, John Tweddell
Monster Hunter by Downes, Jonathan

Fortean Words

The Centre for Fortean Zoology has for several years led the field in Fortean publishing. CFZ Press is the only publishing company specialising in books on monsters and mystery animals. CFZ Press has published more books on this subject than any other company in history and has attracted such well known authors as Andy Roberts, Nick Redfern, Michael Newton, Dr Karl Shuker, Neil Arnold, Dr Darren Naish, Jon Downes, Ken Gerhard and Richard Freeman.

Now CFZ Press are launching a new imprint. Fortean Words is a new line of books dealing with Fortean subjects other than cryptozoology, which is - after all - the subject the CFZ are best known for. Fortean Words is being launched with a spectacular multi-volume series called *Haunted Skies* which covers British UFO sightings between 1940 and 2010. Former policeman John Hanson and his long-suffering partner Dawn Holloway have compiled a peerless library of sighting reports, many that have not been made public before.

Other forthcoming books include a look at the Berwyn Mountains UFO case by renowned Fortean Andy Roberts and a series of books by transatlantic researcher Nick Redfern.

CFZ Press are dedicated to maintaining the fine quality of their works with Fortean Words. New authors tackling new subjects will always be encouraged, and we hope that our books will continue to be as ground breaking and popular as ever.

Haunted Skies Volume One 1940-1959 by John Hanson and Dawn Holloway
Haunted Skies Volume Two 1960-1965 by John Hanson and Dawn Holloway
Haunted Skies Volume Three 1965-1967 by John Hanson and Dawn Holloway
Haunted Skies Volume Four 1968-1971 by John Hanson and Dawn Holloway
Grave Concerns by Kai Roberts

Police and the Paranormal by Andy Owens
Dead of Night by Lee Walker
Space Girl Dead on Spaghetti Junction - an anthology by Nick Redfern
I Fort the Lore - an anthology by Paul Screeton
UFO Down - the Berwyn Mountains UFO Crash by Andy Roberts

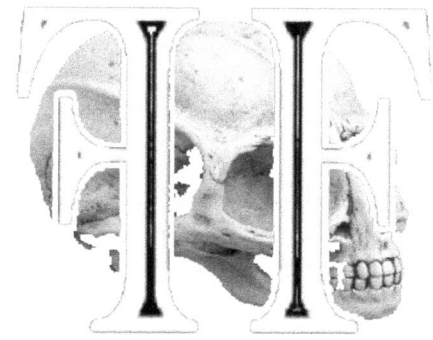

Fortean Fiction

Just before Christmas 2011, we launched our third imprint, this time dedicated to - let's see if you guessed it from the title - fictional books with a Fortean or cryptozoological theme. We have published a few fictional books in the past, but now think that because of our rising reputation as publishers of quality Forteana, that a dedicated fiction imprint was the order of the day.

We launched with four titles:

Green Unpleasant Land by Richard Freeman
Left Behind by Harriet Wadham
Dark Ness by Tabitca Cope
Snap! By Steven Bredice

www.ingramcontent.com/pod-product-compliance
Lightning Source LLC
Chambersburg PA
CBHW062127160426
43191CB00013B/2223